TAKING SHAPE

For my parents and my students

TAKING SHAPE

A new contract between architecture and nature

Susannah Hagan

Architectural Press

OXFORD   AUCKLAND   BOSTON   JOHANNESBURG   MELBOURNE   NEW DELHI

Architectural Press
An imprint of Butterworth-Heinemann
Linacre House, Jordan Hill, Oxford OX2 8DP
225 Wildwood Avenue, Woburn, MA 01801-2041
A division of Reed Educational and Professional Publishing Ltd

Ⓡ A member of the Reed Elsevier plc group

First published 2001

British Library Cataloguing in Publication Data
Hagan Susannah
    Taking shape: a new contract between architecture and nature
    1. Architecture – Environmental aspects 2. Sustainable development
    I. Title
    720.4'7

Library of Congress Cataloguing in Publication Data
A catalogue record for this book is available from the Library of Congress

ISBN 0 7506 4948 8

Composition by Scribe Design, Gillingham, Kent
Printed and bound in Great Britain by MPG Books Ltd, Bodmin, Cornwall

CONTENTS

Foreword   vii

Acknowledgements   ix

Introduction   x

Part One

1   Defining environmental architecture   **3**

2   The 'new' nature and a new architecture   **16**
   2.1 Introduction   16
   2.2 Ceci n'est pas une pipe   16
   2.3 All about Eve   19
   2.4 Nature redux   21
   2.5 Racinated   24
   2.6 Re-racinated   31
   2.7 The return of the repressed   33
   2.8 The birth of the green   37
   2.9 Blurring the boundaries   42
   2.10 Conclusion   44

3   A post-imperial modernism?   **45**
   3.1 Introduction   45
   3.2 Makers and breakers   46
   3.3 Back to the garden   50
   3.4 Uptown   52
   3.5 A kinder gentler modernism   59

Part Two

4   Ethics and environmental design   **65**
   4.1 Introduction   65
   4.2 Being good   67
   4.3 Being good in buildings   70
   4.4 New is good?   72
   4.5 The good, the bad and the juggled   75

5   Materials and materiality   **77**
   5.1 Introduction   77
   5.2 A lost chance   78

5.3	Telling the truth	83
5.4	Building the truth	86
5.5	Grounded	90
5.6	Conclusion	92

Part Three

6	**Rules of engagement**	**97**
6.1	Introduction	97
6.2	Symbiosis	101
	6.2.1 Paradise regained?	103
	6.2.2 Terra cognita	104
6.3	Differentiation	115
	6.3.1 'You say banana...'	116
	6.3.2 Building 'there'	121
	6.3.3 No 'where'	125
6.4	Visibility	128
	6.4.1 Dreams of dwelling	129
	6.4.2 Between the lines	131
	6.4.3 Open the box	135
	6.4.4 A cooking lesson	137
6.5	Conclusion	145

7	**Doing it**	**147**
7.1	Introduction	147
7.2	Symbiosis: Richard Horden	151
7.3	Differentiation	156
	7.3.1 Climatic differentiation: Ken Yeang	156
	7.3.2 Cultural differentiation: Renzo Piano	158
7.4	Visibility: Emilio Ambasz	161
7.5	Conclusion	163

Part Four

8	**ComplexCity**	**167**
8.1	Introduction	167
8.2	Curvy bits	168
8.3	Cities of the plain	171
8.4	The wild wild Web	175
8.5	On edge	179
8.6	Sustainable heroics?	183
8.7	Flowers of the field	186
8.8	Of mutual benefit	190
8.9	Beyond pricing?	191
8.10	Conclusion	191

Conclusion	193
Bibliography	197
Illustration credits	206
Project credits	208
Index	211

FOREWORD

For those concerned with the future of the environment - built and unbuilt - this book is, in my view, indispensable. *Taking Shape* is at once an intriguing overview of the relationship between architecture and the environment, and a timely manifesto: nothing less than a new vision for the role and meaning of architectural form. It provides a balanced and comprehensive introduction to the concepts and history of environmentalism, and more specifically the creation and operation of a built environment that works with, rather than against climate. It also examines the philosophical, ethical, and cultural debates that underlie the evolving theory of a new relationship between architecture and nature. These include traditional and current definitions of nature and of architecture, shifts of emphasis in concepts of function, structure, and beauty, tensions between the utilitarian and the conceptual, the ethical and the aesthetic, the role of vernacular architecture, heroic Modernism and contemporary forms; and the predicament of urban and ex-urban development.

More importantly, *Taking Shape* identifies the formal potential of environmentally sustainable design for the first time. Previous efforts on the topic have been largely framed by a 'functionalist' point of view, with the primary role of the built environment to solve the problem of sustainability, and architectural form the by-product of this endeavor. This book turns the argument on its head. It argues that aesthetic pleasure is as necessary as ethical concern to the formal embodiment of a society that seeks the greatest good for the maximum number of people. Further, it insists upon the persuasive power of architecture as symbol and proposes environmental sustainability as a major cultural underpinning of architecture. Such an alliance of form and ethics unleashes the exciting possibility that architecture may take new forms both resonant and relevant, with typologies of sustainable form as yet unimagined. Restoring the aesthetic to the realm of necessity, architecture is elevated to a central and visionary role.

In proposing such an alliance, Susannah Hagan seeks to address both the political realities of environmental reform and a crisis of meaning within the architectural community. Coherent policies on the built environment vary widely in developed and developing nations. Although there are mature environmental movements in the US and Europe, there is little consensus on change. As the debate reaches a critical juncture, this book, like the architecture it espouses, will be essential to the arguments - and ultimately the agreement - which will inform public policy and legislation.

In the United States, a frenzy of building activity over the past eight years has left the architectural community with the feeling that architecture may have lost its relevance, and that the expediency of construction has displaced any meaningful discourse about its purpose. What culture is to be addressed? What meaning conveyed? What technology incorporated? And what form might that architecture take in light of shifting ethical positions and the largely untapped potential of digital technologies? At a moment when architecture appears, on the one hand, to pander to current recidivist tastes, and on the other, to be no more than an exercise in style devoid of technical innovation, social responsibility or cultural meaning, this treatise proposes environmental sustainability as a new basis for architectural relevance and experiment.

What is 'sustainability' and how broadly should its net be cast? Can it encompass economic, social and aesthetic concerns even as it pursues environmental balance, a new 'contract' with nature? What is 'natural', and what is 'artificial? How are these ideas intertwined with current notions of beauty and social welfare? Are aesthetic pleasure and ethics irreconcilable? Can architecture provide sustainable shelter and be art? Can an aesthetic of excess embody and inspire fundamental social reform? *Taking Shape* addresses these central questions with passion, lucidity, and conviction. It identifies the need to participate in the formation of a rigorous, visionary agenda to re-imagine architecture as a partner in the pursuit of a new contract with nature. To ignore its message is to risk missing a new relationship between architecture, nature and the built environment.

Paul Florian
Florian Architects
Chicago
January 1, 2001

ACKNOWLEDGEMENTS

I must first thank the three godfathers of this book, Paul Hirst, Simos Yannas and Mark Cousins, without whose intellectual generosity I would never have made my way through the labyrinth of 'sustainability'. This isn't to say any of them necessarily agree with all, or even most, of what I have to say, but they helped me to think about it in ways I couldn't otherwise have done. Stephen Adutt, Peter Salter and Mohsen Mostafavi made it possible for me to teach what I was thinking about, and so develop arguments that would otherwise have remained untested. Mark Dorrian and Tanis Hinchcliffe were there at the very beginning, encouraging me to take the first steps forward, and Paul Florian was there at the end, helping me towards publication. Pippa Lewis and Richard Hill rode to the rescue at a testing moment, as did Samantha Boyce, my exemplary agent. Katherine MacInnes was the one who paved the way at Butterworth-Heinemann; Sian Cryer and Alison Yates were endlessly patient editors, and the meticulous professionalism of Pauline Sones and Susan Hamilton was an education in itself. I must also thank the architects who contributed their time and thoughts to the subject of this book, in particular Brian Ford, Alan Short and Richard Horden.

INTRODUCTION

Neither half of this book's title is self-explanatory, not 'Taking Shape' and not the reference to a 'new contract'. 'Taking Shape' emphasizes the still emergent state of an architecture that is engaging in a new contract of co-operation between built and natural environments, so-called 'sustainable' or 'environmental' architecture. At present, environmental architecture is split between an arcadian minority intent on returning building to a pre-industrial, ideally pre-urban state, and a ratio-nalist majority interested in developing the techniques and technologies of contemporary environmental design, some of which are pre-industrial, most of which are not. The two approaches co-exist within the same ethical framework, share a certain optimism about the possibility of change, and are bolstered intellectually by a heavy reliance on phenomenology as it has been interpreted by architectural theorists. Both use environmentalism as a new meta-narrative that restores the human subject to the centre of moral discourse and a realm of effec-tive action it has not inhabited since the collapse of architectural modernism. From the arcadian minority has come a revival of craft tradi-tions and vernacular techniques for mediating between inside and outside, but it is the rationalist majority who now dominate the field. One has only to look at the proceedings of any conference on environ-mental architecture in the last twenty years to see the overwhelming emphasis on the scientific and quantitative dimensions of the discipline: thermal conductivity of materials, photovoltaic technology, computer simulations, life cycle analysis, and so on.

This science drives much of environmental design, as it both answers a now proven need to operate in the world less destructively, and enables the existing distribution of economic power to remain in place. A proportion of this rationalist camp holds to a utilitarianism that consid-ers any concern with architecture as art to be irrelevant at best, and criminally irresponsible at worst. Another proportion of the rationalists' work looks no different from the neo-modernist architecture it claims to supplant. Between these kinds of practice is a growing number of archi-tects who take what they require from both arcadian and rationalist positions, but subscribe exclusively neither to low nor advanced technologies, 'natural' or synthetic materials, passive or active environ-mental design strategies, expression or operation. They discuss form in the same breath as they discuss energy efficiency. The result is not an architecture generated from a technology, as in principle happened with the Modern Movement, but a technology, or rather a range of technologies, inserted into pre-existing architectures, which are then re-formed to different degrees, according to the rigour with which the environmental agenda is pursued.

Technically, then, this practice is already highly sophisticated, with environmental performance improving constantly. Culturally, it has barely broken the surface of the collective consciousness. If it is perceived at all, it is perceived as conservative, aimed at achieving stasis rather than embracing change. How this has happened, when environmentalism is as much an engine of change as it is a protest against changes that have already occurred, is one of the central questions this book seeks to address. There is no reason why an interest in, and a respect for, the workings of nature should imply a conservatism of thought or architectural form. This conservatism is only one of its incarnations, albeit the dominant one currently. Intellectual and formal innovation are equally possible, but not as yet equally present, within environmental architecture. There is resistance both from those within environmental design who don't want its 'hard' science to be 'softened' by cultural or conceptual considerations, and from those outside who see this reluctance as universal and intrinsic, rather than an accident of history waiting to be reformulated.

In the ideological battle between environmentalism and consumerism, presentation is everything. A practice that is perceived as regressive is at a disadvantage against one that is perceived as innovative, however harmful at some level this innovation may be. But if a new contract between nature and architecture requires a reappraisal of what we build and the way we build it, it is a reappraisal that considers the new to be as essential to the project as the old. While both those inside and outside the environmental fold are aware of the precedents upon which this architecture design draws – classicism, traditional vernacular, humanism, and even mysticism – they are not similarly open to the potential that contemporary thinking in both the arts and sciences has for pushing environmental architecture towards much greater self-consciousness, and as a result, a greater persuasiveness in presenting its case through what it chooses to make visible.

This visibility is crucial in what is a power struggle between those who profit from continued abuse of the physical environment, and those (not all of them human) who suffer from it. Architects are a tiny fraction of the numbers involved in the production of objects, and the increased energy efficiency of their objects will have no impact whatsoever on global climate change in material terms. As exemplars, however, such buildings have a potential value out of all proportion to their numbers. It is for this reason one might be justified in devoting attention to them: architectural production can influence the rest of the building industry.

The 'contract' referred to in the second part of the title is that proposed by environmentalism as it pertains to built culture. In one sense, this contract is not new at all, in that it seeks to re-establish the more co-operative relation between built and 'natural' environments seen in many pre-industrial societies in what is now an industrial and post-industrial world. This less confrontational relation does not require a return to pre-industrial modes of producing and living, however, though some within the environmental movement find this desirable. Very little of this pre-industrial content pertains today in the West, and it is the wishfulness of such a return that provokes a certain impatience with those who call for it on the part of those who do not. This impatience leads to a dismissal of the entire project, because means are confused with ends. Architects pursuing sustainability can and do avail themselves of traditional means of mediating between built and natural environments without in any way subscribing to them as ends, that is, as emblematic of a certain way of life and a return to it.

In fact, environmental design embraces advanced technologies as well as traditional techniques. The character of these advanced technologies derives from different values to those governing the instrumental use of technologies. These values encourages the development of technologies that aren't double-edged swords, as is, for example, genetic engineering, which can be used exploitatively for the redesign of human beings before birth, and benignly for the manufacture of waste-eating bacteria. The first is potentially a dangerous abuse of a little understood power; the second is not. Some, however, may disagree on drawing the distinction here, rather than sooner: between bacteria that appear 'naturally', and those we engineer. So that viewing environmental technology as non-instrumental requires an acceptance of the possibility that technology isn't all intrinsically exploitative, that some of it can be co-operative rather than invasive, for example, photovoltaic cells, which convert solar radiation into electricity and enable buildings to feed off the sun like plants.

Architects in the 1970s and 1980s, who accepted the necessity for some form of environmental design, produced what was called 'green architecture', though the term was still being used by John Farmer in 1994, when he wrote *Green Shift*, an examination of 'the green past of building' (Farmer, 1996: 6). 'Green' has a complex genealogy arising partly out of the environmental movements aligned with the Left in the 1960s (the 'Green' parties that have kept the adjective to date), and partly out of the Flower Power counter-culture movements of the same period. As it emerged in architecture, 'green' came to be associated more with the latter, and lost its connection with a left-leaning critique of the economic and political status quo. As the term 'sustainable' overtook the term 'green' in the late 1980s, much of the counter-culture element was shed, as 'sustainability' can refer as easily to the establishment's answer to the mess it has itself created, as it can to a critique of that establishment. It embraces, in other words, reformer as well as revolutionaries.

The alarm in the 1960s over the environmental effects of modern technology, first sounded by Rachel Carson in her book about the insecticide DDT (*The Silent Spring*, 1962), gave way in the 1970s to alarm over threats to the way of life which that instrumental technology had made possible. When the price of oil was drastically increased by its producer countries in 1974, and again in 1979, the International Energy Agency (IEA) was set up in the West to explore alternative energy sources. Research into alternative technologies was thus begun within the scientific establishment itself, often funded by the industrial establishment, in order to develop technologies that would sustain the status quo – both in terms of standard of living and those profiting from providing it.

By 1987, and the UN World Commission on Environment and Development's Brundtland Report, 'sustainability' was the new buzz word, defined, in the report, as 'development that meets the needs of the present without compromising the ability of future generations to meet their own needs'. Architects open to the environmental message, but unwilling to be associated with the often Luddite tendencies of the Greens, found the progressive science-based version represented by 'sustainability' much easier to accept.

The meaning of the term 'sustainable architecture', however, is not as clear-cut as such a description implies, and is open to a range of contradictory interpretations. These are understandable, as 'sustainable' connotes both a critique of, and a perpetuation of, established practice. Included within 'sustainable architecture', therefore, are architects who are suspicious of architecture-as-form-making, and those who want to protect form-making from the potential reductiveness of environmental design; those who employ only low technologies and those who employ advanced technologies as well; those who think environmental architecture should be formally – though not stylistically – identifiable as such; those who think it should remain a plurality of architectures, and those who think 'architecture' is an irrelevance, when the problem and its solutions are essentially political.

Even within this last view, however, exemplary architecture has a contribution to make – in changing the cultural, if not the meteorological, climate. This is important because if social change doesn't arise democratically from the bottom up, it will be imposed from the top down. Obviously, there is already movement in both directions, but not fast enough to answer what is now expressed in terms of 'environmental crisis'. Indeed, there are those who believe democracy and environmentalism are mutually contradictory, and that only through a draconian concentration of power at the top can the necessary change in consumerism's present direction be effected. Even the more optimistic criticize the possibility of real environmental reform within democracies:

existing economic structures, power structures, and legal/political insti-tutions would remain broadly in place but would be given a new set of policy priorities: ministries would develop energy, transport and indus-trial (etc.) policies within agreed environmental constraints, businesses would be given economic incentives for ecological good conduct...Of course, these hidden assumptions have only to be spelled out for their sociological implausibility to become evident... (Benton, 1994: 38).

These 'hidden assumptions' are far from hidden. They are what is coming to pass in northern Europe, particularly in Germany and Scandinavia, where precisely this kind of democratic reform of institu-tional behaviour is being chosen by the voters. The problem is perhaps different from the one articulated in the above quotation. It is not that such changes are 'implausible' – they are happening – but that they may well prove inadequate to the size of the environmental problem, especially if they are designed essentially to protect existing markets and distributions of wealth. There is much evidence to suggest that this is the case. Governments may go to Earth Summits, but they will not necessarily do anything when they get there:

In Kyoto the insidious influence of the Global Climate Coalition (funded primarily by Shell, Texaco, Ford and the US National Mining Association) resulted in the US government's refusal to sign up to any meaningful [CO_2 emissions] targets... (Howieson and Lawson, 1998: 139).

The vital question for democracies, therefore, is whether they can muster enough political will to avoid environmental meltdown and the martial law that would almost inevitably accompany it. The signs so far are not promising.

In this context, a discussion about the potential of environmentally sustainable architecture seems trivial. There are, however, two assumptions underlying this book. The first is that it is better to contribute to democratic persuasion rather than hasten compulsion, while the choice is still there. The second is that architecture, as the product and the producer of culture, is in a position to persuade. It is highly visible persuasion, the reification of certain social desires, and values, over others. This ideological dimension of the aesthetic, its power to win over and hold, has been ignored, or rejected as suspect, by many of those engaged in environmental design. But as a site for the development and display of a new co-operative contract between built culture and nature, it has a catalysing role to play. The built environment is a very big polluter, the source of 40 to 50 per cent of all carbon dioxide emissions, so that the building, as much as the car, is an environmental hazard. Architecture is useful in this context if it addresses this threat with all the means at its disposal, formal as well as operational.

Concern about architectural form is only just beginning to enter the debate within environmental design itself. The previous lack of concern has been one of the chief disincentives for architects outside environmentalism. One of the first to address the issue was Dean Hawkes in an essay called 'The Language Barrier' in 1992 (Hawkes, 1996). A few years later, a paper given at the 1996 Solar Architecture conference in Berlin[1] suggesting such a perspective be addressed was by no means universally welcomed, nor was a keynote speech at the 1998 PLEA conference in Lisbon on the same subject.[2] In all three cases, it was environmental architecture as cultural expression, and cultural expression as a self-conscious process in its own right, rather than as a by-product of a material production, that was the focus of interest. This book seeks to explore it in greater depth, within the confines of western architectural theory and practice, particularly that of western Europe. This is in part because I am more familiar with environmental design in

---

1. See Hagan, Susannah (1996). 'The Tree in the Machine: Making an Architecture out of a Technology'. In *Solar Energy in Architecture and Urban Planning*, Proceedings of the 4th European Conference on Solar Architecture, Berlin, April 1996, pp. 266–69, Felmersham: H.S. Stephens & Associates.
2. See Nicoletti, Manfredo (1998). 'Passive Systems and Architectural Expression'. In *Environmentally Friendly Cities*, Proceedings of PLEA 98, pp. 13–22, London: James and James (Science Publishers) Ltd.

western Europe than anywhere else, and partly because there is more of it relative to anywhere else.

The directly political and institutional aspects of environmental design have been dealt with cursorily. There is a very large literature on the politics, political implications, and implementation of 'environmental sustainability'. There is, however, little written on the cultural implications of environmentally sustainable architecture. John Farmer's book *Green Shift* (1996) was the first to examine environmental architecture's historical antecedents and present diversity in any detail – so that a wide-ranging examination of the subject, particularly with regard to the future, is long overdue.

The term 'sustainable' is used as if its meaning is obvious, whereas in fact its meaning depends almost entirely on who is speaking. What, then, is 'environmental' or 'sustainable' architecture'? Is it the plurality of existing architectures made more environmentally sustainable? Or do these become something other as they engage with an environmental agenda? Where does one draw the line between those architects who have allowed their previous strategies to be sufficiently modified by environmental concerns to achieve an acceptable level of energy efficiency, and those who have not; between those who have addressed environmentally sustainable operation exclusively, those who have addressed the expression of the relation between nature and architecture exclusively, and those who are beginning to address both? Such line-drawing requires criteria for judgement. What could they be, and from where could they be drawn? How is one to decide what is more important in environmental terms – architecture[3] that *expresses* its sustainable condition more successfully than it *operates*[4] sustainably, or vice versa?

In answer, this book suggests three criteria to consider, and to consider with: 'symbiosis', 'differentiation' and 'visibility' (re-presentation). They denote three modes of engagement with environmental design. 'Symbiosis', that is, a more co-operative material relation between building and environment, is a prerequisite for environmental sustainability. All buildings, by law, will eventually be required to meet the levels of energy efficiency now only published as guidelines in this country by the Building Research Establishment (BRE). Within this symbiotic parameter, however, architectures can – and do – maintain their existing identities. The second criterion, 'differentiation', begins to re-form existing forms as the architectural is further influenced by the environmental. The third criterion, 'visibility', suggests the possibility of new forms, or the yoking of certain existing formal experiments to environmental modes of operation. Architects are free to choose the level of intensity at which they engage with environmental design, but increasingly, as environmental legislation arrives from the European Union, engage they must.

---

3. The use here of the word 'architecture', rather than 'building', is quite deliberate. Architecture is both rarer than building, and usually carries intentional meaning. Both these characteristics are crucial to the book's argument.
4. For the sake of economy, I understand 'operate' to include construction, so that the word refers, not just to the building's running, but to building as an operation within the physical environment.

In constructing these criteria, I have relied on contemporary architectural theory as much as on present environmental practice, and am immensely indebted to both. This was both necessary and strategic: currently, those engaged in environmental architecture are critical of theorizing they consider too onanistic to be of any help in their undertaking; and those engaged in experimental theory and practice are dismissive of the lack of any widespread architectural reflexivity within environmental architecture. There is also a more profound and apparently intractable difference between the two groups: those architects involved in environmental design tend to be intellectually and emotionally disposed towards unity, order, continuity, ontology and stability, whether they are arcadians or rationalists. Their models of nature are old ones: in the case of the arcadians, of nature as something animate and powerful, which is to be respected; in the case of the rationalists, of something susceptible to empirical measurement, an unconsciously ironic continuation of the very scientific methods that enabled us to damage the environment in the first place. (Though the means have a general similarity, however, the ends are diametrically opposed: environmental design aspires to co-operation rather than exploitation.) Those architects, critics and theorists characterized as 'avant-garde' (Eisenman, Libeskind, Gehry, Kipnis, Lynn, etc.), whatever that means when 'the new' is immediately commodified, tend to be intellectually and emotionally open to tolerating, if not actively embracing, discontinuity, heterogeneity, fragmentation, complexity and instability. Their model of nature draws heavily on theories of complexity or at least on an interest in going beyond Enclidean geometry, and their architecture tends towards an impatience with the conventionally orthogonal and an unapologetic interest in novel form-making.

It is the intention of this book to examine whether these two partial views of the same reality – the environmental and the aesthetically experimental – are mutually exclusive, matter and anti-matter, or whether they can inform each other to produce a possible model for architecture that exists only embryonically at present, an inclusive architecture that embraces both operation and formal expression within an environmental framework. Without attending to operation, environmentally 'sustainable' architecture fails to qualify as sustainable at all. Without considering expression as well, it will remain, at its least reflexive, 'sustainable building', and at its more reflexive, the by-product of the visibility of various environmental devices, whether traditional or contemporary: stack vents, solar chimneys, buffer zones, etc. The importance of moving beyond this 'accidental visibility' stands in direct proportion to the importance one attaches to the ideological battle between those who respond to environmentalism's moral imperative, and those who resent or reject it. The book is, therefore, a bridging exercise between environmental design and architecture-as-cultural-expression, intended to contribute to the development of a more self-consciously visible environmental practice. Potentially, environmental architecture could occupy much the same ground as the 'New Architecture' of the Modern Movement did, or at least was originally intended to occupy:

Catch phrases like 'functionalism' (die neue Sachlikeit) and 'fitness for purpose = beauty' have had the effect of making [the New Architecture] purely one-sided...[S]uperficial minds do not perceive that the New Architecture is a bridge uniting opposite poles of thought...[T]he aesthetic satisfaction of the human soul...is just as important as the material (Gropius, 1971: 23–24).

The book is divided into four parts. Part 1 consists of three chapters, and seeks to place environmental architecture within a datum of history and theory that includes the contemporary as well as the historical.

Chapter 1 (Defining environmental architecture) governs the rest of the inquiry, and explores in more detail some of the issues touched upon in this introduction. It discusses the present emphasis within environmental design on the building as physical object (achieving acceptable environmental performance) rather than the building as cultural artefact, and asks whether this bias should necessarily be the case. The consequences of broadening the domain to embrace ideas usually considered irrelevant to it are explored here.

Chapter 2 (The 'new' nature and a new architecture) traces architecture's historical relationship with various religious and scientific models of nature, culminating in that currently presented by theories of complexity. Consistent with the argument that environmental architecture has as much, if not more, to learn from the present as it does from the past, the implications for environmental architecture of this new model of nature are explored, implications that challenge our preconceptions about architecture as much as those about nature.

Chapter 3 (A 'post-imperial' modernism?) asks whether the project of modernism is finished, or whether it is moving into another phase. Contained within this is a more specific question about the position of environmentalism within intellectual history. Is it another 'ism' to add to the rest, following the collapse of modernism? Or is it a more mature stage of modernism itself, in which the burden of universal applicability is again taken up, this time with a much more sophisticated acknowledgement of local variation, the recognition of which it depends on for its practical success?

Part 2 of the book consists of two chapters that address historical/theoretical issues raised by environmental design in general, and environmental architecture in particular. Chapter 4 (Ethics and environmental design) examines the environmental challenge to assumptions about the value of the new common to architecture, modernism and consumerism. The new generally requires more energy to produce than the reconstitution of the old. Because of this, what is perceived as a virtue is now recast as ethically questionable. Which is more important, novelty or survival? Is it justifiable to frame the question in such an extreme form? Is it really a question of 'either/or'?

Chapter 5 (Materials and materiality) examines the way in which emphasis on the building as physical object revalues the materiality of architecture more successfully than, say, architectural phenomenology and its poetics of place. Environmentalism gives a different scientific and ethical weight to the act of building, with a new set of social meanings connected to the particular way in which an architectural idea is embodied.

Part 3 of the book is devoted to suggesting criteria by which to identify – and produce – environmental architecture, that is, to identify existing production, and produce more ideologically effective work. These criteria are acceptable in their totality only if one accepts that environmental design can and should be developed in this direction. The three criteria are examined in two chapters. Chapter 6 (Rules of engagement) is devoted to their historical sources and cultural implications, and Chapter 7 (Doing it) to the case studies that embody one or more of the suggested criteria. It is the intention with these two chapters to bridge the culturally imposed gap between theory and practice, and to develop a theory, a 'way of seeing', in the service of a new practice. So that although theory and practice seem to be artificially divided into separate chapters, the division is there only to be ignored, since, both chapters are hybrids, with practice permeating the chapter on theoretical sources, and theory permeating the chapter on current and future practice.

As mentioned above, the three suggested criteria are 'symbiosis', 'differentiation' and 'visibility'. 'Symbiosis' is the *sine qua non* of environmental architecture. The building must achieve a reactive, rather than oppositional, relation to the environment, replacing or supplementing fossil fuel-driven technologies with renewable energy-driven ones, and/or passive environmental design techniques. The cultural and environmental implications of the range of strategies available are examined in Chapters 6 and 7.

The criterion of 'differentiation' is posed as a question: if, within the universal end of achieving symbiosis between built and natural environments, the adoption of vernacular passive design techniques leads to a formal differentiation between buildings of one climate zone and another, should this differentiation be extended to a conscious expression of cultural variation as well? Post-structuralist thought has urged a recognition of the invalidity of any meta-narrative, architectural or otherwise. Does the meta-narrative of environmentalism escape this censure by being founded on difference, on a multiplicity of versions and applications of itself? If the ends are agreed upon only at the most general of levels, does the fragmentation of means save it from the naive oversimplification of other meta-narratives? Can it be, in other words, as general *and* particular as, say, psychoanalysis, rather than simply as general as, say, Marxism? The question is explored in both Chapters 6 and 7, through architectural examples that demonstrate a variety of built responses to this question.

The criterion of 'visibility' addresses both the need for environmental architecture to become more self-consciously visible at this stage in its development, and possible models for accomplishing this. These models, which are the product of looking to nature conceptually rather than operationally, are deliberately provocative, standing as they do outside not only the formal concerns, but the ethical framework of most architects presently developing environmental architecture. The ideas and the architecture presented in this section are thus a means of challenging both sides of this yoking together: those who privilege the environmentally utilitarian and those who privilege the conceptual.

Part 4 consists of one chapter, entitled ComplexCity. This chapter cannot begin to do justice to such a vast and proliferating subject. It is restricted, therefore, to looking at ways in which the new models of nature have a bearing, not only on contemporary architectural theory and practice, but also, potentially, on sustainable urban development. Historical precedents and contemporary examples that seek to contain and control growth are contrasted with new ideas of self-organization. Intervention is contrasted with a biology-driven *laissez-faire* approach that is, in part at least, a reaction against the failures of modernist interventions in the city.

On one level, the content of this book should be of no lasting value. It is predicated on the danger of continued fossil fuel use and overexploitation of natural resources. This will either change or end in environmental – and social – meltdown. We are in a transitional phase, the outcome of which will be influenced, not by ruminations such as this, but by new sustainable technologies becoming profitable enough quickly enough for us to change direction in time, as the political will to do this before the economic benefits are clear is conspicuously lacking. It is against this background of environmental convulsion that ideas about the role and importance of architecture must be weighed, and necessarily be found wanting.

On a deeper level, the content of this book may last a little longer, as it addresses, through the lens of architecture, a larger cultural debate between a definition of liberty as consumer choice, and of ethics as an obligation to the health – perhaps even the survival – of the community; between a view of progress as unsustainable, and of sustainability as unprogressive, and, at its most fundamental, between those who look forward and those who look back. In seeking to address both sides, this book may fail to reach either. Nevertheless, it's still better to wave, in the hope not too many of us will drown.

PART ONE

1 DEFINING ENVIRONMENTAL ARCHITECTURE

It may be true that one has to choose between ethics and aesthetics, but whichever one chooses, one will always find the other at the end of the road.
Jean-Luc Godard

Environmental architecture is currently more widely referred to as 'sustainable architecture', and was formerly more widely referred to as 'green architecture'. The vagueness and ambiguity of the word 'sustainable' makes the term 'sustainable architecture' equally vague and ambiguous. There are, after all, many forms of sustainability – economic, political and social, as well as environmental – and what is 'sustainable' for one group is not necessarily sustainable for another. 'Social sustainability', for example, could apply equally to societal organization that permits the continuation of a status quo, or to the universal provision of the necessities of life which would disrupt the status quo. 'Economic sustainability', within the context of architecture, could refer to a client's profit margin or to a regulation of property speculation. The term 'sustainable' is, therefore, unstable, largely because of the instability of point of view. The car, as currently powered, is economically sustainable, but environmentally, and often socially, unsustainable. To qualify as thoroughly 'sustainable', the car would have to be environmentally and socially, as well as economically, sustainable. In fact, environmental sustainability, that is, our treating the environment in such a way as to perpetuate its health and consequently our own, is often portrayed by its opponents as a threat to economic and social sustainability, in that it criticizes many existing environmentally harmful industries, and therefore threatens jobs.

When applied to architecture, the term 'sustainable' currently refers to environmental sustainability. Swept up in the concern for the environment, however, is an accompanying concern for social sustainability, as this implies public health and a fairer distribution of physical resources and physical risks. Economic sustainability, in the sense of value for money or return on investment, is also implicit within environmental sustainability, and increasingly easy to demonstrate with built examples. Unpacking some of the meanings in the first half of the term 'sustainable architecture' does not render it transparent, however, as it refers not to one, but to a spectrum of architectures, from the traditional vernacular (which tends to be environmentally sustainable by default), to existing-architectures-made-more-sustainable, to environmental determinism, to those few architects who are pushing environmental design into reflexivity, that is, into self-conscious expression of its more symbiotic relation with the natural environment. Though all these architectures are party to a new contract between nature and architecture, only those at the reflexive end of the spectrum are concerned with representing, as well as enacting this.

Those already involved in 'sustainable architecture' maintain that the distinction 'sustainable' is temporary, as one day all architectures will be environmentally sustainable. The question is, will existing-architectures-made-more-sustainable, modernist and post-modernist, be able to remain as they are, or will they inevitably be re-formed by the exigencies of environmental design? Contrary to popular misconception, this is presently the choice of the architect. I say 'presently' because at the moment rigorous environmental performance targets are largely voluntary. If, or rather when, they become both compulsory and demanding, it may be harder to avoid their affecting the design. An architect like Mario Cucinella (Plate 1 and Fig. 1.1) chooses to keep his environmentalism discreet; his office building in Recanati, Italy, for example, is a variation on the theme of the elegant modernist glass box. Michael Hopkins combines environmental design and contextualism, as in the Inland Revenue Headquarters in Nottingham (Plate 2). Short Ford Associates, on the other hand, chose to push the marriage of environmentalism and historicism to a flamboyant and highly self-conscious extreme in the Queens Building at De Montfort University, Leicester (Plate 3 and Fig. 1.2). Different again is Emilio Ambasz, who chooses to pursue an architecture that both expresses and enacts a symbiotic relation between built and natural environments (Plate 4). Environmental architecture, in other words, is environmental architecture*s*, a plurality of approaches with some emphasizing performance over appearance, and some, appearance over performance.

Affecting the architect's choice will be the degree to which energy efficiency and economy of means are a greater priority than any of the others involved in the design process. If they are the most important consideration, then the architecture will inevitably reflect its supremacy

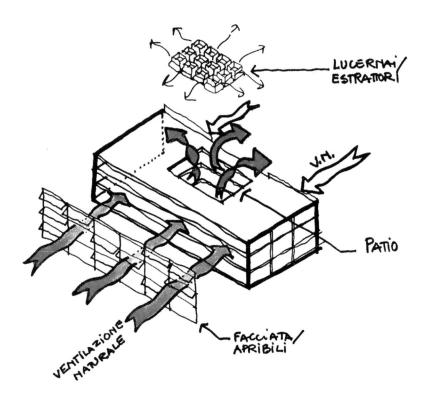

Fig. 1.1
iGuzzini Illuminazione Headquarters, Recanati: diagram of natural ventilation system, MCA.

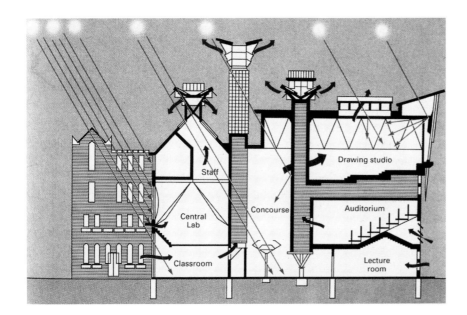

Fig. 1.2
Queens Building, De Montfort University,
Leicester: section showing environmental
strategy, Short Ford Associates.

– in configuration, in choice of materials, in techniques and technologies employed. If it is secondary to other considerations, like an established architectural identity or a dialogue with architectural history, then it will not be allowed to dominate design decisions. One of the reasons the architectural expression of environmental sustainability has not been universally welcomed in environmental circles is that representing a new contract between nature and architecture does not in any way imply the architect has successfully signed up to it. In other words, the building may speak of a new regard for nature-as-model and still operate in an entirely conventional way, guzzling fossil fuels. Frank Gehry's non-linear, snakeskin-clad designs (Plate 5), or Peter Eisenman's explorations of topography and tectonic plates (Fig. 1.3) may represent such an engagement, but this interest is not extended to renegotiating the material relation between such architecture and nature. In other words, the imitation remains aesthetic instead of expanding to include operation as well – at least so far. In what may be a turning point in the relation of such non-linear architecture to the materiality of nature, Greg Lynn and Michael McInturf have designed a visitors' centre for the Austrian Mineral Oil Company in Schwechat, Austria (Figs. 1.4–5) that not only incorporates photovoltaic panels on its roofs, but claims to expose them to maximum solar radiation through the very thing that damns such designs in the eyes of many: their formal novelty.

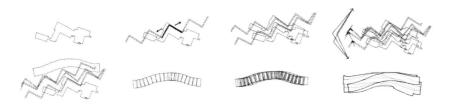

Fig. 1.3
Aronoff Centre for Design and Art,
University of Cincinnati: shifts in plan,
Eisenman Architects.

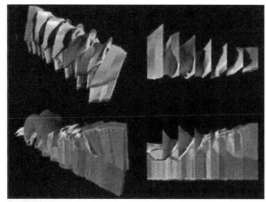
Fig. 1.4 (a)

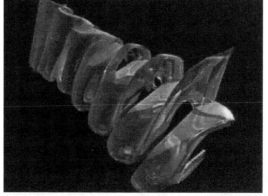
Fig. 1.4 (b)

Fig. 1.5 (a)

Figs. 1.4–5
Visitors' Reception, Austrian Mineral Oil Company, Schwechat, Austria, Greg Lynn, GLFORM.

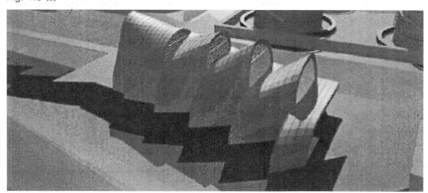
Fig. 1.5 (b)

To reverse the equation, then: can and should a concern with expression be included with operation in the development of environmental architectures, or is it an energy-expensive irrelevance? Even outside sustainability, a discussion of aesthetics is difficult, if not impossible: 'Why...when we continue to honour *firmitas* and *commoditas*, do we assiduously avoid *venustas*?' (Bloomer, 1993: 3). Part of the difficulty, surely, is 'the strong relation between beauty and power' (Bloomer, 1993: 3), the historical power of an establishment able to dictate what it is permissible to consider beautiful. To be cultivated is, since the Greeks, to be a member of an élite educated to recognize the beautiful in permitted places: in certain sites of cultural production, in certain human beings, in certain aspects of nature.

Fig. 1.6
Infants' School, Crosara, Italy, Synergia.

The concept of the sublime so expanded aesthetics, or 'judgements of taste' (Baumgarten), that it became more and more difficult to discuss such judgements and assume there was both comprehension of, and consensus on, one's judgement. Beauty, since the Greeks, had integrity. It was whole, bounded, coherent, harmonious and true:

For Aristotle, the beautiful object is the one which has the ideal structure of an object; it has the form of a totality...clear and distinct...Any addition or subtraction from the object would ruin its form (Cousins, 1994: 61).

This indeed is Alberti's definition of beauty: a composition that would be incomplete and therefore unharmonious if an element of its composition were removed. This harmony was important because it reflected the divine order of the heavens, which was also readable in nature. Beauty and divinity were traditionally linked, which is why beauty and truth were linked both from the classical world until at least the nineteenth century. The perfect order of the beautiful object represented a truth about the universe: that it too is ordered perfectly – by God. As in Keats' 1820 poem *Ode to a Grecian Urn*:

When old age shall this generation waste,
Thou [the urn] shalt remain, in midst of other woe
Than ours, a friend to man, to whom thou say'st,
'Beauty is truth, truth beauty,' – that is all
Ye know on earth, and all ye need to know.

The shock of claims that the category of the aesthetic could also be applied to the amorphous and chaotic aspects of nature – storms, mountain ranges, the sea – must have been intense when they were first made. For Mark Cousins, the admission of the sublime – the inchoate – into aesthetic discourse does not negate the equation of beauty with totality; the totality is merely shifted from what is beheld (the coherent object) to the beholder (the coherent subject, contemplating the incoherent from a distance safe enough to preserve the subject as a totality). To the less subtle observer, however, what changed with the emergence of the sublime as a category was what was visible: the inclusion of the hitherto not-beautiful within aesthetics, and the subsequent collapse of the category itself. So that in suggesting the aesthetic as worthy of consideration within environmental design, one cannot conclude that 'beautiful buildings' will necessarily result, that is, buildings that are beautiful according to traditional definitions of closure, order and totality. The aesthetic can and does contain the 'sublime' as well as the 'beautiful' within the present plurality. The architecture of deconstruction, of folding, of non-linearity are three of its embodiments, and are found 'ugly', that is, 'out of place' (Cousins, 1994: 61), by those who view the 'place' of architecture – and what has a place within architecture – traditionally.

As beauty became more and more disassociated from a divine order, it was viewed as less and less necessary a part of the Vitruvian triad, an attribute superfluous to requirements. Whereas the relation between form and some kind of practical function, whether structural or programmatic, remained safely within the realm of necessity, the relation between form and not-function did not. An excessiveness began to haunt architectural expression, which for some came to constitute beauty:

The Vitruvian triad has always put beauty in a...condition of necessity, but it is not. It is something displaced...Beauty really summarises aura and excess (Eisenman, 1993: 131).

Interestingly, this view of beauty as exceeding the bounds of necessity can find its legitimation in nature just as easily as the Aristotelean definition, which sees beauty as a necessary part of the divine and natural order:

the living world shows a multiplicity of forms that cannot be explained by any possible need for the preservation of the species. But it is a characteristic of life, of plasmatic substance, the unmistakable stamp borne by the shape of a species, a stamp that can show excess...It is the form that is there simply for its own sake and thus represents the essence of the self (Speidel, 1991: 19).

Within environmental terms, it is the moving of beauty from the realm of necessity into the realm of excess that brings it into conflict with environmental ethics, and it is one of the contentions of this book that aesthetic pleasure, if not conventional 'beauty', not only can, but should be returned to the realm of necessity, and so be contained within, or at least compatible with, environmental ethics.

This is already the case at the arcadian end of environmental architecture, insofar as nature is both good and beautiful. Culture-as-beauty is conceivable within this view only as it imitates the beauty of nature. Hence the devotion to 'natural' settings and 'natural' materials at this end of the spectrum, and a championing of traditional vernacular architecture. This construct is of no help in admitting much contemporary architectural practice within the parameters of environmental architecture. Too much of the present plurality of architectures, sustainable or not, stands outside the traditional definition of beauty. Instead, they must be judged as producing in the receiver – or not – a certain 'aesthetic pleasure', a much more liberal category than beauty. This pleasure, which ostensibly has no purpose but to be itself, is a quality architects pursue without naming it, again whether they are also pursuing environmental sustainability or not. Architects like Mario Cucinella are quite relaxed about the degree to which their designs will achieve optimum environmental performance. For them, design is more than environmental design, and 'the environment' is more than a set of energy exchanges; it is also a cultural formation. Sergio Los, on the other hand, while not a determinist, is much more exigent environmentally (Fig. 1.6). He is impatient with architecture that is always 'asking for visibility', and paying an environmental price as a consequence. For him, the first commandment is, 'Don't waste shapes'.[1] The term 'waste' is loaded, however. It is this very 'waste', this excess, which constitutes beauty for some. And conversely most architects, indeed most people, consider beauty 'necessary' to their lives immediately their 'bellies are full'.

Even on a utilitarian level, is 'shape' (or form) a useful environmental yardstick? The Phileban blocks of mainstream modernism, or the International Style functionalism that preceded it certainly did not 'waste shapes', but nor, as built, were they environmentally sustainable. Los has in mind the arbitrary complexities of deconstruction, which have been pursued with unapologetic 'visibility'. But this pursuit, surely, is culturally, if not environmentally legitimated? The desire for visibility, for identity, is present historically in almost all high architecture. This is, surely, part of the role of architecture? It once gave us highly visible palaces and churches; it now gives us highly visible palaces of culture. Are the complex forms of Frank Gehry in the Bilbao Guggenheim Museum or Peter Eisenman in the Aronoff Centre really a 'waste of shapes'? Perhaps their very complexity could one day contribute to successful environmental performance. Environmental design can push the architect towards a high degree of formal differentiation in pursuit of a climatically mediating building envelope. Is it beyond the bounds of

1. Sergio Los in a lecture given to the Energy and Environment Programme of the Architectural Association, 25 February 1998.

possibility that the forms which now appear arbitrary could one day be grounded in a serious consideration of the building-as-environmental-response as well as cultural artefact? Is complexity in and of itself unsustainable, or is it merely that the computer programs presently used to predict environmental performance are still too crude to model anything but the rectilinear and the simple? Nature is complex. Why shouldn't an architecture once again modelled on that nature be equally complex, not only in operation, but in form?

Again, one is forced back upon the necessity of drawing a line between the environmentally acceptable and unacceptable. Where does the line lie in architecture? And how much of what is culturally acceptable, at least within the culture of architecture itself, is environmentally unsustainable? Environmental design works with climate rather than against it, using available air and/or earth and/or water to cool, and solar radiation and recovered heat to warm. An ever-increasing range of techniques and technologies have been either uncovered or discovered to achieve 'low energy' buildings, that is, buildings consuming a low amount of fossil fuel relative to conventional buildings of the same size and function. Many of the techniques are traditional, some of the technologies highly advanced, and choices between the poles of tradition and innovation are not necessarily made for purely environmental reasons. There is an ideological agenda driving an architect who opts for an earth roof over one loaded with photovoltaics (silicon cells that convert solar radiation into electricity). Environmental design has its own logic, much of it ethically driven. Those architects rigorous enough to follow this logic to its conclusion tend towards an environmental determinism, some of it quite elegant, in which form and strategy are kept as simple as possible. For them, it would be unethical to do otherwise.

In what is probably still the best known and most widely disseminated book on the subject, Brenda and Robert Vale's *Green Architecture*, the authors develop a form of 'green utilitarianism' that places environmental design within a clear moral framework. The Vales take as a paradigm the cabin in the woods built by the nineteenth-century American Transcendentalist Henry David Thoreau, described in his book *On Walden Pond*. Thoreau says: '[T]hey can do without architecture who have no olives nor wines in the cellar' (Vale, 1991: 12). The Vales comment:

Thoreau's recognition of the subservience of art to the equitable access to resources, so that all may be adequately fed and sheltered, must underlie any green approach to architecture (Vale, 1991: 12).

Thoreau's injunction carries certain implications about architecture that the Vales then echo when they call for 'the subservience of art to the equitable access to resources'. The first implication is that the definition of architecture is the Ruskinian one of art added to building, rather than of art (beauty) as an essential component of the Vitruvian triad. Thoreau does not say 'they can do without *shelter* who have no olives nor wines in the cellar', but 'they can do without *architecture*'. The two are not synonymous. Architecture is excess. To Ruskin, acceptable excess; to many environmental designers, unacceptable excess. The second implication is that art is not necessary to life the way shelter is. Shelter is on the same level of necessity as food (it is the 'cellar' where the food is stored); architecture (as art) is not. Furthermore, everyone must have shelter before we embellish it with the art of architecture. The degree to which the built environment is sustainable is therefore the degree to which it manages to adequately shelter every man, woman and child on the planet, and this sheltering is not the province of architecture. This 'green utilitarianism' seems to require either that we put the art of architecture to one side until all are sheltered, or redefine architecture exclusively *as* shelter. Either way, the conventional view of architecture as shelter *and* art, or at least artful shelter, is lost. It is the same kind of thinking which condemns the 'waste of shapes', and poses a direct challenge to the priorities of most architects. There is an important point here, but one that concerns building in general rather than architecture in particular, and that is the environmental unsustainability of almost all 'shelter'. The built fabric, as it presently stands in a city like London or New York, is haemorrhaging energy. Architecture's contribution to rendering this more sustainable lies less in its commitment to 'adequacy' than to being exemplary, and thus by necessity, visible.

The question, then, is not whether the art of architecture carries any value within the parameters of environmentalism, but whether environmental architecture can afford *not* to value the art of architecture. Can such an architecture be culturally, as well as environmentally, sustainable without it? After all, the 'environment' is more than just the biosphere, into which we must now fit or die. It is also the 'built environment', a cultural as well as a physical entity. Can architects pursuing sustainability afford to address only the environmental aspect of the built environment when it is qualitative as well as quantitative? There is not, and probably never will be, a voice to prescribe for an 'Environmental Movement' the way Le Corbusier prescribed for the Modern Movement, concentrating in the equivalent of the 'Five Points' a similarly rich mix of agendas, experiments and technologies in order to bring them to the forefront of cultural consciousness. Sustainable pluralism will no doubt continue to pursue universal environmental ends through a variety of stylistic and technical means. Nevertheless, the bringing into full cultural consciousness of this variety is long overdue. Prejudice against the potential of environmental architecture, let alone its present production, is still widespread, even in countries like England, where its practices are entering the mainstream.

The range of strategies available to those engaged in environmental architecture is rarely appreciated by those outside it, many of whom caricature the part as the whole. They view 'environmental architecture', like 'green architecture' before it, as part of yet another 'back to nature' movement in which we all weave our own clothes and villages. For such sceptics, 'environmental architecture' connotes a narrowing of horizons, an abdication of ambition and imagination, and a self-imposed restriction to a palette of twigs and thatch. There are, certainly, people within the spectrum of environmental practice, the Permaculturists, for example (Mollison, 1996), who repudiate modernity, and, usually, the city, but they represent one view among many. Environmentalism, like any narrative, from Marxism to feminism, is a broad church, with many different 'sects' within it. The majority of those pursuing sustainability in architecture would fail to recognize themselves in an anti-modern description. Indeed, these architects could be more accurately described as developing a form of 'post-imperial' or 'post-instrumental' modernism; one that achieves a much more calibrated relationship with a nature recognized as highly differentiated as well as universal.

The social and environmental agendas of 'green utilitarianism' are framed in the languages of ethics and of crisis: the whole world is homeless; the whole globe is warming; what are you doing about it? The moral superiority of an architecture defined solely in terms of necessity poses a challenge to those who are as concerned with form as they are with environmental crisis. Should they, and the sceptics outside who share these concerns, be dismissed as hopelessly in love with 'the plunge backward,...the foundering in the "happy era" of bourgeois *Kultur*' (Tafuri, 1987: 63)? Or is it possible to reconcile ethics and aesthetics outside of an environmental functionalism, in which use and expression are, as nearly as possible, one? Is the greatest good for the greatest number purely a material good, or is the pleasure to be had from the built environment not as important as the pleasure to be had from the natural one? Isn't this pleasure, which inspires at least some of us to protect nature, equally important as an inspiration to protect built culture? Is the plastic and/or chromatic invention of Gothic or Mannerist or Baroque architecture, or indeed contemporary non-linear architecture, not as worthy of value as the extravagant plastic and chromatic invention of nature – the blinding variety of tropical birds, the insane diversity of bugs? Or is the superabundance of natural invention to be similarly excluded from 'the necessary'? If biodiversity is so precious, why isn't built diversity?

This is hardly the first time that ethics and aesthetics have been presented as opposing domains. Kierkegaard's part-confessional, part-philosophical book *Either/Or* (1843) is an anatomy of this opposition, its very title suggesting the impossibility of reconciliation between the two. The character 'A' is a young man, who, in the first volume, particularly 'Diary of a Seducer', extols the aesthetic life. In the second volume, the character 'B', an older man, defends the ethical life in a series of letters to A. Readers are to choose for themselves which argument seems to them stronger: either/or. This choice is not in itself a moral one. The aesthetic is not evil to ethics' good. The choice is whether to view life in terms of moral choices or not.[2] What is important here is the recasting of the aesthetic, not as detached from 'seeing life in terms of moral choices', but detached from seeing those moral choices as universally legitimate and rationally legitimizable.

For Gianni Vattimo, on the other hand, this aesthetic, and for him postmodern, denial of the possibility of universal legitimation, and the recognition of the equal validity of the Other – other cultures, other values – does not negate ethics, but *is* an ethics in its own right:

2. 'The choice between the ethical and the aesthetic is not the choice between good and evil, it is the choice whether or not to choose in terms of good and evil' (MacIntyre, 1996: 40).

The notion of 'beautiful' in this instance cannot be referred back to Kant's aesthetics, inasmuch as beauty is not defined by objective criteria...What, then, is the criterion?...[T]he only way of finding criteria consists in appealing to memory...to...indications we have inherited from the past (Vattimo, 1988: 75).

This sounds dangerously close to a rationale for historicism, but what Vattimo is endeavouring to do is replace the metaphysical concept of beauty as a legitimation for the architectural project with 'the voices of different communities, speaking not only from the past, but from the present too' (Vattimo, 1988: 76). Beauty as traditionally defined in the West is replaced by 'aesthetic value', and wholeness by fragmentation. Architecture that has aesthetic value is architecture legitimated through its expression of this 'multiplicity' of communities, through its aesthetic expression of an ethical recognition of the Other. Vattimo's recasting of beauty as 'aesthetic value' allows the aesthetic to re-enter the world through the ethos of community. The point is reinforced, albeit unwittingly, by Jerome Stolnitz in an essay called 'The Aesthetic Attitude'. This he defines as 'disinterested and sympathetic attention to, and contemplation of, any object of awareness whatever, for its own sake alone' (Stolnitz, 1998: 80). The thrust of this definition is one of non-instrumentality, of viewing the Other as an end in him (it) self, rather than a means to our ends, precisely what Kant defined as the *ethical* attitude. The history of western ethics is the history of the extension of this attitude to a wider and wider selection of Others: from the chief or king to the aristocracy, then to all landowning men, then to all men, then to women, then to children, and now to nature, or more precisely, the biosphere, the 'thin film of life' that covers the planet. Nature, from an ethical and aesthetic point of view, should now be given the same 'disinterested and sympathetic attention...for its own sake alone'. The value of nature as a thing-in-itself is something the art of architecture is as capable of recognizing as environmental design is. So that from whichever direction architects begin, they can finish by including both as different aspects of the same non-instrumental attitude towards nature. This overlapping of the aesthetic and the ethical in their ways of viewing the world is of vital importance if the aesthetic is to be restored to the realm of necessity, rather than seen as an optional extra.

Although one would not want to repeat the mistake of the Modern Movement in thinking architecture can create social change, there is a case to be made for it being able to contribute to social change by making its emergence visible. This visibility could encourage further, or more rapid change, as self-conscious form is given to less conscious cultural shifts. Architecture cannot speak about such change. It is a visual not a verbal language, with all the crudeness that suggests. Nevertheless, forms can have extraordinary power – to interrogate, provoke and inspire. To dismiss this power as irrelevant to the present ideological battle is to fight with one hand tied. There is no reason, if most architecture serves the status quo, why other architecture cannot serve as critiques of the status quo:

'counterhegemony' is to be understood in purely superstructural terms, as the elaboration of a set of ideas, countervalues, cultural styles, that are...anticipatory in the sense that they 'correspond' to a material, institutional base that has not yet 'in reality' been secured by political revolution itself (Jameson, 1985: 69).

Current environmental architecture could certainly be viewed as 'strategic pockets...within the older system' (Jameson, 1985: 70), and it is my view that they can be helped to become the norm if an alliance is effected between ethics and aesthetics, content and form. The environmental project within architecture needs the self-consciousness of 'art' as much as any new narrative does. From this point of view is not the art of architecture that is the luxury, but the attempt to keep environmental design either purely utilitarian or a counter-culture cult. Those determined to drive buildings down to some bedrock of 'thing-ness', in which only certain of their aspects are significant, miss the point that however simply it is framed, environmental architecture is also ideological – in some forms, a counter-ideology to the prevailing consumerist one, in others, co-opted by the political and economic establishment.

By 'ideology', I don't mean a Marxist 'false consciousness', but 'the process of production of meanings, signs and values in social life' (Eagleton, 1991: 1). To ignore this dimension is to ignore architecture's role in the above process, in this case, the role of environmental architecture in a critique of the still dominant 'meanings, signs and values' of consumerism, as it is manifested within architecture itself. This critique will be successful only if it wins over more people than it alienates, and it will win over only if architecture is allowed to be 'art' as well as shelter. In order to produce forms capable of communicating the environmental enterprise inspirationally, acknowledgement must be made, difficult for utilitarians, of the power of aesthetic pleasure. It was the aesthetic, as well as the economic and social implications of the new building technology that drove the Modern Movement at the beginning of the twentieth century, and it is the aesthetic as well as the economic and social implications of 'post-imperial' building technologies that could potentially drive an 'Environmental Movement' at the end of it. It is not 'shelter' that is going to address this aesthetic – and ideological – dimension, any more than it is 'shelter' which is developing the application of advanced environmental building technologies.

The whole point of the environmental project is, surely, to transform mainstream society. Nothing less will be effective. This means, of course, that it will often be pursued in ways unacceptable to radicals, ways that seek to redirect, rather than dismantle, the status quo. But perhaps this too is necessary. The status quo is the cause of our environmental problems. Its modification is achievable. Its eradication is not – unless it destroys itself, a distinct possibility according to some environmentalists. In the built environment this kind of redirection can be furthered by architects, not only specifying and designing the building's fabric and services in particular ways, but also expressing architecture's capacity to transform itself. This is its ideological message: not that architecture can transform society, but that it can transform itself, and as architecture does, so, perhaps, can other forms of production.

At the beginning of the twentieth century, Le Corbusier warned, 'architecture or revolution'. At the end of the century, we know 'architecture' doesn't have the power to be an equivalent term to 'reform'. So we can't say in the current context, 'architecture or pollution'. The ideas developed in architecture for the benefit of the built environment won't 'save the world', but they may help save the built environment. In so doing, architectural practice could regain a moral and practical authority it hasn't had for thirty years. What is clear from the work of those already inhabiting this 'both/and' domain of ethics and aesthetics is the groundedness of an architecture that holds both environmental design and architectural expression in tension, neither privileged over the other. This is vital if the term 'environmental architecture' (as architectures-in-general) is to be anything but an oxymoron.

2 THE 'NEW' NATURE AND A NEW ARCHITECTURE

2.1 Introduction

One cannot pursue a discussion of a new contract between architecture and nature without examining the extraordinarily complex cluster of meanings associated with the word 'nature'. Indeed, one cannot discuss nature free of quotation marks without examining the word itself, its difference from the word 'environment', and its use in the binary opposition 'nature/culture'. There is, for example, the nature that is outside us – the biosphere – and that which is inside us – 'human nature'. We refer to the Grand Canyon and to Hyde Park as nature. We say certain acts are not 'natural', and speak authoritatively about what 'nature intended'. Ecologists describe an empirically measured nature, and poets and explorers used to celebrate conquering 'her'. It is an amorphous word that assumes an intuitive understanding of the particular way in which a speaker is using it.[1] This chapter will confine itself primarily to a discussion of nature in terms of architecture, and concentrate on another model of nature from the one classical physics presents us with: complexity. For the first time in our history, we are able, technically, to begin to imitate nature's complexity on an operational level. What has been for centuries implicit in the making of our landscapes and the selective breeding of plants and livestock – that the distinction between nature and culture is often impossible to make – is now explicit. This blurring exists both in our continued interventions in nature – plants that grow plastic, cloned sheep – and in our 'interventions in culture' – submarines that move like fish, robots that learn like humans. Architecture, which has always held an ambiguous position between nature and culture, is moving towards an even greater ambiguity as it pursues environmental sustainability.

2.2 Ceci n'est pas une pipe

To talk about 'environmental architecture', that is, architecture which contributes to allowing nature to physically sustain us, we first have to

---

1. Kate Soper's book *What is Nature?* (1995) is a generous and rigorous account of the contemporary debate.

define what we mean by nature. It is two things: a material reality and a cultural construct. The two exist in parallel, but they are not, and never can be, the same thing. As material reality, nature exists as both that which is outside us and that which contains us. It was here before we emerged, and it will be here when we submerge. It is the given, both stable and unstable – trees, uranium, the weather, tectonic plates, DNA, the carbon-based universe, etc. This definition of nature-as-given comes down clearly on the side of those who argue that there is an objective phenomenon outside our various views of it. A phenomenon that measurably suffers when we inflict too much damage on it, that gives up some of its secrets to those who rigorously search for them, and that is independent of our views of it, whether scientific or religious.

It is the view of nature as measurable and quantifiable that is referred to in the term 'environment', material surroundings that include not just the 'natural' environment – bees, trees, sky, etc. – but the built environment as well, with its own measurable physical properties, its own atmospheres, its own micro-climates. It is these two domains that the non-vitalist version of ecology[2] seeks to understand, as they affect our activities and we affect theirs. Like all science, environmental science aspires to a position of objectivity. Nature as cultural construct – religious, artistic, historical – is not of interest to it, although the measurable relationship between us and the material world is also a construct, and contributes to the mutation of cultural constructs. The connection between temperatures inside and outside a building may not stir anyone's passions, but that between the ozone layer and our industrial processes certainly does. Vast vested interests are at stake, industrial and political, and a change in practice is expensive in many ways. Any weight the environmental argument carries derives, not from ethics, but from science: the environmental debate is predicated on our ability to quantify what 'we' are doing to 'it'. Its relevance for those vested interests lies solely in the economic implications of what 'we' are doing to 'it'.

In this 'realist' view, nature is that 'to whose laws we are always subject, even as we harness them to human purposes, and whose processes we can neither escape nor destroy' (Soper, 1995: 155–56). It is not possible for even the most committed 'idealist', for whom nature is an entirely cultural construct, to ignore a dimension of reality to nature independent of his or her linguistic overlays:

[I]t is not language that has a hole in its ozone layer; and the 'real' thing continues to be polluted and degraded even as we refine our deconstructive insights on the level of the signifier (Soper, 1995: 151).

On the other hand, only the cultural constructs of nature are truly knowable, because we make them. Historically, we have always

---

2. The word 'ecology' was coined by the German biologist Ernst Haeckel (1834–1919) from the ancient Greek 'oikos', meaning household. Haeckel himself held to the vitalist view of nature as alive, a view most recently elaborated by certain interpreters of James Lovelock's 'Gaia theory'. Other ecologists view this vitalism as unjustified, and pursue ecology as an empirical science. For an appraisal of Haeckel's vitalism and its links to nationalism and Nazism, see Pepper (1999: 184–88).

projected different interpretative models onto nature: it was made by God in six days; it is the product of the Big Bang; it is a dangerous harpy; it is a bountiful mother; it works like clockwork; it is permanently on the edge of chaos; it is what we should return to; it is what we have evolved away from; it is full of gods and goddesses; it is an inanimate source of raw materials. Kate Soper, however, in her book *What is Nature?*, warns realists against being as exclusive as idealists. The latter's refusal to accept the autonomy of the unknowable (unknowable as a thing-in-itself), should not provoke a refusal in the former to ignore nature-as-construct, a marked tendency in much environmental analysis. Both realist and idealist views of nature are essential to a fully developed environmentalism, as it is our cultural constructs of nature that encourage or inhibit various behaviours towards it.

Both views are also essential to an architecture that is intent upon establishing a new relationship with nature. As our powers of observation have improved through improvements in the instruments used to do the observing – the telescope, the microscope, the computer – so we have seen more and differently, and our view of nature has changed accordingly. This has caused us to review our position within that nature, and, eventually, the architecture that expresses that position. In, for example, Vitruvius in the first century BC, Alberti in the fifteenth century, Laugier in the eighteenth century, Ruskin in the nineteenth century, Aalto in the early twentieth century and Calatrava in the late twentieth century, the urge is the same: to ground architecture in a particular view of nature. However, their views were, and are, often radically different from each other. There is, first and foremost, the difference between the religious 'top-down' model of nature, and the Darwinian 'bottom-up' model. In the first, order flows from the mind of God down through the Great Chain of Being to the lowliest one-celled organisms. There is a unity in creation because it flows from a single source. In Darwin's model, order arises from one-celled organisms. They evolve into more complex life forms in a state of mutual dependence. The unity lies in the interconnectedness of this bottom-up proliferation. A dynamic, non-teleological model thus replaces the fixed all-at-once-for-all-time model of the Bible. The very idea of an 'ecosystem' is one of parts forming an interactive whole. What links the religious and Darwinian apprehensions of this whole is the idea of pattern, form, and an aesthetic dimension to the empirical.

Today we have our own projections. These take two main forms: the unreconstructed modernist version, in which nature is viewed as a source of raw materials and instrumental knowledge, and the increasingly influential environmental model, in which nature is viewed as a number of almost ungraspably complex interrelated systems in which we are included, and upon which we are, and will always be, dependent. These opposing views are, since the development of complexity theory in the 1960s, united in one new and fundamental way: in neither case can the historically clear distinction between 'nature' and 'culture' any longer be made with conviction, as the two are increasingly perceived as folded into each other. Such is the scale of transformation of nature by culture that the division between nature as that which is given, and culture as the sum total of that which we make, is becoming obsolete at the very moment when environmentalists are demanding we recognize and protect that given. Both are true, and neither is the whole truth.

2.3 All about Eve

The roots of culture have of course always lain in nature, literally, in the way something like agriculture has transformed the wilderness into cultivated fields, and metaphorically, in the way nature has served, for example, as a model for the religious mythology of death and rebirth in the coming of spring after winter. Historically, in the West, this binary – nature/culture – has been bound up with another unequally valued binary – female/male, which may have some bearing on the prevalent perception of environmentalism as 'soft' scientifically and intellectually. That is, nature, in the West, has been seen as female and inferior, and culture has been seen as male and superior. This has had disastrous consequences, for women and nature. In the *Timaeus,* Plato sought to explain the origins and structure of the universe, and in so doing, gendered the explanation, so that the creation of the world and its staggering variety begins with ideal 'Form', and enters the world as material objects through the 'Chora'. Form is described as male, the father of and model for the material object. The Chora is female, 'a kind of womb for material existence' (Gross, 1994: 22), the 'place or space' which functions as receptacle, mother and nurse. For Plato, the abstract ideal Form is superior to the mere container that is the Chora, as the male is superior to the female.

Christianity improved neither the lot of women nor of nature. In the *Book of Genesis,* it was Adam's task to name all living things in the Garden of Eden as a sign of mastery over them. Eve interrupted this work by conversing with a serpent and provoking humankind's expulsion from the Garden. Woman was blamed for the Fall, the fall of nature as much as of 'man', as what was once gentle and immortal became hostile and ultimately fatal. We die, and woman, though bearer and sustainer of life, was condemned as the cause of our mortality. It is not surprising, therefore, that in this view, which has informed western culture since the Middle Ages, woman and nature are conflated:

Women are identified with nature and the realm of the physical...men are identified with the 'human' and the realm of the mental...Whatever is identified with nature and the realm of the physical is inferior to...whatever is identified with the 'human' and the realm of the mental, or conversely, the latter as superior to the former (Warren, 1990: 129–30).

In other words, women are devalued because nature is devalued, and the identification of the former with the latter is no innocent analogy. The female reproductive role ties women to the animal world in a way that men can avoid. Women are literally left 'holding the baby', and 'all she is allowed to do' is artfully transmuted into 'all she can do'. The more this division was enforced, the more empirically true it became, confirming as 'natural' something that was originally a cultural construct.

The outside became the domain of men, and the interior, the domain of women, themselves possessed of 'interiors'. Thus it should come as no surprise to hear, in one of his incarnations, one of the greatest of the architectural modernists, Le Corbusier, impatient with nature when compared with culture, with matter when compared with the mind, with the female when compared with the male: 'Man undermines and hacks at Nature. He opposes himself to her' (Le Corbusier, 1987: 24). Nature, the organic, represents disorder, chaos, unpredictability – those aspects of materiality ignored and devalued by Newtonian science and Cartesian thought and systematically shunned by the Enlightenment, to which Le Corbusier was heir.

The concern, in the later twentieth century, to redress the balance between a female nature and a male culture gave rise, in the 1970s, to a form of environmentalism called 'ecofeminism'. Its adherents, whatever their differences, are united in a common conviction that if nature as well as women had been devalued as a result of the 'logic of domination' (Le Corbusier, 1987: 24), then nature, as well as women, must be revalued, and 'environmentalists and feminists must be allies' (Davion, 1994: 11). The same 'structures of patriarchy' that exploit and oppress women exploit and oppress nature:

[T]hose fighting to save the environment should, as a matter of consistency, be working to overthrow patriarchy, and those working to overthrow patriarchy should be fighting to save the environment. At a conceptual level, these fights are inextricably interconnected (Davion, 1994: 11).

There is a conflict in this enterprise, however.[3] If one is attacking the 'feminizing of nature', then the simultaneous revaluing of both women and nature maintains the very historical equation of women with nature that is under attack. Indeed, some ecofeminists go further, and actively reinforce the connection between women and nature, seeking to celebrate rather than sever it. Women's intuitive, physical connection with 'Mother Earth' is posited as superior to the destructiveness of 'male' instrumental reason, which exploits nature. Ecofeminists and environmentalists may be 'natural' allies, but the ideological contradiction within ecofeminism suggests that other feminists and environmentalists may not be.

The same dilemma is found within architecture: how to break the historical associations between nature and the female, architecture and the male: 'Construction is a sublime male poetry...If civilisation had been left in female hands, we would still be living in grass huts' (Paglia, 1990: 38). The collapse of these binary opposites may in fact happen, not through conscious acts of cultural deconstruction, but through the mutation of the nature/culture binary into undreamed-of hybrids. Without these opposing categories, the identification of nature, and environmentalism, with the devalued female will be much more difficult. In meditating upon the garden, Jennifer Bloomer sees just this complex

---

3. For a more detailed discussion of this, see 'Nature and Sexual Politics' in Soper (1995).

'both/and', in a location where many binaries come together and mix (Plate 6):

In the garden we are in the space of nature and culture, form and matter, concrete and abstract, exterior and interior. And, significantly, we are in a space of the feminine and the masculine in which assignments of value flicker and oscillate in locales both esoteric and mundane (Bloomer, 1996: 22).

Environmental architecture could be viewed as achieving the same kind of inclusiveness as the garden, producing buildings that are as ambiguous and multivalent as the landscapes in which they are placed. For this to happen, however, a much greater awareness of the old divisions and their dissolution is necessary within the practice of environmental design. Even on the operational level, with which so much of it is concerned, there is a resonance to be had from the ability of hardware such as photovoltaics (Plates 7–8) to inhabit the domain of natural process in a way it has never been able to before, enabling buildings to feed off the sun like plants.

2.4 Nature redux

The loss of differentiation between the domains of nature and culture makes defining them in terms of their differences increasingly problematic, even if we see ourselves as separate, and thus different, from nature. Reyner Banham articulates the logical extreme of this modernist view in his introduction to *Theory and Design in the First Machine Age*:

Our accession to almost unlimited supplies of energy is balanced against the possibility of making our planet uninhabitable, but this is balanced, as we stand on the threshold of space, by the growing possibility of quitting our island earth and letting down roots elsewhere (Banham, 1975: introduction).

In other words, that which technology messes up, technology can fix, even if it's a fix of last resort: the abandonment of the planet in spaceships.

Within the modernist framework, the embeddedness of culture in nature can be, and often is, invasive rather than co-operative, a relentless endeavour to control how and what nature produces. Very often what first appeared as a benefit to us later developed into a danger to us, for example, the mutation of animal husbandry into factory farming. So that although there is a blurring of the boundaries between culture and nature in the results of these activities, a distinction is maintained between the actor (culture) and the acted-upon (nature), with the first privileged over the second. It is important to note, however, that the relationship between nature and culture has always been more ambiguous than any generalization could indicate. For example, although building was always intended as shelter – that is, as protection from nature – and although the city became an artificial environment of its own, consuming and often asset-stripping nature, the traditional role of architecture has been to imitate nature in various ways. Imitation is a very different activity from domination, and runs throughout the history of architecture, including the Modern Movement. When the rhetoric of the machine was at its most strident, there were architects like Wright, Neutra, Scharoun and Aalto insisting on nature remaining a model for architecture. Even Le Corbusier, that most eloquent celebrant of the rationality of the machine, could not prevent, at the same time, a traditional regard for nature from erupting into his own work.

For all his talk of it, however, Le Corbusier's view is a universalized one. Nature is 'Nature' with a capital 'N'. It consists of health-giving sunshine, fresh air and trees. As Dorothée Imbert demonstrates in her book *The Modernist Garden in France*, this leaves one with a generalized nature suitable for a new universal architecture, the International Style:

Architecture was placed in what I consider a paysage-type, *a generic landscape framed by calculated openings... (Imbert, 1993: 148).*

Of the five points of a new architecture proposed by Le Corbusier, the first two – pilotis and roof gardens – effaced the imprint of the building and the garden on the surrounding landscape...Once the specific identity of the garden was removed and the landscape typified, all sites became interchangeable (Imbert, 1993: 166).

It was the specificity of different landscapes, different topographies, different climates, and high degree of differentiation in the biosphere, from weather to species, that modernism ignored. Understandably it addressed what we have in common, not what separates us. Nature had value only insofar as it was universal, as the products of the machine were universal, products that were to include buildings.

At the same time, other modernists recognized that this industrial model of universal standardization was inadequate. Aalto was interested in the more complex example nature could set. In his case, it was the extraordinary variety generated from the unit of the cell, in contrast to the monotony of mass production, that he looked to:

Nature herself is the best standardisation committee in the world. But in nature, standardisation is almost exclusively applied to the smallest possible unit, the cell. This results in millions of different combinations that never become schematic...The same path should be followed by standardisation in architecture (Aalto, 1986: 221).

This fragment at first seems to be another modernist imposition of the mechanical metaphor upon nature. And yet, although Aalto's observation is couched in these terms, he is looking *to* nature for guidance, to its subversion of our crude ideas about standardization. For him, this diversity operated at the scale of the room, which for him resembled the organic cell.[4] After all, the word itself is used both biologically and architecturally.

---

4. See Porphyrios (1982).

Aalto's friend, the artist Moholy-Nagy, provided him with the theoretical ammunition to defend his shift within modernism from a law-abiding International Style to an architecture that imitated nature rather than the machine. While teaching at the Bauhaus, Moholy-Nagy wrote a book entitled *von material zu architektur* (1929), in which he was concerned to point out to his students that if they pursued functionalism the correct way, that is, with a comprehensive understanding of task, tools and material, then their designs, 'even without studying a natural model' would nevertheless be 'confirmed as agreeing with nature's own creations' (Moholy-Nagy in Schildt, 1986: 219). In other words, Bauhaus students would find themselves imitating the laws of nature 'naturally', by imitating the way nature 'thinks'. The version of nature imitated, consciously or unconsciously, is nature as 'structures, processes and causal powers that...provide the objects of study of the natural sciences' (Soper, 1995: 155).

Like Moholy-Nagy and Aalto, Richard Neutra dared to suggest that we might be the losers in seeing nature as an imitation of culture (for example, nature-as-clockwork), rather than culture as an imitation of nature. In both cases, 'nature' is a cultural construct, but the first devalues it and the second doesn't:

We have tended to indulge in a crude and naive fragmentation of the world fabric..., reducing life to a jumble of discrete parts...This...may be

Fig. 2.1
Edgar J. Kaufmann Desert House, Palm Springs, California, 1946, Richard Neutra.

a practical hypothesis in coming up with technologies that are transiently useful or impressive, but...the world is not a lifeless machine that can simply be...tinkered with here and there (Neutra, 1989: 33).

Long before chaos theory, Neutra had an intuition of an underlying complexity in nature, which could serve as a model for a more complex and 'natural' way of organizing space that might enrich modernism (Fig. 2.1):

In nature there are flowing transitions and dynamic connections between all phenomena. Only man has imagined an intellectual antithesis, giving everything a...category or classification[5] (Neutra, 1989: 15).

What is of interest in this quote is the distinction Neutra sets up: the 'discrete part' versus the 'flowing transition'. The first is static, the second, dynamic. The first is easy to delineate, because fixed; the second is much more difficult, because fluid. This fluidity is a different aspect to be drawn from nature, an intuition of what science will begin to explore from Einstein onwards, and what a number of architects are now interested in expressing: relativity, instability and complexity. This model bears no resemblance to the nature that classical – and modernist – architecture looked to, which embodied balance, stability and linear order.

2.5 Racinated

The practice of architecture imitating a nature that was itself an imitation of the divine order was developed in writings by Plato and Aristotle, and reached its architectural apogee in the Renaissance, in the writings and designs of Alberti. In Alberti's treatise *On the Art of Building* (1452), beauty was found in a kind of numerology. Those numerical relations arrived at through empirical observation of nature were by far the most dominant, for the natural world was the model for the beauty he sought to create in the built world:

our ancestors learned through observation of Nature herself...Among the odd and even numbers, some are found more frequently in Nature...[T]hese have been adopted by architects when composing parts of their buildings... (Alberti, 1991: 303–34).

What Alberti's architecture imitated was not the material world as such, but the perceived mathematical structure of the material world, the proportions and harmonic ratios that one could see in nature. With this idea, one could include architecture as an art imitating nature, for although it did not depict it (except decoratively), architecture did imitate the proportional laws found there (Fig. 2.2). The sets of harmonic relations found in nature are thus vital for the work of the Renaissance

---

5. This closely parallels Moholy-Nagy's language: 'Harmony does not lie in an aesthetic formula, but in organic, undisruptedly flowing function' (Moholy-Nagy, 1986: 219).

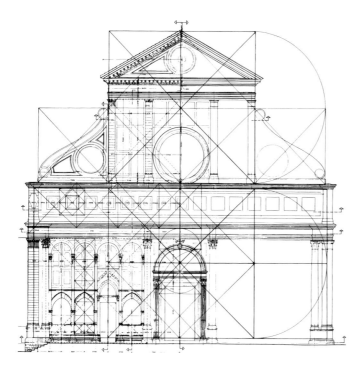

Fig. 2.2
S. Maria Novella, Florence, 1470, Alberti:
elevation showing proportional
relationships.

architect, in particular, the relation of the parts of the human body to the whole: '...the building may be considered as being made up of close-fitting smaller buildings, joined together like members of the whole body' (Alberti, 1991: 8).

What is important is that during the Renaissance, the cultural norm was for people to see themselves as part of nature, not separate and superior. Indeed nature, as a manifestation of the mind of God, could be viewed in this sense as superior to culture, which could only ever be the manifestations of the mind of man. For Alberti and his contemporaries, both art and nature were governed by 'concinnitas', an overarching harmony between the parts and the whole, the ordering principle that keeps numbers – and members – in certain relationships to one another. The desire was to make men's work as 'natural' and inevitable as God's, and as such this integration applied on both a formal and a functional level. In Aristotle, each part was essential to the whole, not only in terms of composition, but also function: '[I]n some way the body exists for the soul, and the parts of the body for those functions to which they are naturally adapted' (Aristotle, 1911: 645).

The ties between God, nature and architecture were loosened by Claude Perrault in the seventeenth century in an act of extraordinary intellectual daring. Claude was the brother of Charles Perrault, one of the founders of the French Royal Academy of Science (1666), which, together with its English counterpart – the Royal Society – under Isaac Newton, was to begin to draw a line between science and religion in the West. In the same spirit, Claude Perrault rejected both ancient Vitruvian and Renaissance Albertian dogma, declaring architecture to be neither given directly by God, nor inferred from a divine order perceivable in nature: 'Man has no proportion and no relation with the heavenly bodies...infinitely distant from us' (Perrault in Perez-Gomez, 1983: 26).

To demonstrate this newly secularized classicism, Perrault then proceeded to develop a new universally applicable proportional system of his own, 'no longer linked with that of a cosmological scheme...' (Perez-Gomez, 1983: 26). It was man-made, or 'arbitrary', as Perrault termed it. Not surprisingly, he was dubbed a 'modern', as opposed to the 'ancients', who clung to the notion of a divinely ordered architecture.

As Newton demonstrated the universal law of gravitation in his *Principia Mathematica* (1687), which reconciled the seemingly immutable motion of the stars with the mutable motions on earth, and Thomas Hobbes (1588–1679) transformed the machine-as-fact into the machine-as-metaphor and imposed it upon nature, and Francis Bacon reduced nature to 'a storehouse of matter', nature ceased to be animated, an end in itself, with its own imperatives. As a result, it began to lose its power as a model for cultural production – in every sphere, that is, except architecture. A century after Newton, at the very time instrumental modernism was coming into its own, the Abbé Laugier was writing a treatise on architecture (*Essai sur l'architecture*, 1753) demonstrating, on no archeological evidence whatsoever, the origins of classical architecture. This purportedly arose from a primitive hut that itself arose directly from nature. In other words, culture was still being validated through nature, or what this eighteenth-century theorist imagined nature to be: a guide for the classical Orders. In the *Essai*, 'the ethical validation for architecture remains the same – that architecture conforms to 'nature' – but the restriction to prosaic materials or...imitation of natural forms...dissolves into...architectural language that is an abstraction' (McClung, 1983: 118). This abstract language consists of 'a vocabulary of specific structural relationships' (McClung, 1983: 118), those between column, entablature and pediment. 'To legitimise neoclassicism as the only proper style' (McClung, 1983: 118), Laugier's primitive hut, made out of columnar trees still rooted in the ground, has a pediment made with their branches, and an entablature made out of still more branches, to give a pure classical architecture of column, not wall.

The little hut which I have...described is the type on which all the magnificences of architecture are elaborated...Never has there been a principle more fruitful in its consequences; with it as a guide it is easy to distinguish those parts which are essential components of an order of architecture from those parts which are only introduced through necessity or added by caprice (Laugier, 1977: 2).

The highly sophisticated neo-classical architecture of eighteenth-century France was not 'natural' in the sense of being primitive or rough. It was natural in the sense that it abstracted organizational principles from a primitive and rough model (the hut), much as Alberti abstracted certain proportional relationships from nature. The thinking is the same in all these examples, however: nature is that which is already there, the source of legitimation for those things which are not already there: the things we make. The more closely culture resembled nature, either literally or metaphorically, the more right it had to exist, because it was following the laws of the (God) given (Plate 9). This was the closest one got to escaping the arbitrary condition of human creation. It was an attempt literally to 'ground' arguments for choosing one option over another in design.

One could use Laugier's 'structural proof' to justify forms of architecture other than classical, of course. Sir James Hall was at pains to demonstrate the 'naturalness', that is the sole legitimacy, of Gothic rather than classical architecture (Fig. 2.3). On a journey through France in 1785, he saw peasants 'collecting the long rods or poles which they make use of to support their vines...It occurred to me that a rustic hut might be constructed from such rods...bearing a resemblance to the works of Gothic architecture' (Hall, 1797: 12). When Hall returned home, he carried out an experiment, building a Gothic church out of ash wood poles and willow rods, tying the rods to the poles and bending the poles towards each other until they touched at the top, and thus arriving at the three main characteristics of Gothic architecture: the clustered column, the pointed arch and the branching roof. The poles rooted and

Fig. 2.3
Sir James Hall, *Origins of Gothic Architecture*, 1797.

sprouted, 'producing leaves...exactly where they occur in stonework' (Hall, 1797: 25). He thus proved, to his own satisfaction at least, that Gothic architecture had wooden (or woodland) origins, and was therefore as natural and unquestionable as its classical rival.

Despite these intellectually dubious exercises, nature continued, and continues, to play a role in the generation of architecture, often in the guise of 'organic architecture'.

[T]he term 'organic analogy'...involves a...metaphorical comparison of works of art with the phenomena of nature, and is concerned with aesthetic qualities rather than with strictly scientific parallels... (Steadman, 1979: 7).

Fig. 2.4
Doric and Ionic orders on the reconstructed Stoa, Athens.

Fig. 2.5
La Sagrada Familia, Barcelona, Gaudi:
decorative shells.

In this sense, the classical orders are 'organic' in their relating of architecture to nature-as-human-body, with Doric columns analogous in their strength and simplicity to the ideal of the male body, and Ionic columns analogous in their delicacy and attenuation to the ideal of the female body, etc. (Vitruvius) (Fig. 2.4). This equation between the 'natural body' and architecture is still there in the twentieth century, with Le Corbusier's 'Modulor'.

The disposition of parts within the whole of any organism is, of course, closely connected to function: the function of the parts and the functioning of the whole. Function in an organism covers every activity from digestion to reproduction to standing up. So that if one moves away from an architecture imitating nature formally (Fig. 2.5 and Plate 10), one can still imitate it by imitating patterns of structure, that is, by imitating the function of 'standing up', something that buildings must also perform successfully. Steadman refers to this as the 'anatomical analogy':

In its most naive expression the anatomical analogy as applied to buildings takes the form of a simple metaphorical comparison of the skeleton of the animal with the supporting structural framework of columns and beams or piers and vaults (Steadman, 1979: 41).

The analogy surfaced as early as J.-R. Perronet's 1770 comparison of the structure of Gothic cathedrals with the skeletons of animals, and was vividly apparent with the advent of modern building materials, which made the structural skeleton a commonplace rather than an exceptional event:

For Le Corbusier..., the traditional load-bearing wall construction of stone is to be compared with the restricting external bony shell of the tortoise or lobster. By contrast, the modern free-standing type of columnar structure of concrete or steel would correspond to an internal skeleton, while the screen walls...would be equivalent to...skin (Steadman, 1979: 41).

In contrast to Le Corbusier's use of analogy, the work of the contemporary Spanish architect Santiago Calatrava is an almost literal representation of structures found in nature. That is, the structural frameworks of many of his buildings, not only function like animal skeletons, but strongly resemble them as well (Figs. 2.6–7). He keeps the skeleton of a dog in his office, but is at pains to point out that the formal representation of animal skeletons is an aesthetic preference, and not dictated by the imitation of their function. He insists, furthermore, that he is as much influenced by the work of Candela and Gaudi as he is by the observation of nature. Nevertheless, the figurative aspect of Calatrava's work reveals a profound understanding of statics as it is transferrable from nature to architecture:

I believe that the professional activity of an engineer lies mainly in the development of analytical models which describe nature in a realistic way. Working with isostatic structures inevitably leads one to sketching nature (Calatrava, 1993).

Calatrava's structural functionalism, then, is derived from nature, and has an aesthetic dimension, as indeed it has in nature. In both, the forms have a beauty that can be seen as deriving from the perfect fit between their configuration and their task. Conversely, the beauty of the forms could be seen as something 'in excess' of that task, so that Calatrava could be claimed by utilitarians and formalists alike. There is nothing particularly 'environmental' in this correspondence between organic and non-organic skeletons, but the fact that the correspondence is made indicates a certain valuing of nature that does have environmental implications, in that such valuing could be nudged towards operation as well as configuration.

2.6 Re-racinated

For the English architect and academic John Frazer, such ideas creak with age, though he does acknowledge Goethe as a precursor, in his *Naturphilosophie*, an unwitting anticipation of the common genetic foundation of life. Frazer himself engages with this genetic structure in terms of nature-as-information rather than with a structural, organizational or representational model (Plate 11):

How does nature encode information in DNA, and make form which is capable of response, development and evolution?...I've been preoccupied for thirty years by how information is to be encoded in architectural design, not only to answer technical questions but the formal issues...the generation of form itself (Frazer, 1993: 21).

Despite the newness of the computer technology that makes such a project even conceivable, the engine behind it is Darwinian: '...I see the computer as an evolutionary accelerator' (Frazer, 1993: 24). Frazer is not the first to be fascinated by the prospect of speeding up product evolution. Mass production was the first indication that dramatically speedier development was possible, a phenomenon observed by Le Corbusier,

Figs. 2.6–7
City of Arts and Sciences, Valencia,
Santiago Calatrava: skeletal structure.

but misinterpreted. His famous comparison of the Greek temple and the automobile missed the point (Le Corbusier, 1986: 134–35): while recognizable taxonomically as a 'type' of transportation (four wheels, chassis, windscreen, seats, etc.), the car, unlike the temple, never reached a point of perfection, but continued – and continues – to evolve, pushed by the market.

Frazer is trying to develop an architecture driven by the same informational codes that drive organisms. Computer programs are made to function in much the same way as DNA, and in an analogous environment. He talks of 'divergent evolution' and 'natural selection' and 'survival of the fittest in engineering terms' (Frazer, 1993: 21). The only reason we can't yet design something like a dolphin is not because we are still devaluing nature, but because we still lag behind it: 'it's completely beyond man to design anything at that level of sophistication. We don't have the technique' (Frazer, 1993: 21). Frazer's ambition is to develop buildings that receive information through their fabric as we do through our skin, that learn from their mistakes and transmit that feedback into a 'gene pool' for future buildings.

The results so far are visible only on the computer screen, and while rich and intriguing, bear no resemblance to anything conventionally described as 'architecture', even Deconstructive architecture. Rather than redefining his inventions, Frazer would prefer to reinvent architecture, and

abandon talk about meaning. Buildings have meaning only in the sense that dolphins have meaning: a theological argument about the purpose of life. In my own work I would never use the words language or meaning... (Frazer, 1993: 22).

Even if architects could design free of hermeneutic intention, however, reception is beyond their control. Frazer's own work, whether he intends it or not, carries both explicit and implicit cultural meanings. However mute or ambiguous architectural form may be, meanings accrue to it like barnacles to a hull.

So, although 'architecture' as we know it disappears in Frazer's computer-generated structures, he is nevertheless carrying on the architectural tradition of imitating nature. What is new and crucial is that he is imitating it on an operational level. By 'operational' I am not referring to simple functions like isostasis, but to the dynamic self-organizing activity characteristic of all non-linear phenomena in nature, from the brain to the weather. Frazer's engineered genetics (as opposed to genetic engineering) grapples with the *generation* of complex structures. As such, his work poses a profound challenge to any architecture attempting to imitate this alternative model of a non-linear nature. The immutability and predictability guaranteed by classical science lends itself 'naturally' both to the stasis of architecture, and the statics of building engineering. And though there have been attempts by architects such as Frank Gehry and Peter Eisenman to escape the formal predictability of this stasis, their buildings are still physically static. They are complex in form, but not in operation, and thus still miss the essence of complexity in nature: non-linear change over time. In organisms, this can be very rapid if one is looking at feedback systems within the organism, rather than the evolution of the organism as a whole. Buildings like Gehry's or Eisenman's can only be 'stills' of what is a dynamic process because that, so far at least, is the 'nature' of architecture.

The design for the Nunotani Headquarters in Tokyo represents a phenomenon that is found all over the world: tectonic plates and their instability (Plate 12), but the crucial elements of movement and transformation inherent in tectonic plates are missing. In seeking to represent them in a static building, one is in fact denying their identifying characteristic. A set of super-imposed freeze-frames of motion is just that: frozen, a contradiction in terms. Nevertheless, there is in both Gehry and Eisenman, an interest in and understanding of an emergent model of nature that does not exist in environmental architecture, which is still embedded in classical science and its emphasis on the conventionally measurable:

There is a new theory of nature emerging today – one based on dynamics, complexity, discontinuities and events – and a new (though still inchoate) architecture that embraces these same fundamental rhythms of fundamental becoming...Oscillation...will be a veritable engine driving a morphogenetic machine in a new non-linear world in which nothing is predictable save transformation *itself (Kwinter, 1993: 91).*

Can buildings imitate the new paradigm of nature any more closely? Is there any point to their doing so? In order to answer these questions, the paradigm itself requires further examination. What is this 'new' theory that has led to this 'new' paradigm? In what ways are the science and the paradigm 'revolutionary'? In what ways do they change our perceptions of culture as well as nature, and more specifically, our perceptions of architecture?

2.7 The return of the repressed

By the time the Modern Movement was finally catching up with seventeenth-century science and exploring the building-as-machine in imitation of the universe-as-machine, the science of the twentieth century was undergoing a major paradigm shift, from the projection of nature-as-clockwork to a new projection of nature as relative, dynamic and uncertain. Though its claims to total objectivity are discredited, the western empirical tradition of enquiry into the physical world has enabled us to transform what we have observed, and observe what we have transformed, the two locked in an indivisible tangle of mutual influence denied by classical science:

Einstein emphasised that science had to be independent of the existence of any observer. This led him to deny the reality of time as irreversibility, as evolution. On the contrary, Tagore maintained that even if absolute truth could exist, it would be inaccessible to the human mind...Whatever we call reality, it is revealed to us only through the active construction in which we participate (Prigogine and Stengers, 1985: 293).

That there is a 'new' science qualitatively different from classical science (classical physics) was categorically asserted by the Nobel Prize-winning chemist Ilya Prigogine as early as 1979 in the book he wrote with Isabelle Stengers, *La nouvelle alliance*. This provoked heated debate in Europe between those who held physical laws were universal, immutable, reversible and therefore timeless, and those, usually in the biological sciences, who maintained that the laws of classical physics swept to one side that which it could not measure, but which characterized life for all of us: change as well as stasis, becoming as well as being, uncertainty as well as predictability, and above all, the 'arrow of time', which makes growing young, for example, an impossibility:

This is the question of the relation between being and becoming, between permanence and change...Is change, whereby things are born and die, imposed from the outside on some kind of inert matter? Or is it the result of the intrinsic and independent activity of matter? Seventeenth century science arose in opposition to the biological model of a spontaneous organisation of natural beings (Prigogine and Stengers, 1985: 291).

This seventeenth-century view is still with us, particularly in physics, and particularly among those physicists still striving for a Grand Unified Theory:

One of the main sources of fascination in modern science was precisely the feeling that it had discovered eternal laws at the core of nature's transformations and thus had exorcised time and becoming (Prigogine and Stengers, 1985: 291–92).

Even Einstein, who first brought uncertainty into this secure edifice with the theory of relativity, would not countenance the idea that it had begun a process of undoing our faith both in predictable order and the possibility of knowing it: 'our vision of nature is undergoing a radical change toward the multiple, the temporal, and the complex' (Prigogine and Stengers, 1985: 292). These are no longer considered illusions, with an immutable reality lying behind. On the contrary, they are increasingly viewed as the most important part of this reality, so that the exception to the rule is not the irreversible (mutability) but the reversible (the unchanging). Prigogine and Stengers are inclusive, however. They do not suggest rejecting classical physics and the model of nature as stable and predictable and replacing it with chaos, but of reconciling dynamics with the Second Law of Thermodynamics: 'We must accept a pluralistic world in which reversible and irreversible processes coexist' (Prigogine and Stengers, 1985: 257).

The Second Law of Thermodynamics makes time of central importance in science by maintaining that the universe is constantly losing energy over time. Its state at one moment is therefore different from its state at another moment: it has less and less energy. In other words, the universe evolves; it becomes different, and the development of this difference is irreversible. This continuous loss of energy is called entropy,[6] which gives rise to two contradictory phenomena. On the one hand, as energy is lost, there is less of it to maintain complex systems – of chemicals, of organisms, etc. – so there is less complexity and less diversity. On the other hand, Darwin's theory of evolution demonstrates convincingly that despite entropy, complex systems continue to develop, indeed, may be developing in response to entropy. Such systems are not static; they too change over time, and are often in a state called 'far-from-equilibrium'. It is this state that is being explored in certain scientific circles, and which is transforming our view of nature:

We now know that far from equilibrium, new types of structures may originate spontaneously. In far-from-equilibrium conditions, we may have transformation from disorder...into order. New dynamic states of matter may originate, states that reflect the interaction of a given system with its surroundings (Prigogine and Stengers, 1985: 12).

The life sciences, and their knowledge of change through time (evolution), are on the ascendant. Physics, which once dismissed these sciences as the study of ephemeral aberrances, must adjust to the new priorities of a new scientific age. 'A new unity is emerging: irreversibility is a source of order at all levels. Irreversibility is the mechanism that brings order out of chaos' (Prigogine and Stengers, 1985: 292).

This presents us with a paradigm much more gradated than sets of binary opposites held in tension: order and disorder, predictability and unpredictability, etc. Order actually seems to emerge out of disorder, just as disorder obliterates order when the intensity of a reaction is raised. The science Neutra criticized as 'crude and naive fragmentation' is itself beginning to reject such fragmentation:

[C]haos theorists...feel that they are turning back a trend in science toward reductionism, the analysis of systems in terms of their constituent parts: quarks, chromosomes or neurons... (Gleick, 1994: 5).

Chaos theory studies the way hitherto immeasurably irregular phenomena once dismissed by classical science as 'chaotic' actually contain an order within them, only discernible in the 1960s once the computer was powerful enough to track it. These 'chaotic' phenomena include everything from river flows to cigar smoke, hurricanes to variations in the orbits of the planets. In focusing on smaller and smaller particles of matter, classical physics has tended to lose sight of the fact that the carefully mapped behaviour of one water molecule, for example, changes radically and unpredictably when the numbers are increased to the size of a river. Millions of molecules become qualitatively different, a complex and unpredictable system on 'the edge of chaos' (Waldrop, 1994: 12), but never tipping into it.

This is the new 'balance of nature', not a fixed and stable entity, in which order dominates disorder, but an interlocking series of dynamic

---

6. 'Entropy is the rule...; all energy is destined to be degraded, but physical systems are becoming more ordered on earth, while life systems continue to evolve towards greater order, greater complexity, less randomness...' (McHarg, 1971: 53).

systems in which order and disorder pull at each other continuously: 'The edge of chaos is where life has enough stability to sustain itself and enough creativity to deserve the name of life' (Waldrop, 1994: 12). Neither order nor disorder is privileged, rather it is the movement between them that creates an ever-metamorphosing biosphere in which there is an order, but a vastly more subtle one than nature-as-clockwork:

Nature forms patterns. Some are orderly in space but disorderly in time, others are orderly in time but disorderly in space. Some patterns are fractal, exhibiting structures self-similar in scale. Others give rise to steady states or oscillating ones... (Gleick, 1994: 308).

The unpredictable dynamism of nature is usually illustrated by the example of the 'butterfly effect', the idea that a butterfly moving its wings today on one side of the world can set in motion a series of events that results in a storm the next month on the other side of the world. This so-called 'sensitive dependence on initial conditions' means small variations at one end of the scale can have an enormous effect at the other, and is 'an inescapable consequence of the way small scales [are] intertwined with large' (Gleick, 1994: 3). It is this dynamism in nature, rather than the much more easily imitated stasis and stability, with which architecture is now able to negotiate a position, not only formally but operationally. In fact, it is probably much easier to establish on the level of operation, and gives environmental architecture an advantage, since the environmentally designed building is intended to react dynamically to changing conditions, sun-tracking photovoltaic panels and louvres being cases in point.

To the extent that the irreversibility of nature has become scientifically respectable, complexity is 'new', but we have always had an intuitive, phenomenological understanding of it. Does this 'new' science, then, have implications for a new relation between nature and culture? Prigogine and Stengers caution against too literal a correspondence being made between complex systems in nature and human society:

It is not surprising that the entropy metaphor has tempted a number of writers dealing with social or economic problems. Obviously here we have to be careful; human beings are not dynamic objects... (Prigogine and Stengers, 1985: 298).

Nevertheless, it is fair to say that human society, like the animate world surrounding it, has evolved from simpler forms of organization to more complex, some of which persist, others of which decay, and that there are fruitful analogies to be made between the mechanisms of order and disorder in both human society and in nature.

In his book *One Thousand Years of Nonlinear History*, Manuel de Landa rejects analogy and declares the non-linear correspondence between nature and culture to be literally true: culture, like nature, is the result of flows of energy and matter coagulating into certain configurations at certain times, whether they be human bodies, mountains or cities:

human culture and society (considered as dynamical systems) are no different from the self-organised processes that inhabit the atmosphere and hydrosphere (wind circuits, hurricanes), or, for that matter, no different from lavas and magmas, which as self-assembled conveyor belts drive plate tectonics... (de Landa, 1997: 55).

De Landa's language is almost shocking in its uncompromising equation of the workings of nature with those of culture. The text is sprinkled with caveats and provisos, warning, like Prigogine and Stengers, that culture is non-materialist as well as materialist, but the thrust of the argument asserts the contrary. Regardless of whether one agrees with the extremity of this position, however, it is highly significant as evidence of the restoration of nature as the dominant paradigm for culture. In fact, in this view, culture is literally part of nature, operating according to the same laws and the same lawlessness. Richard Dawkins' populist social Darwinism goes even further, absorbing individual human behaviour into a crude genetic determinism (Dawkins, 1989). The only defence of the continued relevance of the will and consciousness of culture seems to be to reassert the difference between it and nature:

the dualist strategy of thinking about 'nature' and 'society' (or 'culture') as qualitatively distinct realms offers one obvious and unambiguous way of resisting biological determinism...Nature/society dualism is a way of...insisting that society plays its own independent role (Benton, 1994: 28).

This is crucial for makers of material culture like architects. Do they have responsibility for what they make, or are they mere conduits for self-organizing cultural imperatives that once coagulated into the Modern Movement and may now coagulate into environmental architecture? In revaluing nature, are we in danger of devaluing culture by denying it any autonomy? To merely reverse the relationship within a binary is to get precisely nowhere – or worse, to get somewhere even worse (see Chapter 8).

2.8 The birth of the green

If nature is again in a position to influence architecture as much, if not more than any other cultural domain, how is this to be manifested? If, as this chapter suggests, the division between nature and culture is becoming increasingly blurred, how can 'nature' be a clear paradigm at all? The answer lies in the cause of this loss of demarcation. There is a blur because culture is able increasingly to understand and imitate the *operations* of nature. This imitation is of a very different order from mimicking the way that parts of it look, or are organized. It is the flexibility, the reactive and transformational capacities of the organic that scientists are now seeking to emulate in materials, computers and robotics, rather than the traditional idea of the organic as forms that ape those found in nature, or as the use of 'natural' materials, or as a perfectly organized whole in which all the parts are essential and proportionally related. In 'biomimesis', scientists look at everything from the way the brain learns through trial and error, so that robots may do the same, to the way a fish moves through the water, so that submarines can become similarly flexible and energy efficient:

The apparent veil between the organic and the manufactured has crumpled to reveal that the two really are, and always have been, of one being...[There is a] common soul between organic communities we know of as organisms and ecologies, and their manufactured counterparts of robots, corporations, economies and computer circuits... (Kelly, 1994: 3).

This suggests a radical reappraisal of the building as physical object, and consequently, of the relationship between architecture and nature. John Frazer is both closer to it and further away than, say, Gehry or Eisenman. Closer, in that he is attempting to approach design in terms of 'active' rather than inert matter; further away, in that this evolutionary architecture can't, or can't yet, be built. What, then, is possible if we stay within the parameters of that which is buildable, however 'deconstructed'? Present environmental architecture imitates the organic in its adaptation to differing climatic and physical conditions, as this is immediately achievable within existing environmental and architectural economies. Dynamic operation is being explored by those formerly dedicated to older mechanical technologies, architects like Richard Rogers and Norman Foster, but it is still in its infancy: a few condition-sensitive moving parts run by computers that can barely cope with even this level of complexity. A new generation of materials and systems is required to begin to realize in built form Frazer's 'living' computer creations:

The ultimate smart structure would design itself. Imagine a bridge which accretes materials as vehicles move over it and it is blown by the wind. It detects the areas where it is overstretched...and adds material until the deformation falls back within a prescribed limit...The paradigm is our own skeleton (Beukers and van Hinte, 1999: 47).

Neither the formal experiment of Eisenman, however, nor the technophilia of Foster and Rogers embraces all aspects of nature-as-complexity. Both, in their widely divergent ways, over-generalize in environmental terms. This generalization is valuable, in that it enables us to perceive something that would otherwise remain implicit, and therefore invisible, within the particular. But such generalization excludes another aspect of complexity-within-nature: differentiation. In this context, differentiation refers to different ecosystems in different climates and different topographies. By emerging from the (differentiated) ground up, vernacular architecture has traditionally embodied the differentiation found in nature. Industrial technology, on the other hand, is incapable of differentiating without conscious efforts to inflect itself. 'Operationalists' like Rogers and Foster do not see the need to do so, and are replacing universal mechanical technology with a new universal 'green' technology of photovoltaic cells, reactive glazing and computers. The results, like Foster's Reichstag resurrection, at first gave little visibility to the profound cultural shift such a technological shift implies (Plate 13). In later projects of both Foster and Rogers, however, there are significant changes in the palette of materials used, and thus in the message being conveyed. For example, the use of wood by these architects is markedly on the increase (Plate 14). Limiting the degree of architectural transformation – particularly in choice of materials – reduces the environmental benefit of such buildings. Why do it? To preserve an established architectural identity, or a particular kind of performance, over maximum energy efficiency. When scientists pursuing biomimesis produce artificial 'smart skins' that act successfully like living skin, which are impermeable to water and permeable to air, heal themselves, and grow an insulating layer when needed and shed it when not, these 'High Tech' architects will no doubt be the first to experiment with them. When technologies are developed that enable the building to track the sun like a flower, moving around to face it or hide from it, opening up or closing down to allow or exclude more solar gain; when, in short, buildings have the technological capacity to regulate themselves automatically to maintain internal equilibrium the way organisms do, these architects will doubtless lead the way, but where? 'Where Chaos begins, classical science stops' (Gleick, 1994: 3), and, perhaps, where nature-as-complexity begins, conventional assumptions about architecture stop.

Such claims of an end to architecture-as-we-know-it have been made before, most recently by those who experimented with deconstruction. Those claims, however, were made on the basis of formal disruptions. Underneath, the buildings remained resolutely conventional in their pursuit of an ordered internal environment, in the consumption of fossil fuels to this end, and in the economic and political relationships that made the production of such a 'rebellion' possible, with such work almost always commissioned by institutional (i.e. establishment) clients. In fact, the work currently being produced by Foster, Rogers, Grimshaw, Future Systems, etc., dubbed 'Eco-Tech' by Catherine Slessor (1998), embodies a more profound shift away from 'imperial modernism' than either historicist or deconstructive post-modernism. Though no less embedded in the political and economic status quo, 'Eco-Tech' seeks a different relationship between building and physical environment from the conventional one, and achieves it by trying to push high technology past its 'imperial' phase, rather than abandoning it altogether. An enormous amount of research goes into these projects. In fact, the only reason we can discuss buildings as miniature power stations, putting new clean energy into the grid, is because some of these architects have picked up the R&D ball and run with it (Figs. 2.8–9). 'Eco-Tech', however, is only a beginning, some exigent environmentalists would say a false start, in establishing a more symbiotic relation between the built and natural environments. The model of nature-as-complexity suggests possible directions for architecture that environmental architecture, whatever its stripe, has barely begun to entertain.

In his book *Out of Control*, Kevin Kelly (1994) outlines what he calls the 'Nine Laws of God'. These govern what he calls 'the incubation of somethings from nothing', and are therefore certainly applicable to buildings. The commandments which could have some bearing on the

Fig. 2.8
The Turbine Tower, Tokyo, Richard Rogers Partnership: research project with Ove Arup and Partners and Imperial College.

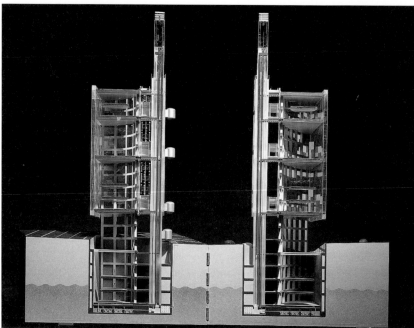

Fig. 2.9
The Turbine Tower: section models showing thermal response of building in summer (left) and winter (right). On the winter model, wind turbines can be seen sitting between the aerodynamically designed office building and the service core.

building-as-physical-object, and by extension, the-building-as-cultural-object, instruct architects to (1) 'control from the bottom up', (2) 'maximize the fringes', (3) 'have multiple goals', and (4) 'seek persistent disequilibrium'.

(1) 'Control from the bottom up'

When everything is connected to everything in a distributed network, everything happens at once. When everything happens at once, wide and fast-moving problems simply route around any central authority. Therefore overall governance must arise from the most humble independent acts done locally in parallel, and not from a central command (Kelly, 1994: 469).

If applied to architecture on a technical level, this law means that one no longer tries to control, centrally and crudely, the overall internal conditions of a building. Instead, local sensors, informing a computer-controlled Building Management System (BMS), would enable the building to react locally to variable conditions, for example, to those on the north side as opposed to those on the south side. These multiplicitous local reactions would minimize energy expenditure and loss by organizing themselves into an intricately balanced overall reaction to external conditions: an overheating south side would provide heat for an underheated north side, for example.

(2) 'Maximize the fringes'

A diverse heterogeneous entity...can adapt to the world in a thousand daily mini-revolutions, staying in a state of permanent, but never fatal churning. Diversity favors...the outskirts...moments of chaos...In economic, ecological, evolutionary and institutional models, a healthy fringe speeds adaptation, increases resilience, and is almost always the source of innovations (Kelly, 1994: 469).

In other words, the rewards of the first law mentioned are spelled out in this second one: a building with a system of local, continuous compensatory reactions will provide greater adaptation, resilience and energy efficiency than a generalized model.

(3) 'Have multiple goals'

Simple machines can be efficient, but complex adaptive machinery cannot be. A complicated structure has many masters and none of them can be served exclusively (Kelly, 1994: 469).

A quite radical reconceiving of the building's task is implicit here. A conventional machine has one or several fixed tasks and performs them. It is a closed system: it does what it is designed to do. Once fixed, the machine will not respond to other tasks. There is thus a finitude in both machine and task. Similarly, in a conventional building of any kind, the task, both formal and environmental, is to defend the closed system. A 'free-running' building aims only for a range of temperatures that achieve a less precise level of comfort. An open, as opposed to a sealed, building cannot do otherwise. It makes itself vulnerable to external conditions in a way sealed buildings deliberately avoid. This multiplies the variables it must react to.

(4) 'Seek persistent disequilibrium'

Equilibrium is death. Yet unless a system stabilises to an equilibrium point, it is no better than an explosion and just as soon dead. A nothing, then, is both equilibrium and disequilibrium. A something is persistent disequilibrium – a continuous state of surfing on the edge between never stopping and never falling (Kelly, 1994: 469).

Disequilibrium is forced upon a building if it seeks to adapt to, rather than oppose, change. I am not referring here to demountable buildings, but to buildings, which, although enduring, may have constantly metamorphosing forms rather than a fixed configuration. Elements may be culturally identifiable, but in a reactive building, internal consistency may well be achieved through external flexibility. That is, if an environmental equilibrium is wanted inside, it may be achieved by a persistent formal disequilibrium outside. This does not necessarily imply the building *looks* like an organism, but that it *operates* like one. Amoebic forms are of interest to a certain group of architects exploring non-linearity (see Chapter 6), but are by no means the only option. A 'biomimetic' building implies a self-regulating operational order that emerges from the edges, rather than being imposed from the centre, but that in no way determines the form. There is no one design 'solution', no style that is dictated by nature-as-complexity. Architects would have as much autonomy and as many choices as they do now.

2.9 Blurring the boundaries

The analogies between the operations of the biosphere and the operations of various aspects of our culture ('robots, corporations, economies and computer circuits' (Kelly, 1994: 3)) seem to undermine, if not negate, the oppositional definitions of culture and nature set out at the beginning of this essay. If culture has unwittingly been operating like nature, how can it be claimed they are fundamentally different from one another? In fact, the definition of nature as 'given' and culture as 'manufactured' in no way contradicts a perceived operational correspondence. Complexity theory merely undermines the modernist conclusion that because nature and culture are produced in different ways, they are irreconcilably opposed, something that modernism itself is rendering obsolete through some of its new technologies. The new paradigm of nature actually pushes us, not back to a pre-industrial relationship, with the manufactured again contained within 'natural limits', but forward, into unmapped terrain, where manufacture redefines 'natural limits' by taking operations found in nature and reproduces them within the realm of the artificial. If the biomimetic becomes the norm, then the old opposition becomes a continuum, with the entirely manufactured at one end (e.g. computers), and the entirely given at the other (e.g. oceans).

There is, then, a growing world of objects that belongs both to nature and to culture, an area where the two domains overlap, and in overlapping, form something new. The hybrid, the object in nature modified by our intervention, has been with us since the beginning of culture. The synthetic, the object manufactured from materials that bear no resemblance to their original state, has not. The biomimetic, in which the manufactured is modelled on operations in nature, is very recent indeed. A name has already been coined for part of this ambiguous new domain: the bionic, 'mechanical systems that function like living beings' (OED), and is capable of providing great benefit to us, and no great harm to anything else.

No longer structured by the polarity of public and private, the cyborg defines a technological polis based partly on a revolution of social relations in the oikos, *the household. Nature and culture are reworked; the one can no longer be the resource for appropriation or incorporation by the other (Haraway, 1991).*

This sounds positive: a reassessment of entrenched social relations and distributions of power now necessitated by the appearance of creatures (cyborgs) that cross the boundaries set up to enforce those relations and distributions. There are, however, dangers:

Late twentieth century machines have made thoroughly ambiguous the difference between natural and artificial, mind and body, self-developing and externally designed...Our machines are disturbingly alive, and we ourselves frighteningly inert (Haraway, 1989: 176).

Does one, in this analysis, classify buildings as 'machines' or as extensions of ourselves, that is, as inert or alive? Environmental architecture is certainly supposed to function as if it were alive, and ultimately could become fully bionic:

After thousands of years of...soldering, forging and burning inanimate matter to create useful things, we are now splicing, recombining, inserting and stitching living material into economic utilities. We are moving from the age of pyrotechnology to the age of biotechnology (Rifkin, 1998: 41).

Who is to say that in the future, fibres or skins won't be grown to clad buildings,[7] or that structure won't be self-repairing, like bones? These kinds of biomimetic advances through genetic engineering are, surely, to be welcomed? They are the sunny side of the brave new world of designer babies so many fear, which, far from rendering us paraplegics serviced by machines, enables us to engage with the material world in a far more subtle and informed way than hitherto.

---

7. 'The United States Army is inserting genes into bacteria that are similar to the genes used by orb-weaving spiders to make silk. Spider's silk is among the strongest fibres known to exist. Scientists hope to grow the silk gene-producing bacteria in industrial vats and harvest it for use in products ranging from aircraft parts to bullet-proof vests' (Rifkin, 1998: 43).

2.10 Conclusion

The oppositions between culture and nature, so importantly and brutally drawn up by modernism, are dissolving again, not into a return to what was, but a transformation of it. Culture emerged from nature; now it's being submerged in culture, but a material culture increasingly modelled on the *modus operandi* of nature. The division between the living organism and the machine continues to collapse. With machines, possibly even buildings, on the verge of being able to learn, react and adapt, with humans able to replace parts of themselves with some of these machines, and with nature further reordered by synthetic ecosystems, the division between culture and nature will be less and less discernible. The embrace of advanced 'bio-logic' by technology speaks of a newfound maturity on the level of invention. Whether this maturity can be extended to its application in the world is entirely up to us. In architecture, constructing a culture that is nature that is culture will be the most remarkable model we have yet had.

3 A POST-IMPERIAL MODERNISM?

3.1 Introduction

As nature becomes, through the science that has exploited and continues to exploit it, once again a model for imitation by culture, modernism, as characterized by instrumental rationality, is acquiring the potential to bring about the negation of its initial condition: the master/slave relation between itself and nature (Fig. 3.1). Aspects of western culture have changed dramatically since the late 1960s, but these changes, instead of being cast as 'post-modern' could as easily be viewed as the beginning of a new stage of modernism: a 'post-imperial' or, in Ulrich Beck's terminology, 'reflexive' modernism (Beck, 1992).

Since the eighteenth century, the promised 'liberty, equality and fraternity' of the Enlightenment became diverted into a culture of expertise, in which the 'haves' controlled knowledge as well as wealth, and many of the marginalized did not manage to make heard their claims to a withheld legitimacy until the twentieth century. The marginalized can be seen, therefore, not as the beneficiaries of a post-modernism that takes them into account, but as a modernizing wave within modernism itself, trying to push it past where it had stalled:

Modernity has...taken over the role of its counterpart – the tradition to be overcome, the natural constraint to be mastered (Beck, 1992: 185).

Hence Beck's term 'reflexive': modernism has replaced nature as that which is to be overcome by modernism. Environmental architecture could be viewed as one aspect of modernism overcoming itself: the built environment on its way to overcoming its exploitation of the natural environment.

The environmental lobby, though by no means the only group providing a critique of the dangers of exploitation, is one of the most vocal. Much of its criticism is science-based, turning on science the scepticism science uses on all endeavours but its own. Unreflexive science has produced a society qualitatively different from the industrial society that preceded it:

While all earlier cultures and phases of social development confronted threats, in various ways, society today is confronted by itself through its dealings with risks (Beck, 1992: 183).

Fig. 3.1
Entrance to new section of La Sagrada Familia, Gaudi.

For Beck, those with enough knowledge to criticize are without power; and those with power are immune from criticism. The industries fed by instrumental science take no responsibility for the risks they produce as side-effects (e.g. radiation from nuclear energy), and those in or outside such industries and outside government critical of the risks have no means of compelling accountability. Those doing the criticizing include scientists, however, scientists who have crossed over from doing instrumental science to measuring the effects of that instrumentality, and developing new technologies with fewer environmental side-effects. Until mainstream science can criticize itself from within the way environmental science criticizes it from without, and whistle-blowing is not merely tolerated but actively encouraged inside risk-producing industries, we will continue to be the greatest danger to our species:

concealed risks...can suddenly change into social risk situations of such seriousness [e.g. BSE] that it becomes inconceivable how the thoughtlessness of industrial society could have been handled so poorly – politically and not just techno-scientifically (Beck, 1992: 227).

It is the purpose of this chapter to examine modernism as that for which environmentalism in general, and environmental design in particular, are proposing themselves as a possible future: as a different meta-narrative in the first case, and as a different means of producing material culture in the second, both of which are both implicit within modernism itself.

3.2 Makers and breakers

The above assertion is contentious, but the ground for it was laid by Jurgen Habermas, probably modernism's best-known apologist. Habermas does not accept that 'purposive rationality' has become 'overblown into a totality, [abolishing] the distinction between what claims validity and what is useful for self-preservation' (Habermas, 1987a: 119). Modernism has been characterized as encouraging a systematically exploitative relation between nature and culture. It could be argued, however, that human development has always involved the exploitation of the environment. Civilizations have risen by extracting what they wanted from nature with increasing efficiency, and fallen because they over-extracted. The main reason modernism, rather than 'human nature', stands accused is because technology since the eighteenth century has become so much more powerful than its earlier versions, and with an increase in power has come an increase in destructiveness. Had we had the means earlier to transform the given as widely and swiftly as we can now, this 'destructiveness' would have made itself felt earlier. In other words, the drive to control the physical environment, to use it as a means to our ends, is as old and fundamental a cultural phenomenon as the necessity, so far at least, of living within its limits.

These two positions, of domination and co-operation, informed modernism as they informed the social attitudes that preceded its emergence, but in inverse proportion. Within modernism, instrumentality grew and grew, a monstrous child that now threatens the existence of its parents, though at its inception it was perceived as vital to that existence, and indeed was. In classical Greece, 'techne' was interpreted as a form of benign, rather than malign, systematization. *Techne* means literally craft, art or science – 'technique', since what you cannot conquer you have to find a way around. Ingenuity within the limited means at one's disposal thus became associated with *techne*, but that is to reduce its complexity as a term.

It is certainly associated with a grappling with limits, and in its widest interpretation, could be viewed as 'culture', the sum total of our efforts to protect ourselves from the contingencies of nature, standing in opposition to '*tuche*', luck. *Techne* encompasses everything from crafts such as house or boat building, to arts such as dancing or music playing, to sciences such as mathematics or astronomy. In *The Fragility of Goodness*, Martha Nussbaum (1989) cites four features common to all these forms of *techne*: universality, teachability, precision and concern with explanation. Such criteria, however, do not lead to consensus, in ancient Greece or now. Nussbaum describes two versions of *techne* found in Plato's *Protagoras*: that of Protagoras himself, and that of Socrates. Socrates' definition favours the sciences, the more practical and effective kinds, those that can measure and be measured: '[W]hat is measurable or commensurable is graspable, knowable, in order, good; what is without measure is boundless, elusive, chaotic, threatening, bad' (Nussbaum, 1989: 107). Socrates was, in fact, pushing *techne* towards a fraction of itself: technology. Heidegger describes it as well as anyone:

One says: Technology is a means to an end. The other says: Technology is a human activity. The two definitions of technology belong together...The manufacture and utilization of equipment, tools and machines, the manufactured and used things themselves, and the needs and ends they serve, all belong to what technology is...Technology itself is a contrivance, or, in Latin, an instrumentum. *The current conception of technology, according to which it is a means and a human activity, can therefore be called the instrumental and anthropological definition of technology (Heidegger, 1977: 4–5).*

The Socratic *techne* increases our control over the contingencies of the physical environment and thus excludes the arts. These too concern measurement – rhythm, proportion, harmonics – but as an end in itself, not as a means to some practical end.

Protagoras, on the other hand, defends *techne*'s original complexity. This is what Nussbaum refers to as a '*bona fide techne*': 'qualitative, plural in its ends, and in which the art activities themselves constitute the end' (Nussbaum, 1989: 99). It is less 'effective' than instrumental *techne* (technology). That is, it has less effect on the physical environment, and as such may be exactly what we require at this point in our species' history. Socratic *techne* won out justifiably over Protagoras' version in ancient Greece: life was unremittingly harsh and dangerous. Today, we can see the ethical and environmental price we paid for that crucial turn towards a directed rationality. Perhaps it's time to return to a *techne* that contains the possibility of an 'internal end' (Nussbaum,

1989: 98) after centuries of 'external ends'. We have become too expert in using the environment as raw material.

Is there any other way for modern technology to operate, however, given that its project is to ceaselessly overcome limitations – of knowledge, of praxis, of the flesh? Architecturally, could a more Protagoran technology become the norm, and what would it be like? It could be argued that architecture is already Protagoran, containing both applied science and art, a means to an end (shelter) and an end in itself (form). A certain level of technology is required to construct it, but it need not be one powerful enough to over-consume resources or pollute. With pre-industrial building we were forced to observe the physical limits of the 'natural materials' being used. There were not at our disposal the synthetic materials that now enable us to defy almost any constructional limit. A modernist would ask what possible virtue there could be in accepting limits, and what possible rationality in accepting limits one can break. The answer lies in the price one is prepared to pay for breaking them. For instance, most nineteenth-century industrialists were quite happy to pay the price of a maimed and diseased workforce in the interests of the new mass production. When this direct human cost became less acceptable, the environmental cost was, and still is, discounted, and with it, the indirect human cost.

At the beginning of the twentieth century, the idea that the physical environment merited as much respect as human society was not even entertained. Use was never viewed as abuse. Le Corbusier, for example, is full of the infectious Hegelian euphoria of the 1920s: 'The fruits of civilization only ripen when all its technical resources are evolved...[M]an is capable of perfection' (Le Corbusier, 1987: 30, 48). This triumph of culture was conceivable as a result of the scientific revolution in seventeenth-century England, and the philosophical revolution in seventeenth-century France. Between the materialism of Francis Bacon (1561–1626) and the idealism of René Descartes (1596–1650), not much of an animate nature was left standing. Bacon saw it as raw material, and Descartes as something that existed only insofar as the human mind existed to perceive it, its reality impossible to prove without God's guarantee. By the seventeenth century, therefore, nature was something irretrievably 'other' in the West. We were separated from it twice over: materially and conceptually.

The acceleration away from nature increased geometrically during the nineteenth and twentieth centuries (as did nostalgia about it) and produced as much anxiety as optimism. During this time, the word 'alienation' is used as often as 'progress'. Baudelaire, in his cycle of poems about nineteenth-century Paris, *Les Fleurs du Mal*, was the archetypal voice of the new alienated 'modern man', a counterpoint to the optimists who saw it as 'the best of times'. The argument between utopians and dystopians filled the arts and literature, a variation on the eternal battle between conservatives and progressives: those who believe change can only make things worse, and those who believe it is the only way to make things better. For the purposes of this discussion, I have borrowed William McClung's terminology in his book *The Architecture of Paradise*, and call the former 'arcadians' and the latter 'utopians', as it has a semantic connection with the present discussion on nature and culture.

Within architectural modernism, classification is not quite so simple as arcadian/anti-modernist, utopian/modernist, though certainly such a division could be found. The Modern Movement wrestled with nature in a number of ways. Wright, for example, for all his reliance on modernity in the form of the car for the success of his ideal city (Fig. 3.2), was an arcadian at heart. For him, the good man was the one 'amply able to off-set the big city of today': the one who would live in, if not build himself, what he calls the 'organic building', an echo of the primitive hut in conception: '[I]t is in the nature of an organic building to grow from its site, come out of the ground into the light...A building dignified as a tree in the midst of nature' (Wright, 1971: 49–50). Modernity was merely the means by which the Usonian citizen could return to nature. Sant'Elia and his fellow Futurists, on the other hand, pursued a form of urban supremacism, with not even a blade of grass appearing in any of Sant'Elia's drawings of the Città Nuova (Fig. 3.3). Le Corbusier is too complex and contradictory to pigeon-hole. The success of his urban visions depended heavily on an integration of nature with his Cartesian forms. Arcadia and utopia were drawn together, their imagery more potent combined than separated.

3.3 Back to the garden

'Arcadians', historically, were those who saw us as part of nature, and subject to its laws, whereas 'utopians' saw us as separate from – and superior to – nature. Obviously we are separate in one sense: we are conscious of ourselves in a way the rest of nature does not seem to be. In the West, the Bible carries a metaphorical, if not a literal, truth. Adam and Eve's eating of the apple from the tree of knowledge led to their expulsion from the Garden of Eden, where they had been fed and protected by God and lived at one with nature. The expulsion from Eden, the Fall, can be seen as a fable about the gaining of self-consciousness. At some point in our psychological development, both as a species and as individuals, we are able to look at ourselves and say we are part of nature. The minute we can say it, we are no longer part of it in the same way. We are separated by an awareness of 'us' and 'it'. In this account of the Eden myth, every human being goes through this loss of paradise when they leave infancy and slowly become aware of themselves as discrete entities, separate from the mother and from Mother Nature.

Culture, then, became necessary the moment we ceased living as animals, and started living as humans, or, metaphorically, when we were cast out of a benign Eden and into a hostile wilderness. We had to feed and clothe and shelter ourselves with the products of our own invention. The 'ideas of shelter, of house, of hearth and home reflect man's struggle to regain some of the protective features of the Garden' (Quantrill, 1987: 21). At first, then, culture was protective, and, on a technical level, reactive, coping with, rather than trying to control nature. The very word 'culture' demonstrates just how closely bound up with nature it originally was. It and the word 'cultivation' come from the Latin *cultivare*, to bestow labour, to train and develop, to promote growth, whether of crops or the mind. It is, however, as much a taming activity

Fig. 3.2
Living City, 1958, Frank Lloyd Wright.

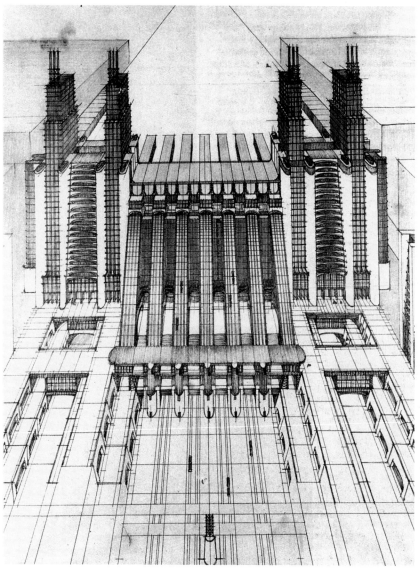

Fig. 3.3
Central Railway Station and Airport of La Città Nuova, 1913–14, Antonio Sant'Elia.

as a promotional one. 'Cultivation' channels growth in certain directions and not others, towards the order of the human and away from the contingency of nature. Increasing success with this agenda produced two kinds of reactions, sometimes in the same person. The first was a growing appreciation of nature 'in the raw' as we became safer from its more common dangers, the Romantic cultivation of the sublime being a case in point. The second reaction was a desire to capitalize on our success and subjugate nature further, to make a 'second nature', produced entirely by us, and ostensibly, entirely predictable. Again, the split between what nature provides and what we make is absolute, as if nature were not the source of what we make.

Arcadians oppose this conception of culture as independent of nature. For them, such an imagined separation is what has allowed culture to 'spoil' nature. Architecture, as the house of this culture, is justifiable only insofar as it imitates nature, and various foundation myths reinforce this. In architecture, one of the first of these is the Vitruvian myth about architecture's origins (Fig. 3.4). According to this, men and women 'bred like wild beasts in woods and caves and groves, and eked out their lives with wild food' (Vitruvius, 1960: 38). To begin with, they imitated the shelters of birds and animals. Then, 'by their own reasoning', they built 'better dwellings' (Vitruvius, 1960: 38–39). Here, culture quite clearly emerges out of nature, and is justified by this source. The primitive hut is an improvement on 'the shelters of birds and animals', but is nevertheless still connected to them. It is 'a document of the naturalness and necessity of the act of building' (McClung, 1983: 93). Animals build shelters. So do we.

Fig. 3.4
Vitruvius: the primitive hut.

Animals use what is to hand in nature. So did we. The primitive hut represents 'the search for an art that in Aristotle's sense completes or fulfills nature without violating her' (McClung, 1983: 114). To arcadians then, architecture as a manifestation of culture is tolerable if it 'can be seen as essentially "natural" by virtue of perceived submission to natural laws, or by virtue of the unaltered state of its materials (which refer us directly to their source in nature)' (McClung, 1983: 116). So that the less worked-upon a building is, the rougher, the cruder, the more 'natural' its materials, the nearer it is to our lost union with nature. Artifice has thus been associated historically with the 'unnatural', the corrupt, an equation seen in the poetry of both ancient Rome and eighteenth-century London, to name but two, in which the city is portrayed as complex and sinful, and the countryside as simple and wholesome.

3.4 Uptown

In his book *The Architecture of Paradise*, William McClung describes the cultural evolution from arcadia to utopia in this way:

As a general pattern it may be said that to the extent that Paradise is of the past, it is arcadian and open;...to the extent that Paradise signifies the Paradise to come, it is urban and conspicuously fortified...The history of Paradise is the history of the loss of belief in the possibility of the pastoral, that is, of unelaborated nature benign without reservation, limitation or threat (McClung, 1983: 19).

The celestial city embodies the consciousness of history, of process, and of threat... (McClung, 1983: 103).

I would qualify this model. It is not that the pastoral *per se* has been rejected, even in this naïve form, but that those who have shifted to an idea of culture-as-salvation have done so after 'a loss of belief in the possibility of the pastoral'. Arcadia still lives as a future in the minds of many in the environmental movement, but not in the minds of the utopians within it or outside it. The latter tend to mistrust nature, which is both beneficent, maternal, joyous, pure, the work of God, and cruel, devouring, grim, dirty, and 'fallen'.

The distinction between a penitential [arcadian] and a triumphant [utopian] framework for celestial space implies a shift of emphasis from a post-lapsarian to a presalvationist structure (McClung, 1983: 82).

Where arcadians look back to Eden, and urge us to repent our presumptuous civilization (in particular its technology) in order to regain that perfection, utopians look forward to an inorganic paradise that does not yet exist. To look towards the ideal city is to think we are improvable, and that what we make can – or will – eventually rival anything God (or nature) made.

The utopian desire to break away from nature is probably as ancient as our desire to be at one with it. Both impulses exist congruently within western culture. In biblical legend, Adam's son Cain built the first city in response to being banished into the wilderness for murdering his brother Abel. This was in order to benefit from 'the companionship of his extended family and friends, and provide protection from thieves and murderers, counteracting the post-Garden sense of abandonment and isolation' (Quantrill, 1987: 26). That is myth. Fact shows the Middle Ages obsessed with the Heavenly City, formal precursor to the secularized ideal city of the Italian Renaissance. The Heavenly City was a city in the sky, where God, Christ and the saints lived in eternal bliss, and which would descend to earth at the Second Coming and the end of time. In its depictions, this city might contain a walled garden, but both city and garden were subjected to the Euclidean order of culture. European medieval and Renaissance gardens were rigidly geometric: squares of planting set out along uncompromisingly ordered paths.

The story of the Tower of Babel would seem to be another arcadian narrative, equating culture with a fatal defiance of the laws of God and nature. In building a tower to the clouds, utopians were doing something 'unnatural', outside accepted limits, which resulted in their losing a unity that stood for all the others – a universal language. But at the same time the population was pelted with minatory parables about construction, the City of God was being developed as a powerful image of perfection. Often, the configuration is an almost exact illustration of the Heavenly City in the Book of Revelation:

And there came to me one of the seven angels saying, Come hither, I will show thee the bride, the Lamb's wife.

And he carried me away in the spirit to a great and high mountain, and showed me that great city, the holy Jerusalem, descending out of heaven from God...And her light was like unto a stone most precious,...and had a wall great and high, and had twelve gates, and at the gates twelve angels... (Book of Revelation, 21.9–21).

The beauty of the Heavenly City is a mineral beauty, as far from the Garden and the taint of fallen nature as it was then possible to get. The perfect square, the circle, the implied cube, the divisions into 24, 12 and 4, all these are part of a neo-Platonic belief in the connection between intellectual order on earth and the divine order above, an order that is to be imposed through men on a chaotic nature. In arcadia, contrarily, one submits to a benign nature's rule. The view of nature informs the form of culture aspired to.

The fact that in the real world, cities were often much more chaotic than nature only served to make architects even more determined to impose a crystalline order, from Filarete's Sforzina (1457) (Fig. 3.5) to Le Corbusier's Ville Contemporaine (1924) (Fig. 3.6). Le Corbusier's version bears a strong resemblance, both in form and verbal description, to the visionary city of the Bible.[1] Instead of jewels, there is jewel-like glass,

---

1. 'The ecstatic quality of the 1920's projects in particular, derives from the architect's submission to the aesthetic of the machine; their visual rhetoric of purity, brilliance, gigantism and replication bears out the language of "implacable" and "infallible" forms, lifting a utopian project into a metaphor for Paradise...' (McClung, 1983: 135).

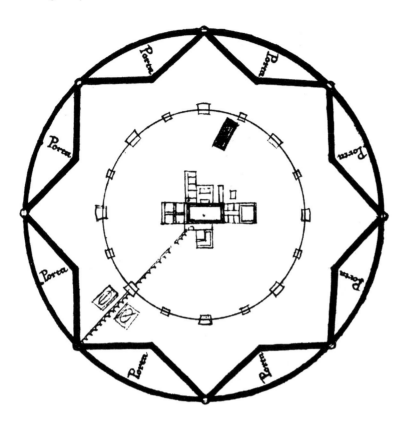

Fig. 3.5
Plan of the ideal city of Sforzina, Filarete.

but the promise is still the same: salvation-through-culture. Le Corbusier's language in *The City of Tomorrow* sounds like the Book of Revelation:

Light streams about us on these heights (Le Corbusier, 1987: 86).

[T]he skyscrapers raise immense geometrical facades all of glass, and in them is reflected the blue glory of the sky...Immense but radiant prisms (Le Corbusier, 1987: 177–78).

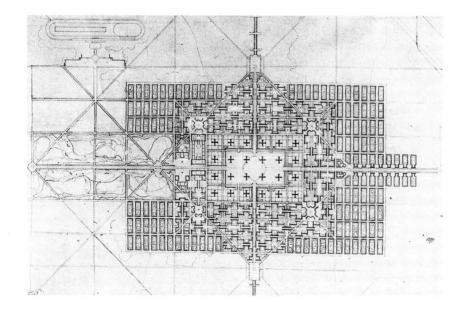

Fig. 3.6
La Ville Contemporaine: plan, 1924, Le Corbusier.

For him, the geometric, the orthogonal, whenever they appear in history, represent the triumph of order over chaos, reason over the irrational, the will over inertia, man over nature.

Le Corbusier's cultural triumphalism was both preceded and exceeded by the Italian Futurists. Their founding manifesto, published in *Le Figaro* in 1909, submerged any doubts they might have had in an almost hysterical enthusiasm for the new era of the modern industrial city. The manifesto's author, Filippo Tommaso Marinetti, wanted a complete break with the past, demanding the immediate destruction of all of Italy's museums, libraries, galleries and palaces. His demands were echoed in 1914 by Antonio Sant'Elia in his own manifesto, *Futurist Architecture,* and in the designs he exhibited for a city of the future, the 'Città Nuova' (see Fig. 3.3), shown at the 'Nuove Tendenze' exhibition that same year. The 'modern' building of 1914 was to be like 'a gigantic machine', built of 'cement, iron and glass, without ornament', and 'brutish in its mechanical simplicity' (Sant'Elia, 1988: 302). This radical new city, made up of such buildings-as-machines, was to be demolished and rebuilt by each succeeding generation to ensure permanent cultural revolution.

A new humanity was to inhabit these ever-new places. Death and mechanization are very closely linked in Futurism, betraying an anxiety Futurists will not consciously acknowledge. Marinetti describes speeding in his car, itself an icon of early-twentieth-century modernity, as being like 'a corpse in a coffin'. In a world ruthlessly renewing itself every generation, to die young was mere politeness, leaving the next wave of humanity unencumbered by the previous one. Nature has vanished from the Futurist city, which sits in limbo, 'liberated' from landscape and vegetation. There is no relationship with nature other than an implicit one: nature as a source of energy and raw materials. The future is man-made, with all the distortions that implies. Technology is so utterly dominant here that everything is machine-made. This obliteration of physical nature is to lead to a transformation of human nature. Marinetti says in another manifesto *Man Multiplied and the Reign of the Machine*:

[W]e must prepare for the immanent and inevitable identification of men with motors...[W]e aspire to the creation of a non-human type in whom will be abolished moral pain, kindness, affection and love, the only poisons that corrode our inexhaustible vital energy; the only breakers in the circuit of our powerful electric physiology (Marinetti, 1991: 99).

The Futurists wanted to prepare the way for a 'mechanical man with replaceable parts', a man liberated from 'the idea of death, and thus from death itself' (Marinetti, 1991: 99), not to mention a man who would fit the new modernity rather than the new modernity having to fit man.[2] This agenda continues today, through bionics and genetic engineering,

2. 'Among all the historical avant-garde movements...the problem was to plan the disappearance of the subject; to cancel the anguish caused by the pathetic...resistance of the individual to the structures of domination as...paradise on earth...' (Tafuri, 1987: 73).

as the limits of nature are once again defied in the most extreme form of modernist utopianism: the denial of death, the one limit nature has put upon us we have so far been unable to escape.

Not all those who accepted the inevitability of the Machine Age were happy about it. The dark side of nineteenth- and twentieth-century machine technology was perceived from its inception. Fritz Lang's 1927 silent film *Metropolis* is typical of a dystopic view contrary to the Futurists'. The metropolis of the title is half old-fashioned Babylon, half city of the future (based on the Manhattan of the twenties), with a ruling élite living above ground in towering skyscrapers, and the masses living underground, slaves to the machines that keep the city operating (Fig. 3.7). A clearer vision of the terrible fate of the proletariat assembled for mass production would be hard to find outside Zola.

Fig. 3.7
The Tower of Babel, *Metropolis*, 1927, Fritz Lang.

The overt critique is socialist, with technology presented as a means of control – of nature and the masses. As one can extract energy from nature with increasing efficiency, so one can extract it from human beings. One of *Metropolis*' chief interests, however, lies in the way the pre-industrial world and its religious values run through the narrative as another kind of critique of the new Machine Age. This is apparent in such scenes as the one entitled 'Moloch', a false god in the Old Testament who demanded human sacrifice. In the film, Moloch is a gigantic machine that kills the workers forced to operate it (Fig. 3.8). Similarly, the huge control tower is called 'The New Tower of Babel'. Just as the biblical builders of Babel lost a universal unity, so Lang alludes, with his control tower, to those aspects of modernism that also

Fig. 3.8
Moloch, *Metropolis*, 1927, Fritz Lang.

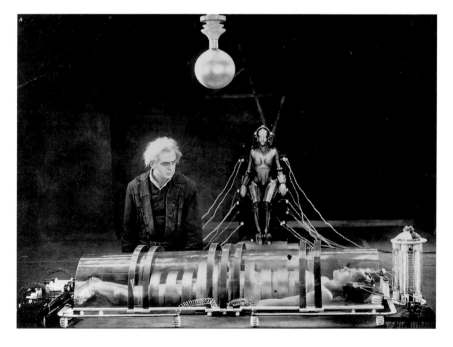

Fig. 3.9
Rotwang the inventor, *Metropolis*, 1927,
Fritz Lang.

involve loss: loss of autonomy, identity, humanity – even life. The men
and women of the 'masses' are reduced to their mechanical tasks. In
one climactic scene, the inventor and villain, Rotwang, takes the
heroine prisoner, and with much pseudo-scientific hocus-pocus, transfers his newly created 'female' robot into the heroine's body, effect-
ing, in a literal way, the take-over of the human – and humanism – by
the machine (Fig. 3.9). For Lang and many others this was a depress-
ing prospect, not, as for the Futurists, an exhilarating one. It was the
price of our new powers the dystopic view dwelled on, usually in social
or psychological terms rather than environmental ones, though life for

the masses underground in *Metropolis* is obviously physically damaging as well.

At the beginning of the twentieth century, however, the optimists were either more numerous or more vocal or both. Like Italy's Futurists, Russia's Constructivists looked ahead with shining eyes, fortified by the possibilities inherent in a political revolution as well as a technological one. Pessimism was out of the question:

But where is the 'poetry and romance' of life to be found in this mechanised hell? the frightened reader will ask. In the very same place, of course. In the sounds and noises of the new town...and in the characteristics of the new style, firmly welded to modern life and clearly reflected in monumentally dynamic works of architecture (Ginzburg, 1982: 118).

Art and architecture were nothing if they were not 'something that perfectly fulfills the requirements and concepts of a given place and epoch' (Ginzburg, 1982: 42), and in the early twentieth century these were predominantly rational and mechanical.

In the 1920s, for the more *sachlichkeit* (objectivity)-oriented proponents of the Modern Movement – Gropius, Hilberseimer, Stam, Meyer, etc. – the machine was the symbol of all that was desirable, both as a thing-in-itself – powerful, fast, enabling – and as the product of a process in which the contingent was minimized and the rational maximized, recast in the language of organic composition:

There is no part or element of the machine that does not occupy a particular place, position or role in the overall scheme, and that is not the product of absolute necessity (Ginzburg, 1982: 86).

These are the products of modern science, these objects of an utterly faultless internal logic, attaining a state of total explicability human beings can only dream of – and aspire to. To make modern society function as near to perfect rationality as the modern machine was now to be the goal of everyone in it. That which defined the best machines could as easily be applied to the best architecture: 'Nothing can be either added to or taken from it without disrupting the whole' (Ginzburg, 1982: 86). Mechanics and aesthetics are suddenly, startlingly, brought together:

What we encounter in the machine, essentially and primarily, is the clearest expression of the ideal of harmonious creation, which long ago was formulated by the first Italian theoretician, Alberti (Ginzburg, 1982: 86).

For Alberti, however, the model of this *concinnitas* was nature, not the machine. In architecture it took three hundred years after it had happened in science for the machine to supplant nature as the paradigm for material culture. This 'supplanting' is in fact a crude usurpation by the mechanical of some aspects of the 'natural', as can be seen in Ginzburg's reference to Alberti above. Nor is it to say that buildings should look like machines. That was never the point. Instead, they were to be designed according to the criteria by which machines were designed. Creation, despite Ginzburg's caveats about the 'insolubility of the creative process', was to be scientific, 'an exact response to a firmly postulated problem' (Ginzburg, 1982: 86). The qualitative, in other words, was to become quantitative, as architecture was brought into the realm of the instrumental.

Modernist 'rationalism', however, was not particularly rational. The battle between those whose irrationality was implicit and those in whom it was explicit is discussed in Antony Vidler's 'Homes for Cyborgs' (1996):

The well-known antipathy of André Breton to Le Corbusier reflected the more general opposition of Surrealism to Modernism. For Breton, modernist functionalism was 'the most unhappy dream of the collective unconscious'... (Vidler, 1996: 42).

Interestingly, the surrealists' architectural counter-suggestions could have come from any contemporary arcadian, though predictably, the surrealists' return to Mother Nature had a heavier emphasis on 'Mother' than on 'Nature'. Vidler quotes Tristan Tzara,[3] the erstwhile Dadaist, at some length:

The architecture of the future will be intra-uterine...From the cave (for man inhabits the earth, 'the mother'), through the Eskimo yurt, the intermediary form between grotto and tent (...which one enters through cavities with vaginal forms) through to the conical...hut..., the dwelling symbolises pre-natal comfort (Vidler, 1996: 43).

Irrational or not, rationalism was identified with modernism, and critics of its 'rationality' themselves ran the risk of being dismissed as 'irrational' – and still do. Environmentalists are certainly vulnerable to this dismissal, which provokes some of them to embrace the irrational with defiant wholeheartedness (e.g. Gaia as the guiding *spiritus mundi*), and others to clothe themselves in modernism's science and technology in order to acquire legitimacy.

3.5 A kinder gentler modernism

Environmental architecture is thus a product of reaction as well as action, defining itself in contrast to a demonized mainstream modernism. 'Demonized' because the rich contradictions within modernism itself, particularly the ambivalent attitude towards nature, are ignored in favour of a caricature drawn from its most unpopular aspects: its reductive universality, its infatuation with industrial production, its juvenile presumption. The work of Mies van der Rohe in such buildings as the Seagram Building (1958) and Lake Shore Drive Towers (1948–51) is the arch-instan-

---

3. See Tristan Tzara (1993). 'D'un certain automatisme du gout'. *Minotaure*, 3–4, December, 81–84.

tiation of these tragic flaws: abstract, technology-driven, hyper-'rational'. The relationship between modernism and environmental architecture is more ambiguous than this, however, because the cluster of values and strategies typifying architectural modernism are still held dear by some of those now claiming sustainability.

The technological agenda of early architectural modernism, for example, is there for all to see in the writings of Walter Gropius, in which architecture is directly connected to the forces of industrial production that have contributed to the present environmental anxiety. In *The New Architecture and the Bauhaus* and *Scope of Total Architecture,* he calls for architects to return to the site of production, in his case, the factory floor. He wants them to '1) join the building industry and...take part in influencing and forming all those component parts for building, and 2)...compose beautiful buildings from these industrialised parts' (Gropius, 1956: 88). An architect like Norman Foster can be seen following these commandments to the letter, and for the same reasons. Indeed, all the architects dubbed 'high tech' pride themselves on just this kind of engagement with an industrialized building process:

All too often designers act in isolation, leaving other specialists to 'make it work'...The scope for really integrated teams with wide-ranging skills is considerable. Current divisions between design and production will be reduced, involving the designer in new and exciting roles closely allied to industry (Foster, 1992: 25).

The intention is not merely to preserve the supremacy of architects in the face of changing technology, but to increase their scope. For modernists past and present, architects are not just engineers or artists, they are co-ordinators, and co-ordinators, not just of building projects, but of society itself.

Richard Rogers, writing on the sustainable city, holds to this view, and to the celebration of technology that was one of its foundations. Some of the technology being celebrated has changed radically, however, and the rhetoric has had to keep in step. In his Reith lectures and his book *Cities for a Small Planet* (1997), Rogers, while remaining within modernism, is critical of its dominant incarnation: 'If cities are undermining the ecological balance of the planet, it is our patterns of social and economic behaviour that are the root cause...' (Rogers, 1997: 5). Equally unequivocal is the belief, first, that change is possible, change that will enable the marginalized (the poor, the environment) to claim their due, and second, that this change is within the province of modernism itself:

My cause for optimism is derived from three factors: the spread of ecological awareness, of communications technology and of automated production. All are contributing conditions for the development of environmentally aware and socially responsible post-industrial urban culture (Rogers, 1997: 5).

Two of these 'factors', communications technology and automated production, are also vast and profitable industries whose own energy consumption and economic relations are not entirely sustainable.

This tension between vision and reality is present in the architecture, not only of Rogers, but of all those developing 'Eco-Tech'. There is a clear intention to improve the environmental performance of their buildings, and at the same time a desire not to stray too far from their previous practice and its embeddedness in the corporate status quo. Perhaps, for this very reason, these modernists can only go so far and no further with a 'reflexive' modernism. Radical critique has to come from the disenfranchised themselves. Nevertheless, one has to acknowledge the efforts those 'high tech' architects who have recognized the dangers of continuing to build in an environmentally exploitative manner. Although their work may indicate only the first stage in the development of a 'post-imperial' modernism, it is an all-important stage. Their very reluctance to allow their architectural identity to be diluted or diverted by the implications of energy efficiency has meant that they have been able to hold onto powerful commercial and institutional clients, who are reassured by the familiarity of the house style – a Trojan horse bringing change into a hostile camp.

Other architects, however, generally the uninformed, have not been open to the potential for change and innovation implicit within environmental sustainability. They are convinced that the exigencies of environmental design pose an ominous threat to their creative freedom, such as it is. Curiously, this view is epitomized in the pages of the journal *Living Marxism*. While much of the left has moved on to address environmental as well as social sustainability, *Living Marxism* lingers in some Victorian time warp in its critique of contemporary culture:

Our aim is to set a new agenda for now, by...tackling the biggest barrier to changing society today – what the Manifesto *[for a World Fit for People] describes as 'the culture of limits'...Whether the discussion is about the economy, the environment, science or social policy, there is a common assumption that there are strict limits to what we can or should do; that we are no longer capable of making much progress...We need a revolution in outlook, so that we can continue to advance and give new scope to human creativity.*[4]

This distortion, first, of the nature of these limits, and second, of the relation between these limits and creativity, is as old-fashioned as it is misleading. Such polemic reinforces the primary association of modernism with the breaking of limits, and this breaking of limits as the only authentic form of creativity. A rejection of indiscriminate limit-breaking, however, does not automatically mean a rejection of 'progress' and a return to the trees, but a rejection of some of those aspects of modernist thinking that are dangerously immature, particularly our relation to nature.[5] The question in architectural terms is whether such recognition is the beginning of a further stage of modernism, or the beginning of a transformative process that will reconstruct architectural modernism beyond the point where one can call it such. At present, sustainable practice contains both possibilities.

---

4. Advertisement in *Living Marxism*, March 1991, for *Manifesto for a World Fit for People*.
5. See Freya Matthews (1994), *The Ecological Self*, in which she discusses the need for now recognizing nature as self-realizing, and therefore a self, requiring the same self-control from us as is required in relation to other human beings.

PART TWO

4 ETHICS AND ENVIRONMENTAL DESIGN

4.1 Introduction

The Modern Movement and the environmental movement have at least one thing in common: an ethical agenda. This is framed in different ways, with the Modern Movement viewing the environmental by way of the social, if at all, and the environmental movement viewing the social largely by way of the environment. Architectural modernism, as it has survived the onslaughts of historicism and deconstruction, has largely divested itself of its ethical agenda, having failed to produce what it promised socially, and largely addressed itself to its own iconography and/or to advancing technology. The work of Jean Nouvel, the Office of Metropolitan Architecture (OMA) or I. M. Pei, for example, referred to by Marc Augé (1995) as 'Supermodernity', is nothing more than another rehearsal of the concerns of modernism minus the ethical dimension. Environmental architecture, however, whether that descended from modernism or repudiations of it, has resurrected an ethical agenda, one derived from the moral framework of environmentalism.

At its simplest, environmental ethics maintain that the instrumental exploitation of nature as a means to our ends must be replaced with a view of nature as an end in itself, with its own imperatives from which we cannot stand apart. That said, it is not possible to encapsulate environmental thinking quite so neatly. There is a deep division in attitudes to nature and humankind within it that produces very different analyses of our present condition:

note the extensive difference between all those arguments that stress the 'intrinsic' and non-instrumental value of nature, and call upon us to preserve it as an end in itself, and those that emphasise the value of nature as an essential means of the preservation and enhancement of human life, and thus the duty we have to conserve its resources for future generations (Soper, 1995: 259).

The 'naturalism' of the first view, which sets us within, rather than above, the order of nature, is typical of so-called 'deep ecology', and alien to the political left, which, if it addresses nature at all, addresses it on the basis of the second of Soper's distinctions, as a 'humanized' phenomenon, remade for our benefit.[1] Deep ecologists like Robert Goodin, Paul Taylor and A. Brennan[2] maintain that the primacy of nature over culture is not derived from its value to us, but from value intrinsic to itself, in which we participate as physical organisms among other physical organisms. The question of how we are to perceive it apart from its value to us is left hanging. The 'socialist' view of nature distributes value only so far as we can perceive value: i.e. to ourselves. Despite these fundamental differences in perspective, however, both ecologists and socialists 'share a commitment to a radical transformation of the moral order' (Benton, 1993: 2–3). The disagreement over the position of human society in relation to nature has obscured the common ground between the two groups, which should produce a united front for change, not self-defeating division (Benton, 1993). What Benton calls 'political ecologists', as opposed to deep ecologists, are as concerned with social justice as those on the left. From either point of view, the physical poisoning and social impoverishment of those who work in polluting industries, and/or have no choice but to live near them, are unacceptable. The deep ecologists, however, have an additional concern: the unacceptable effects on non-human life and ecosystems. For both socialists and ecologists, then, human damage is of profound concern, regardless of whether the human is viewed as more or less important than the rest of the biosphere. For both, a desire to reduce this damage requires a connection to be made between unacceptable environmental conditions and the social structures that bring them about, whether those structures are present capitalist or former communist ones:

to think through the implications of human 'embodiment' and 'embeddedness' [within nature] is to reduce the range of defensible visions of the good life in ways which may begin to offer the possibility of an ordered but still plural social life beyond the material unsustainabilities and social oppressions of the present (Benton, 1993: 104).

This sophisticated defence of choice is not something for which environmental politics is known, tending, as it does, to prescribe one way of life for all. Such a prescription, it could be argued, is much fairer than a variety of ways of life, but requires what universal equality always requires: compulsion. It is the iron hand in the 'good-for-you' glove that alienates many who would otherwise be sympathetic to an environmental ethics that is also a form of social justice. Nevertheless, the idea of 'environmental rights' is one that is finding growing support. These rights are an interesting amalgam of ecological naturalism and socialist humanism, in that they ground their demands for a 'life worth living' in a physical well-

---

1. See Ted Benton (1993: 31–32) re Marx in *Economic and Philosophical Manuscripts*: 'This view of a properly human relation to nature is common to the eighteenth-century practice of landscape-gardening, but extended to the global environment...Marx's vision of a "humanization" of nature is no less anthropocentric than the more characteristically modernist utilitarian view of the domination of nature.'
2. See Robert Goodin (1992). *Green Political Theory*. Oxford: Polity Press; Paul Taylor (1986). *Respect for Nature*. Princeton: Princeton University Press; A. Brennan (1988). *Thinking about Nature*. London: Routledge.

being that necessitates, at the very least, a healthy habitat, while at the same time recognizing that the environmental conditions conducive to such well-being 'cannot be defined independently of the specific patterns of social activity in relation to nature which approach and potentially exceed those limits' (Benton, 1993: 175). These 'patterns of social activity' are different in different societies, and require what any other ethical or legal system requires: a consideration of the particular case as well as the general principle.

4.2 Being good

As political critique, environmentalism claims the moral high ground and commands us to look beyond the economic gains of the exploitation of natural resources to the effect of this exploitation on the wider community, and beyond short-term profit to the fate of future generations. The argument is couched in terms of survival – of both us and the planet – the seriousness of which is intended as legitimation. If environmentalism is a matter of life and death, then who among us would choose death, the death of oneself as well as others? This formulation throws into immediate relief the ambiguous relation between self-interest and altruism that lies at the centre of environmental ethics, as it is at the centre of Judeo-Christian ethics. 'Do unto others as you would have them do unto you' – the ancient command to altruism is already couched in terms of self-interest.

Environmental ethics' claim to universal validity rests on a view of the human-as-embodied contained within a physically sustaining system (nature). As we all share this condition, whatever our cultural differences, we are all equally obligated to protect that which physically sustains us. This obligation, with a nod at Marx, takes the form of 'to each according to their needs, from each according to their use of nature'. The legitimacy of this value system rests, not in transcendence, but on that which such transcendence sought to deny: our animality. From this animality is generated a new transcendence, a moral duty that stands above the self-interest of individuals, corporations and nation states. Such claims to legitimation are far from the Aristotelian concept of ethical claims located within the specific community that formulates them. On purely material grounds, such differentiation is untenable on the level of survival: there is not a community on earth that is not sustained by the earth. Environmentalism, however, recognizes that the particular is as important as the universal, and that the whole is made up of highly differentiated parts, culturally as well as materially. Any new ethical contract between nature and culture will therefore require similarly varied interpretations, and different responses from different societies and different classes – essentially very different duties of care from the 'haves' and the 'have nots'. Despite this disparity in degrees of responsibility, however,

the immense diversity of forms of social relationship and technical means by which humans interact with external nature...should not blind us to the vulnerability of each of those various socio-natural forms to ecological constraints (Benton, 1993: 174).

There are two main obstacles to an acceptance of such an environmental ethics. The first is the debate over the reliability of the science that frames environmental degradation in terms of impending catastrophe. The second is the resistance of nation states to thinking universally. National self-interest was much in evidence at the 1998 Kyoto summit, at which developed nations like the United States sought to exempt themselves from any reduction in their own fossil fuel consumption by trading it off against the lower consumption of developing nations, much to the fury of those developing nations. (Nor does the export of cleaner technologies to developing nations let developed countries off the hook. The latter still need to contribute to a reduction of greenhouse gases as well. The buck cannot be passed to other (weaker) nations.) This refusal to think globally is a refusal to be bound by the universality of environmental ethics, to take responsibility for one's material production and consumption. Other priorities are paraded as ethical commitments in defence of this refusal, for example a commitment to preserving existing jobs. In so far as the employees themselves demand this, it is credible. The same rhetoric in the mouths of their employers suggests a slightly different reading: the preservation of existing corporate entities and their profits.

What is true of nations is equally true of individuals. Although severely restricted in membership, the polis of ancient Greek democracy was the communal bedrock upon which both Platonic and Aristotelian ethics were built. To be a 'good man' in ancient Greece was not to be good in some absolute sense, but to fulfil satisfactorily the role to which one was assigned by the polis (MacIntyre, 1996). In other words, acceptable norms of behaviour towards others were determined by the group, and by the nature of one's position within that group. This model finds little echo in late-twentieth-century democracies, in which citizenship has been replaced by consumerism, and the citizen, with responsibilities as well as rights, replaced by the private individual pursuing private happiness. Like the nation state, the individuals who belong to it perceive the ethical imperatives of environmentalism as a threat to their pursuit of happiness, as that happiness is defined by consumerism. On one level, the happiness of consumerism bears an interesting similarity to the happiness of the ancient Greek concept of virtue, in that both imply a certain material well-being. 'Aristotle's use of this word reflects the strong Greek sense that virtue and happiness, in the sense of prosperity, cannot be entirely divorced' (MacIntyre, 1995: 59). So that to be virtuous is to live well, not only morally, but materially. Consumerism is, however, material happiness run riot. It has broken the limits that prevented it from overtaxing the physical world that is its foundation.

The Aristotelian link between the public and the private good, however, was broken long before. In *Du Contrat Social* (1762), Rousseau was already noting the need to reconstitute institutions that were failing to encourage citizenship in an increasingly atomized society (MacIntyre, 1995: 187). In the late twentieth century, an entire generation in Britain has grown up under Margaret Thatcher's neo-conservative dictum, 'There is no such thing as society'. To this denial of the existence of and need for social cohesion, environmental ethics, like socialism, is implacably opposed. It recognizes both the general concept of 'society', particularly with reference to a global community of interests common to us as a species, and the reality of many different societies with differing interests. It is just this ability to straddle the universal and the particular, the global and the individual, which excites such hostility in certain quarters, for environmental ethics address the individual as directly as they do the state. Responsibility is inescapable. Owning a car, throwing out instead of recycling, not insulating one's roof, all these small domestic acts of defiance carry ethical as well as financial implications, regardless of the state's position.

This is not, however, to diminish the importance of the state within environmental thinking. It is often cast as the enemy, protecting vested interests against grass roots environmental pressure groups. In this 'bottom-up' model, to be environmentally ethical is to be anti-establishment, whether in the form of 'tree-huggers' or the more mainstream Friends of the Earth. And yet the aim of 'bottom-up' lobbying and agitation is very often to provoke 'top-down' change, to pressure the government to legislate for the environmentally ethical, so that those who ignore or resist its requirements are compelled to conform. This is very much the Platonic model. Those who do not choose the good, and they are the majority, have it chosen for them. Sceptics object that no individual or group can know the good better than another, let alone dictate its observance, but the empirical evidence of environmental science makes environmentalism's calls to moral responsibility more compelling than those of its Platonic predecessors, and their referral to some undemonstrable transcendence.

This poses an interesting problem. If at present the ethical is, to some extent at least, socially constituted, that is, if it arises from established social norms, how does one justify the demand to change those norms? On what basis is it possible, since demands for change necessarily stand outside the legitimating power of speaking from inside the establishment? The answer, for Marx, was to address those 'wants and needs which are unsatisfiable within the existing society, wants and needs which demand a new social order' (MacIntyre, 1995: 213). In the case of animal rights, for example, not only are the wants and needs different from those conventionally identified as ours, but the constituencies doing the needing are different as well: species other than our own. If the overriding desire of consumerism is to have, that of environmentalism is to have fairly, as regards both human beings and the biosphere. It is a having that does not harm constituencies in either society or nature. In contrast to socialism, environmentalism casts this fairness more in terms of health than social justice, but as Benton (1993) reminds us, universal health *is* a form of social justice. The wants and needs of certain sectors of society have already been articulated by socialism, communism, and even Christianity. The wants and needs of the biosphere – and the future human and non-human generations dependent upon it – had not been articulated until environmentalism.

How, then, does one persuade those who either cannot see there is a moral choice to be made, or, even more difficult, can see it but refuse to make it? Some of us are endowed with more 'good will' than others. That is, some of us are quite happily inclined towards the ethical, either because we have a greater capacity for altruism (according to neo-

Darwinians, in order to improve our chances of survival), or because we are empathetic enough to genuinely embrace the dictum 'Do as you would be done by', or because we have been effectively inculcated with 'our duty' from an early age. Others of us struggle between 'inclination and duty'. Still others follow their inclinations without conscience.

For political ecologists our universal duty is clear: we have to change our priorities and consequently our behaviour. Those capable of recognizing this duty will embrace it, both in their private lives, and in their lives as citizens. That is, they will do what they can in the everyday world, and campaign for leaders who also recognize this duty. If such a political change comes to pass, then those unable or unwilling to recognize this environmental imperative will be subject to some form of compulsion, financial and/or legal. They will, in other words, be induced to imitate the ethical behaviour they are incapable of freely choosing. Champions of *laissez-faire* economics condemn any such attempt to regulate producers' and consumers' behaviour as 'environmental fascism'. If one believes the environmental analysis of our present position is correct, then such epithets make about as much sense as calling the rule of law 'judicial fascism', in that those who do not choose to are compelled to observe the laws of the land or face the consequences. If one does not believe the environmental analysis of our present position, then it is quite easy to view environmentalism's moral imperative as self-righteous hectoring. With scientific evidence[3] mounting daily in confirmation of global warming, however, it becomes increasingly difficult to present individual or national resistance as rational.

4.3 Being good in buildings

50% of material resources taken from nature are building-related. Over 50% of national waste production comes from the building sector. 40% of the energy consumption in Europe is building-related (Anink, Boonstra and Mak, 1996: 8).

As if this weren't enough, 40 to 50 per cent of the world's greenhouse gas emissions are also produced by the built environment. Given the enormous impact of the built environment upon the natural one, architects cannot avoid for much longer repositioning themselves in relation to their own material production. Within environmentalism, the decisions and actions architects take matter again. Even if most of those in the building industry are still unaware of it, choices as to siting, building configuration, construction methods and materials have environmental, and thus ethical, consequences. Contractors, developers and architects tend to gain awareness of this as legislation interrupts established practice, or, more rarely, as the market demands a change. The

3. 'Through sample drillings in rock, Arctic ice and soil, it has been established that the carbon-dioxide content in the air *never rose above 280 parts per million during the last twelve million years. By 1958 it had risen to 315 parts; to 340 parts by 1988, and to 350 in 1993.* This is the result of burning fossil fuels (coal, oil and gas) and the diminishing of tropical rainforests which absorb large amounts of carbon dioxide as well as producing oxygen' (Papanek, 1995: 22; italics original).

widespread lack of environmental awareness within the building industry presents the architectural profession with the possibility of providing leadership, and recovering some of the moral authority lost during the past thirty years. Within this industry, successful architects have the highest profiles as 'actors in the world'; their decisions are 'exemplary', and can influence clients, contractors and fellow professionals alike.

In order to gain this position of influence, architects need first to educate themselves in order to educate others. The education of clients, however, even if ethically driven, is rarely effective if ethically framed. The priority for most clients is economic. Happily, the economic benefits of 'doing the right thing' are increasingly persuasive:

We are on the verge of a revolution in buildings design. Strategies and materials are at hand that can be integrated into modern buildings that consume much less energy to operate, pollute far less, are much more reliable and livable, and cost no more to construct than buildings based on contemporary practice *(Balcomb, 1998: 33).*

Again, the ambiguous relation between altruism and self-interest is apparent in this dialogue between architect and client, and no doubt between the architect and him or herself. As more environmental architecture goes up, the client can increasingly be persuaded that although a higher initial capital cost may be incurred through commissioning a 'green building', this cost will be paid back again and again in lower running costs. The environmentally ethical argument is put to one side, but does it matter how the client arrives at 'the good' if the results are the same?

The architect's other arena for ethical action is in the design and specification of the building itself. Here, too, motives are mixed. Architects engage with environmental design for a number of reasons, none of which is necessarily explicitly ethical. In a class of architects on the postgraduate Environment and Energy Programme at the Architectural Association in 1998, the range of reasons for choosing the course was more remarkable for its variety than its altruism. One member of this international group thought environmental design would provide him with a methodology that would help with design decisions. Another had worked in an office that had already adopted environmental design, and wanted to acquire greater expertise in it. Another, from India, saw passive cooling techniques as a way of promoting the vernacular solutions of her own country over and against universalizing mechanical services. Another wanted to re-establish the traditional relation between architecture and nature, but in a modern idiom. Another wanted to escape an over-emphasis on the conceptual in architecture, and reground his own work in the material. Another was fascinated by the advanced technology now available within environmental design: photovoltaic panels, smart materials and computer-operated building management systems (BMS). The closest any of the group came to an overtly ethical agenda was one student concerned about the future of over-exploited natural resources.

Architects on a graduate programme are, of course, freer to be frank than architects in practice, where the rhetoric becomes distinctly more moralistic in tone:

the developed world – with its disproportionate ownership of wealth, control of technology and influence over the means of production – bears an inescapable responsibility to make its own economies and cities sustainable... (Rogers, 1997: 174).

Victor Papanek in *The Green Imperative* (1995), goes further, adopting a biblical ring to his exhortations:

*When our designs are succinct statements of purpose, easy to understand, use, maintain and repair, long-lasting, recyclable and benign to the environment, we **inform**.*

*If we design with harmony and balance in mind, working for the good of the weaker members of our society, we **reform**.*

*Being willing to face the consequences of our design interventions, and accepting our social and moral responsibilities, we **give form** (Papanek, 1995: 53).*

Such direct appeals to our better nature alienate as many as they win over. Who are they to tell us? Who are they to prescribe and proscribe? What legitimates them as moral arbiters besides self-appointment? The simplicity of the exhortations annoys rather than inspires, leaving many with the suspicion that the qualifications and complexities of the debate have been swept to one side.

4.4 New is good?

For those architects uninterested in moral imperatives, the main concern about environmental design seems to be with aesthetic limitation. Architectural education, in particular, is still firmly embedded in Enlightenment/Modernist notions of progress, the supplanting of the old with the new (and improved). This has manifested itself in architecture in a drive towards originality – technical and aesthetic. Environmentalism brings with it a reconsideration of what has hitherto been an unchallenged assumption: the desirability of this ever-proliferating new:

The secular, mechanical view of the universe which emerged from the scientific revolution of the 17th century favoured the suspension...of all normative regulation of the concrete forms of human/natural intervention.

Only in recent times, with the growing acknowledgement of environmental outer limits, has this dimension of material culture...been brought back into the scope of normative reflection and practical regulation (Benton, 1993: 177–78).

Within a framework of survival, environmental ethics requires the reintroduction of the idea of 'limits', but of a limited kind. There are limits to certain forms of material exploitation, but within those parameters, the possibilities are limitless. It is a condition described by Benton as 'bounded but unlimited' (Benton, 1993: 177). Architects have not even begun to explore the implications of the 'new' embedded within 'limit', a limit that is material, not intellectual, hampered as they are by the association of the new with the limitless. Why environmental design should be perceived as having more disastrous an effect on creativity than any of the other limitations architects are faced with – of budget, of client demands, of building regulations, etc. – remains a mystery.

The new in architecture in the twentieth century has changed from being communal – a new 'universal' architecture for a new age – to being individual – post-modern pluralism for the consumer age. It no longer carries the salvational connotations it did within the early Modern Movement. Then the new was that which was triumphantly different from the corrupt, failed, decayed old. It was once-and-for-all different, a state of permanent newness in which there was to be no more new, because we had reached the end of the need for the new, the end of linear history. Everything had been achieved. The new was a state of being, not becoming, and architecture, paradoxically, was to acquire through modernism the durability of the old in the form of the unchanging new. Perhaps it is no coincidence that modernist buildings aged so badly. The new materials employed required that they be kept in a state of permanent 'newness', or weathering would soon make them look older than their predecessors (Mostafavi and Leatherbarrow, 1993). Even had it been achieved, one could justifiably ask 'if such a relation to newness conforms to the human desire for renewal' (Levinas, 1997: 128). A modernist utopia predicated on the end of change bears no relation to our condition as living beings defined and stimulated by change.

The pursuit, promoted by capitalist production, of continuously titillating novelty in the service of consumption is not, perhaps, the best counter-model to the 'end of history'. Based on linear time, this view of novelty is one in which the new is the on-the-verge-of-becoming or the just-become (Levinas, 1997). The new loses this newness the longer it remains present in the present, and different classes of object lose their novelty at different rates. New couture barely lasts a season, new cars hardly a year. In contrast, architecture has traditionally attempted to transcend this temporal flow of new into old. Indeed, architecture more or less escaped commodification until the 1970s, when post-modernism encouraged the 'styling' of buildings. This pushed architecture towards consumerism, by privileging style and signification over the tectonic and the social, the architect now in charge of the novel packaging of the building in order to increase its commercial allure. At the same time, environmental design was emerging as a critique of this market-induced acceleration of the consumption of energy, materials and ideas. It placed itself at a certain distance from modernist imperatives of originality, because of the environmental costliness of the new, demanding we consider whether it is necessary at all, or whether energy-efficient refurbishment isn't a greater economy of means. A new building would have to demonstrate distinct environmental advantages to justify it over refurbishment. The desirability of the new was suddenly questionable, not on cultural grounds – for instance, a desire for continuity – but on material/ethical ones. The new carries an environmental price, and as a result, the re-newed, the old made new again, is endowed with an aura it had historically in relation to mythology, but not to material culture. In Christianity's resurrection myth, for example, or science's death-defying genetic engineering, the dead – the utterly unrenewable – shall live again; the ageing – the 'un-new' – shall be young again. Environmental architecture looks to renewal both in the resurrection of historical precedents for environmental control, and in the refurbishment of existing buildings (to higher environmental standards) as one of the most important answers to environmental improvement.

Restrictive though refurbishment is to architects who view architecture primarily as a means of self-expression, there are often compelling arguments in favour of the renewal, rather than replacement of the existing building stock – moral as well as financial arguments. Those who attempt to generalize these into a commandment, however, ignore the overwhelming number of variables concerned in the choice between refurbishment and new-build. Energy is required for the first as well as the second, sometimes more energy if the task is a complex one. On the other hand, even if a new building requires more energy for construction, it may be many times more energy efficient than the refurbished building once it is up and running. On the other hand, a less efficient refurbishment may be justified on other grounds: for example, preserving the social cohesion or visual identity of a particular area. Nevertheless, whatever the complexities of case-by-case assessments, such debates within environmental design demand that architects at least question the desirability – and environmental efficacy – of the new. After all, the power of the new in architecture to effect change is limited by its rarity anyway:

the design of new buildings can contribute only a marginal improvement – only about one per cent of the building stock is newly constructed each year (Hinsley, 1996: 67).

Add to that the fact that only a fraction of this one per cent is designed by architects, and the physical impact of the new is non-existent.

There are those, of course, who deny the possibility of the new. All cultural production stands in some relation to what went before, either in a posture of continuation or of attempted discontinuity. In his book *Studies in Tectonic Culture*, Kenneth Frampton discusses the Portuguese architect, Alvaro Siza. Siza once declared, 'architects don't invent anything, they transform reality'. Etymologically and conceptually, this is a false distinction: invention is not actually invention in these terms. The word derives from the Latin *invenire*, to 'come upon, discover', which suggests that invention isn't creation at all, but the revealing of creation (by God or nature). In this reading, 'originating' is actually beyond us, a divine, rather than human, capacity. All we ever manage is to 'transform reality', that is, rearrange the given. This, in contrast to originating, suggests a re-presenting, or even a re-cycling. The word 'transforming' involves change, but in Siza's view this is only change of given forms and formations, that is, of 'reality', and changing the given is a very different enterprise from creating *ex nihilo*. We can never free ourselves from the 'conditions of emergence', the past and knife-edge present that influence the formation of the future. 'Transforming reality' is task enough, but according to what criteria is this re-formation to be undertaken?

Environmental benefits notwithstanding, it is doubtful whether we can – or should – entirely deny our desire for the new, which is not just about stimulating jaded appetites, or 'wasting' resources. Though there are obvious parallels between the idea of renewal and environmental architecture's commitment to recycling – of materials, of buildings, of techniques – there are also less obvious connections between the new and sustainability. This is important to stress, since outside sustainable practice, environmental architecture is often misrepresented as being conservative to the point of regression, rejecting intellectual and techno-logical change.

While environmental architecture does recycle ideas as old as those found in Vitruvius, it could also, if allowed, engage with the 'newest' science and theory. If environmental architecture is to have a wider cultural relevance, it is as dependent upon the new as the re-newed. The relation of environmental architecture to the new is thus the diffi-cult one of inclusion, embracing the future as well as the past. Even so, the way environmental architecture might anticipate the future stands in direct opposition to the way consumerism views it. The latter needs a future predicated on a linear extension of the present. Sustainability anticipates a future that is a rupture with the present, a shift away from the new-as-novelty to the new-as-renewal of the built and natural environments, a renewal that depends as much on new ideas and techniques as it does on reinstated ones.

4.5 The good, the bad and the juggled

At what point, then, even within the framework of 'bounded but unlim-ited', does the pursuit of the new tip over into excessive environmen-tal cost? Some within environmentalism are very clear that each newness must be environmentally justified. This newness is, of course, material, 'real'. Ideas are environmentally cheap, at least until they lead to things in the world. To this way of thinking, there is material practice that is ethically acceptable and that which is not, and the unnecessary pursuit of the new is ethically unacceptable because of its environmen-tal, and therefore social, consequences.

It is doubtful that those who defined ethics as 'moral science' viewed that science as empirical. Yet that is precisely what is being brought into the domain of ethics through the development of environmental design. By this I mean not so much that the science involved is contained within an ethical framework, though this is so, but that the framework itself is in part constituted by this empirical science. That is, ethical behaviour within architecture has a newly acquired quantitative, as well as quali-tative, basis, or rather, this moral basis can now be quantitatively legit-imated. This is not to say that quantity does not enter into conventional ethical judgement. Our concept of justice, after all, derives quantities of guilt from the quantity of intention judged to have been involved. This is expressed in 'degrees' of murder: 'first degree murder', because entirely intentional, receives a quantitatively greater punishment than 'second degree murder', or manslaughter. The same correspondence between the ethical and the quantitative holds true in environmental design, but the relationship goes further: there are measurable degrees of 'sin', that is, of fossil energy pollution. If this energy were clean, e.g. solar, it would be unproblematic. But for the most part, it is not, and forces ethics into materiality, and materiality into ethics.

In common with religious discourse, environmentalism is saturated with moral judgements about what is 'good' practice, and what is 'bad'. 'Purity' and 'pollution', the results of 'good' and 'bad' practice respectively, connote spiritual cleanliness and uncleanliness as well as literal 'cleanth' and filth. Within the Christian view, literal cleanliness and dirtiness are two of the outward and visible signs of an inward and invisible state of grace, or its lack. Within the environmental view, they are two of the outward and visible signs of an ethical consideration for the community, or its lack. The specification of copper or aluminium, for example, carries not only scientific meaning in terms of the amount of pollution created in their production, but ethical consequences. Is it ethical to put the high performance of copper or aluminium before their quantifiably demonstrable damage to the environment, and thus to the community's health? It is only the scientific analysis of building materials from this particular quantitative perspective that has enabled such a question to be asked, and such an ethical position to be taken or refused. Buildings themselves become such outward and visible signs of moral choices within the environmental hermeneutic, from their configuration and orientation, to the specification of their materials and constructional systems. As a result, architecture's materiality acquires a new, ethical significance. For the first time since the nineteenth century and the storm over the morality of cast iron and plate glass in architecture (see following chapter), materials have returned to a position of the greatest social and cultural importance.

5 MATERIALS AND MATERIALITY

5.1 Introduction

Within the framework of environmental design, we are seeing, not a demand for a 'truth to materials', but for an understanding of a new truth about materials. The new concepts of embodied energy and life cycle analysis (see below) have given material production an ethical weight that is now environmental as well as social. This return to materiality within environmental architecture is at variance with what is perceived to be the increasing 'etherealization' of culture, the result of pervasive electronic mediation: through television, information technology, the Web and virtual reality. The effort on the part of architects like Peter Eisenman and commentators like Paul Virilio has been to understand how this new world of instant replay and disembodied access to any point on the planet is affecting our conceptualizing of time and space, and therefore of architecture:

What...becomes critical is not so much the three dimensions of space, but the fourth dimension of time – more precisely, the dimension of the present...[T]he new technologies are killing 'present' time by isolating it from its here and now, in favour of a commutative elsewhere, but the elsewhere of a 'discreet telepresence' that remains a complete mystery (Virilio, 1997: 10–11).

Though increasing our reach electronically, these 'teletechnologies' literally disable us physically:

Doomed to inertia, the interactive being transfers his natural capacities for movement and displacement to probes and scanners which instantaneously inform him of a remote reality, to the detriment of his own faculties of apprehension of the real, after the example of the para- or quadriplegic who can guide by remote control – teleguide *– his environment, his abode... (Virilio, 1997: 16–17).*

Though true, and shocking, this is a partial picture. It ignores another social trend prevalent in the same wealthy countries where computer ownership is widespread: a profound environmental anxiety and a narcissistic obsession with the body – diet and exercise to produce youthful glamour, high muscle articulation for both sexes, tuned up for self-love and recreational pleasure. The growth of the 'organic' food market, for example, is not only about remaining young and beautiful, but also about staying alive, when industrial farming inadvertently poisons us and genetic engineering is a large question mark. What Virilio therefore misses in his provocative account is the dialectic between the increasing dematerialization of certain aspects of our lives, and the increasing anxiety about their material basis. As the mind flies higher and faster, the body sinks deeper into physical danger.

The same Cartesian split can be seen on a small scale within architecture, in a fascination with the dematerialized products of computer-generated design on the one hand versus a concern about the conditions of the built environment as it is presently constituted on the other. The excitement of cyber-design lies in the creation of new and complex forms. The difficulty lies in realizing them. Cyber-dream and material reality are at present very far away from each other. However much our existence is electronically mediated, that mediation is materially based – a materiality that architecture can not only accept, but defend as equally valuable. At the moment, too much architecture 'pines over and woos this haughty [cyber] technology, whose necessary desire is the obviation of the building' (Bloomer, 1993: 8).

5.2 A lost chance

Battle has been joined before to counter this loss of the 'real'. In the 1970s and early 1980s, phenomenology was borrowed by architecture to enrich the abstraction of mainstream modernism, which, in its universal application of a restricted palette of industrially produced materials, rendered those materials abstract, almost immaterial. Phenomenology, as employed in architecture, was to renew the connection between place and the materials indigenous to that place (Plate 15), using our materiality as a measure of architectural value: 'The body's limits but also its needs are...appealed to as the ultimate standards' (Jameson, 1985: 51). This it has in common with environmental design, where physical 'comfort levels', relative though they are, are paramount in an order of merit centring around the building's environmental performance. Such concepts, for Fredric Jameson, 'involve premises about some eternal "human nature" concealed within the seemingly "verifiable" and scientific data of physiological analysis' (Jameson, 1985: 51). Jameson's critique, and his preference for what he calls the culturally interpreted 'social body', say more about the left's traditional inability to give any credence to nature (as empirically assessed) than it does about the transcendentalism of environmental design. The human body does have universal characteristics, whether or not these constitute part of a 'human nature' – we are born, we thrive, we ail, we die – and these characteristics are as valid as the multiplicity of cultural interpretations projected onto the human body. Nor, in environmental discussions of thermal comfort, for example, are those socially constituted bodies viewed as universally identical. On the contrary, what is considered 'comfortable' in terms of temperature range to, say, Indian bodies, is known to be uncomfortable to northern European bodies. The physical and the empirical have as much validity within discussions of the particularity of the human as the cultural and the conceptual.

The materiality of the world is the means by which, in much phenomenological thinking, we come to know the world. Within this hermeneutic, there is no understanding of the world without physical experience of it, to which the figurative dimension of our language attests ('building an argument', 'scratching the surface', etc.). Stone is harder than the body. Willow wands are more pliant than the body. The body, or rather the dialectic between body and physical world, 'is the foundation for all other things in scientific and prescientific understanding' (Leatherbarrow, 1993: 195). For Heidegger material reality was a given, the foundation of our being. Being was being-in-the-world (*Dasein*), and we have no understanding of existence separate from the world. This world was not the one we discover through science, separated into seemingly autonomous parts by analytical thought, but the one learned of through personal experience in it, the *Lebenswelt* (life-world) of Husserl.

A revalued materiality was resurrected only temporarily by phenomenology, however. The body was subsequently buried again by others – or rather dismembered. Lacan, for example, suggests that the body, like the personality, is constituted through its mirrored reflection from 'pre-mirror stage' fragments, an origin that is repressed, and only comes out in dreams of severed limbs and isolated organs.[1] Such a 'pre-reflective' body is conceptually as 'true' as the beautiful body of humanism. Its adoption as an emblem in the work of architectural deconstruction is as valid as the order of the body-as-whole. In Bernard Tschumi's follies at Parc de la Villette, for example,

the folly stands for a body already conditioned to the terms of dissemination, fragmentation and interior collapse. Implied in every one of [Tschumi's] notations of a space or an object is a body without a centre, in a state of self-acknowledged dispersion...[I]t has finally recognised itself as an object whose finitude is ever in question... (Vidler, 1990: 8).

Where Tschumi takes a stoical view of this fragmentation and loss of centre, Coop Himmelblau takes a romantically heroic stance, splattering the body of architecture all over bourgeois Vienna in acts that are simultaneously self-obliterating and self-commemorating, echoing the extravagance of language found in Futurist writings: 'We want...architecture that bleeds, that exhausts, that whirls and even breaks' (Coop Himmelblau in Vidler, 1990: 8). Such a vision, though full of energy, is full of destructive energy if one is longing for a return to a 'dialogue with tradition', the tradition of material significance of the body and the material world it both inhabits and is defined by. Before architecture's departure into fragmentation, however, phenomenology came closer to re-establishing the value of materiality in twentieth-century architecture

1. See Jacques Lacan (1977). 'Le Stade du Miroir'. In *Ecrits* (Alan Sheridan, trans.), London: Tavistock Publications.

than any other set of ideas before environmental design. At its best, the introduction of this branch of philosophy into architecture in the 1970s produced important and valuable writing: Gaston Bachelard's *The Poetics of Space*, Christian Norberg-Schulz's *Genius Loci: Towards a Phenomenology of Architecture*, and more recently, Kenneth Frampton's *Studies in Tectonic Culture* and Karsten Harries' *The Ethical Function of Architecture*. In direct opposition to much post-structuralist writing on architecture, and its most recent fascination with the dematerializing effect of information technology, phenomenology demands a return – it is always a return – to an emphasis on the material business of making, of tectonics, in the interests of a re-reified community, relocated in identifiable places. Unfortunately for its wider reception within architecture, much of this writing based its arguments on a reductive view of modernism, an outdated view of science, and a nostalgia for a metaphysical architecture (Plate 16):

Stone used to be more than just stone: it also had meaning. Stone spoke and helped architecture to speak...We no longer understand the symbolism of architectural forms. 'On a Greek or Christian building everything originally had a meaning, gesturing towards a higher order of things...' (Harries, 1997: 347).

This kind of transcendent sentimentality is simply and categorically unacceptable to many who might otherwise be tempted to renegotiate a position with the tectonic. Frampton is more secular, and therefore more valuable in bridging the chasm between those who regret and those who accept or actively revel in the loss of a 'higher order'. His suggestion that we reground architecture in the craft and materiality of its construction is echoed by environmental design's preoccupation with the physical/ethical consequences of buildings. Frampton, however, places equal importance upon the representational function of architecture, something environmental design has as yet barely addressed. He seeks to redress an imbalance, not replace one over-valuing with another.

[He] does not wish to deprive architecture of other levels of tectonic expression but rather to reinvest a design with a now largely understated layer of meaning, one perhaps more primitive or primordial in its apprehension (Mallgrave, 1995: xi).

As material object, therefore, the building should communicate to the human-as-embodied, to the body that learns about the physical world, and itself, through direct sensory experience of that world. If there is no 'higher' order, there is still, and always will be, this ontological one on which to ground architectural design.

Architectural interest in phenomenology arose about the same time as, and perhaps in reaction to, the introduction of semiology into architecture. As a philosophical movement, phenomenology is considered by some to be the most important intellectual development of the twentieth century, and by others to encompass so many different philosophical positions, it is as ambiguous a term as 'modernism'. It embraces both the attempt to apprehend 'the thingness of things' (Heidegger) and a rarified idealism in which consciousness itself is the only phenomenon the existence of which we can be certain (Husserl). Somewhere in between stands Merleau-Ponty, who with Sartre developed existential phenomenology, and took up a complex 'both/and' position as regards the world and consciousness. For him, knowledge of the world was acquired through the body, which is neither subject nor object, and which distorts our perceptions of the world. These distortions are only revealed through 'radical reflection', which is in some way qualitatively different from the process of analysis. Analysis splits the complex fields of consciousness into meaningless parts. Radical reflection upon one's consciousness, as influenced or distorted by the body, apparently does not. Architectural theorists understandably turned to Heidegger for guidance, rather than Merleau-Ponty. It was Heidegger, after all, who wrote *Being, Dwelling, Thinking*.

It was the de-materializing semiotic analysis of architecture as a system of signs that occupied many of the most fashionable and/or competent theorists and practitioners in the 1970s and 1980s. This is hardly surprising. It is far easier to use language to discuss language – even a language of visual signs – than to discuss physical experience, much of which is too subjective and ephemeral to survive analysis, or claim objectivity. To assemble a taxonomy of architectural experiences and simultaneously keep them alive, as Norberg-Schulz tried to do in his *Genius Loci: Towards a Phenomenology of Architecture*, is a heroically impossible undertaking. The mouth-watering vernacular examples he gathered were usefully communicable only insofar as they were generalized, while the very act of generalization removed the luscious particularity for which the examples had been chosen in the first place. One cannot prescribe diversity with a book of delightful results; it arises from favourable conditions. It is, therefore, present conditions – cultural, legal, economic – that need addressing, and not the products of past conditions. This view, however, was explicitly rejected by Norberg-Schulz:

[S]ocio-economic conditions are like a picture-frame; they offer a certain 'space' for life to take place, but do not determine its existential meanings...They are determined by the structures of our being-in-the-world... *(Norberg-Schulz, 1980: 60).*

But what are these 'structures of our being-in-the-world' if they are not socio-economic structures? There is only one category left, central to phenomenology: the structures of consciousness itself, which, to Merleau-Ponty, exist at a deeper level than the manifestations of its workings (culture). There are two fundamental problems with this model. The first is the assumption that what is in fact an unresolvable debate over whether consciousness structures the world, or the world structures consciousness, is resolvable. For Norberg-Schulz's assertion to have any validity, consciousness must be viewed as being formed by nature rather than culture. Which means the culture we are born into does not influence the structure of our consciousness. It may influence its content, but not its form.

Even if we accept such a reductive model of consciousness, in doing so we are confronted by a second problem: the only way to go 'deeper' than socio-economic structures is to generalize the human being, to posit universal structures beneath the differentiation of culture. To use this as the foundation of a 'phenomenological' architecture that champions particularity is difficult, for it is only in the domain of culture, that is, of 'socio-economic structures', that this particularity shows itself – in the way things are made and the reasons for their making. This, Norberg-Schulz himself acknowledges:

Character...depends upon how things are made, *and is therefore determined by technical realisation...A phenomenology of place has to comprise the basic modes of construction and their relationship to formal articulation (Norberg-Schulz, 1980: 15).*

'Modes of construction', however, are entirely bound up with socio-economic conditions (Plate 17), whether or not they involve the deep structure of consciousness as well. The reason we don't build hand-crafted buildings any more is that the present socio-economic conditions are entirely different from those in operation when we did. A catalogue of picturesque pre-industrial examples is therefore inadequate for us now. Such contradictions perhaps explain why phenomenology got close, but not close enough, to being a critique with real transformational power, one capable of changing practice.

The recourse to phenomenology was a much-needed antidote to the abstraction infecting much architectural theory at the time, a reminder that the building was a thing-in-itself as well as a signifier in a forest of signifiers.[2] In direct contradiction to semiology, Heidegger insisted on the reality of the referent: 'All significations, including those that are apparently mere verbal meanings, arise from reference to things' (Heidegger, 1982: 197). By the time Heidegger's often impenetrable work reached architecture, however, it had been watered down into a rather wishful agenda:

a simple phenomenology of our everyday environment. Phenomenology in the sense of environmental awareness...is a rediscovery of the world as a totality of interacting, concrete qualities...When this is accomplished we may say that we 'dwell', in the true sense of the word, and become ready to save the earth (Norberg-Schulz, 1988: 16).

What is remarkable about this language is its similarity to that used in much environmental writing, and yet the leap is never made to viewing the building as a truly 'interacting, concrete' thing bound up in a world of 'interacting, concrete' things. The 'thing-ness' of buildings is of interest to this phenomenological school only insofar as it serves a historically conscious material culture. An ecology of materials is never reached. Such a self-conscious poetics is of course useful to the creation of environmental architecture, but the challenge now is to achieve an inclusiveness of signification and environmental performance.

---

2. 'For Kant, the "scandal of philosophy" is that no proof has yet been given of the "existence of things outside of us", but for Heidegger the scandal is "not that this proof has yet to be given, but that such proofs are expected and attempted again and again"' (Inwood, 1995: 347).

5.3 Telling the truth

Choosing to engage with 'materials as facts' requires engaging with some or all of their 'real' properties: density, strength, colour, etc. There is no particular virtue in this, and games played with conventional expectations can and do cause us to reflect upon the 'true' nature of the material being played with. It is merely that in playing this way, the material is dematerialized, in that its 'nature' is distorted, its characteristics masked or reversed. Ruskin condemned such distortions as 'moral delinquency' (Ruskin, 1989: 34) in *The Seven Lamps of Architecture*:

Touching the false representation of material, the question is infinitely more simple [than structural dishonesty], and the law more sweeping; all such imitations are utterly base and inadmissable (Ruskin, 1989: 48).

Such dogmatism arises from a particular view of the relation between nature and culture, a view, first of all, that acknowledges there is a relation, and second, that culture is legitimated by nature. Disguised or synthetic materials, in this construct, obliterate their connection with nature, thus making them 'illegitimate'. If, however, it was just this connection one wanted to sever, in order to celebrate cultural production as autonomous and superior, then it is this very 'illegitimacy', this inability to determine a material's origins, that is desirable. For Gottfried Semper, the disguising or hiding of structural elements by in-fill or decoration was desirable to such a degree that the textiles typical of the in-fill were presented as the one true source of architecture:

Textile Art
A primordial art (Urkunst) *as it were. It alone generates its types from itself or from analogies in nature; all other arts, including architecture, borrow types from this art (Semper, 1989: 175).*

All other arts therefore are re-presentations of this original and originary presence. As we dressed ourselves in textiles, so we dressed our shelters with them. The sight of a woven South Seas hut at the Great Exhibition of 1851 had led Semper to a theory of architecture in which the screen was valued over the structure, and colour was valued over both, for colour was pure representation, at the very least a masking of the 'matter' (structure) beneath, at its most extreme, an obliteration of it (Plates 18–19): 'This annihilation of reality, of the material, is necessary if form is to emerge as a meaningful symbol, as an autonomous creation of man' (Semper, 1989: 131).

The structural is a necessary evil, an unwelcome reminder that culture cannot entirely transcend nature (matter) – the building has to stand up and give shelter. The representational is a discrete and superior aspect; it is that to which structure is literally subservient, hidden underneath applied decoration. The decoration or masking of architecture, with textiles or frescoes or cladding, is the equivalent of decorating the body with clothes, tattoos or paint: it transforms the given, the 'natural', into the cultural, the material into the ephemeral. It is the obverse of Ruskin:

*It is...true that there is no falsity, and much beauty, in the use of exter-
nal colour...But it is not less true, that such practices are essentially
unarchitectural...they divide the work into two parts and kinds, one of
less durability than the other, which dies away...and leaves it...naked and
bare. That enduring noblesse I should, therefore, call truly architectural...
(Ruskin, 1989: 52).*

From here, differences between the two only increase. For Ruskin, truth
to materials means not only expressing the material itself 'naked and
bare', but avoiding the representation of one set of tectonics through
the medium of another – for example, wood techniques expressed in
stone. For Semper, idea does not emerge from material conditions; it
precedes them:

*Just as nature in her variety is yet simple and sparse in her motives,
renewing continually the same forms by modifying them a thousand-
fold...in the same way the technical arts are also based on certain proto-
typical forms (*Urformen*) conditioned by a primordial idea, which always
reappear and yet allow infinite variations conditioned by more closely
determined circumstances (Semper, 1989: 136).*

Such a view is meant to free cultural production from nature, and yet
Semper uses nature as an analogy. He may wish to 'annihilate' matter,
but he, like Aalto after him, looks to nature's evolutionary model for his
cultural one.

In his weightiest text, *Der Stil in den technischen und tektonischen
Kunsten oder praktische Asthetik* (*Style in Industrial and Structural Arts,
or Practical Aesthetics*) (1860–63), Semper develops his theory of imitation, *Stoffwechsel*. In this, idea, in the guise of 'type', precedes
construction – at least after the original development of the type. For
example, he, like other theorists before him, asserts that 'typical'
elements such as classical architecture's columns and entablatures
derived originally from primitive huts – not the invented primitive hut of
Laugier, but anthropologically evidenced primitive huts, such as the one
Semper saw at the Great Exhibition. Since that beginning, these typical
elements have been transferred from wood to stone without difficulty,
divorced from their material genesis. They became part of a symbolic
language that transcended its origin in base matter. As with typical
elements, so with building types: the *parti* was what mattered, that is,
the organizing idea, not the substances through which it was realized.
A cloister could be built of wood, stone or sealing wax. It was of no
importance. What was important was to develop new typologies for the
new age of mass production (by rearranging old ones), and to subordinate the new materials to this old strategy. There was not even the
desire, as there was in Viollet-le-Duc, to allow the new materials to
suggest new forms, to find a new architecture in new physical properties.

Semper's ambivalence about matter is perhaps understandable when
one considers the time at which he is writing. The mid-nineteenth
century saw developments in technology that began to make traditional
ways of judging artefacts highly problematic. The limits on production and

form imposed by the 'nature of materials' and the repertoire of the human hand were being broken both by new techniques of working 'natural' materials, and by the manufacture of new 'industrial' materials, like iron and plate glass. Semper does not fear the loss of certain materials *per se*, but the loss of transferring easily architectural ideas from one set of materials to another. It was as if these industrially produced materials were a block to the usual 'annihilation of matter' by architectural idea:

Where does the depreciation of materials brought about by the machine, by their surrogates, and by so many new inventions lead us? What effect will the depreciation of labour, a result of the same causes, have on the painted, sculpted, and other kinds of decorative work? Naturally, I am not referring to the depreciation in fees, but in meaning, in the idea (Semper, 1989: 138).

Semper rejected the possibility of reproducing a traditional symbolic language within the new dispensation in materiality – industrial mass production. Such a system could reproduce stylistic elements, but mindlessly, and without the contribution of the interpretative hand. Or perhaps he rejected it only for his generation. In 1869 he gave a lecture in Zurich (*On Architectural Style*) in which he looked to the next generation to develop a 'suitable architectural dress' for the big new idea of the century: mass production (Semper, 1989: 284).

The thought that these new materials *were* the big new idea, that expressing them rather than 'dressing' them was the answer, was unthinkable to Semper, but not to Viollet-le-Duc. In the face of industrially produced iron and plate glass, Viollet-le-Duc demanded a truthful acknowledgement both of their difference from 'natural' materials, and the meaning of that difference:

In architecture there are two necessary ways of being true. It must be true according to the programme and true according to the methods of construction. To be true according to the programme is to fulfil, exactly and simply, the conditions imposed by need; to be true according to the methods of construction is to employ the materials according to their qualities and properties... (Viollet-le-Duc, 1959: 382).

Although the Modern Movement was heavily influenced by such French rationalism, Viollet-le-Duc himself never found the new forms to embody his new agenda, and inclined naturally towards the Gothic because of its structural 'honesty'.

The Gothic style is a very clear example of the split in the nineteenth century between those who began to view architecture primarily as tectonics, and those who viewed it primarily as idea. Though, in the *Lamp of Truth*, he echoes Viollet-le-Duc in declaring that good architecture is that which avoids pretending to be what it is not, structurally and materially, Ruskin spurned the architectural use of iron. For him, iron had greater negative symbolic value than it had positive structural benefit, representing all the evils of industrialization, particularly the translation of the hand-work of the human being into mechanical reproduction, denying those who made things the traditional opportunity to express themselves directly through the work of their hands. This, in turn, for Ruskin, denied architecture much of the life it once had: 'things...are noble or ignoble in proportion to the fullness of life which either they themselves enjoy, or of whose action they bear the evidence' (Ruskin, 1989: 148). The use of traditional materials preserved traditional techniques and the traditional ways of life that contained them.

In his concern for the physical as well as the social price industrialization exacted, Ruskin has more in common with contemporary environmentalism than Viollet-le-Duc, who saw the problem as one of appropriate architectural expression, not inappropriate social and environmental cost. Ruskin was appalled by the break with 'nature' the Industrial Revolution dictated:

The very quietness of nature is withdrawn from us;...All vitality is concentrated through those throbbing arteries into the central cities...The only influence which can in any wise there take the place of the woods and fields, is the power of ancient Architecture... (Ruskin, 1989: 198).

But Ruskin's call for a return to 'natural' materials was as unrealistic as his idealization of medieval society. Although the concern for humanity and nature was laudable, his solutions were wishful.

Dismissed as 'materialists' by Semper and Ruskin, architects and theorists like Karl Botticher and Viollet-le-Duc looked to 'base matter' to form the beginning of a new architecture. They did not achieve this: Botticher confined iron to classical forms, and Viollet-le-Duc to Gothic. Nevertheless, as Frampton describes in *Studies in Tectonic Culture*, Botticher wrote a startlingly prophetic passage in 1846 that reversed Semper's order of architectural development. Here, it is materiality that stimulates idea, not idea that transcends materiality:

Our contention that the manner of covering determines every style and its ultimate development is confirmed by monuments of all styles...A new and so far unknown system of covering...can appear only with the adoption of an unknown material, or rather, a material that so far has not been used as a guiding principle. It will have to be a material with physical properties that will permit wider spans, less weight and greater reliability...it must be such as will meet any conceivable spatial or planning need...Such a material is iron...Further testing and greater knowledge of its structural properties will ensure that iron will become the basis for the covering system of the future... (Botticher in Frampton, 1995: 84).

This 'covering', as it evolved into structural steel, will eventually inspire, if not 'determine', a radically new spatial and tectonic economy: the International Style.

5.4   Building the truth

A discussion of materials inevitably encompasses nineteenth-century theorizing, but also new ideas that have a degree of urgency about them not inherent in either the pursuit of truthful expression or semantic games.

As with so much within the domain of environmental sustainability, this new consideration of materials does not inspire – or dictate – a particular aesthetic strategy, but does suggest an ethical one. Materials have a much longer life than the buildings they make. In a sense, they are immortal, neither created nor destroyed, merely transformed from one state to others. They therefore exist in some form before construction and in some form after demolition or decay. This 'eternal' life has environmental and ethical implications. The energy used and pollution produced during the extraction, transformation, transportation and assembly of building materials, their performance during the life of the building, and their possible waste and pollution through dumping after the life of the building, are increasingly unavoidable considerations for the whole of the building industry.

If one repudiates neither modernity nor technological experiment, how does one pursue them sustainably? The industrial processes necessary to manufacture advanced building materials use more energy and create more pollution than the preparation of 'natural' building materials. Performance may be higher using these synthetic materials, an important factor in complex public buildings, but their environmental cost is also higher, and the process of trading off these costs against results is a minefield, mapped less by science than ideology. If you are 'for' modern technology, then you will rationalize your choice of energy expensive materials and technologies. If you are 'against' modern technology, then you will argue in the opposite direction. Governments and big business back modern technology because it is much less of a challenge to the status quo, requiring less reorganization of existing infrastructures and redistribution of power. The same multinational corporations can start manufacturing 'environmentally friendly' products to replace their current, more dubious offerings, whether it be cars, chemicals or glass. The same governments can administer and police the changeover. This is viewed by some as a vital economy of scale, without which a switch to renewable energies is impossible,[3] and by others as the same old vested interests taking over a grassroots drive to escape them.

Whatever direction the solution takes, the problem is the same: our production of wastes far outstrips the environment's ability to absorb them. We produce and consume too much too quickly, and it overwhelms the much slower, more delicate pace of assimilation through natural processes. Environmental accounting provides a framework for assessing this environmental impact at every scale of production. Developed during the 1990s, this 'life cycle analysis' (LCA)[4] is

---

3. 'I have maintained for some time that while small may be beautiful, bigger is likely to be better in terms of reliability and performance. I see the future of solar energy as requiring an opting into the advantages of large-scale industrial processes and technological cooperation, and not in opting out...Individual communes may survive happily in rich countries well-endowed with land, but the energy needs of the vast cities of the world simply cannot be sustained that way. Too often "green dreams" on solar energy are quite out of touch with "green realities"' (Page, 1994: 39).
4. Life cycle analysis was first set out by the World Wildlife Fund (WWF) and the Society of Environmental Toxicology and Chemistry (SETAC) in 1990 and 1993 respectively (see bibliography). 'More recently, the International Standards Organization (ISO) is establishing standards under the ISO 14000 series (Environmental Management Systems). The ISO LCA procedure consists of three phases: Goal Definition and Scoping, Inventory Analysis and Impact Assessment' (Murphy and Hillier, 1997: 78).

a detailed understanding of the impacts incurred during an entire life cycle [of an object], from the extraction of raw materials through manufacturing, use, and eventual recycling or discarding (Van Der Ryn and Cowan, 1996: 91).

The advantage of this environmental assessment method is that it puts the product in an industrial context, and looks inclusively rather than selectively at its environmental impacts. This does not, or does not yet, refer to the life cycle of the building as a whole, only some of its constituent parts. There may always be too many variables to success-fully perform a life cycle analysis on entire buildings, though this would be of more use to the architect (Murphy and Hillier, 1997). Potentially of greatest use to the architect is a Building Research Establishment (BRE) database that is in the process of being assembled. This would provide an LCA of all construction materials.

It is the processes of extraction, manufacturing and transportation that are referred to in the phrase 'embodied energy': the energy it takes to produce a given building material and get it to site. This is measured in kilowatt hours per ton: 'Wood has the least embodied energy at 639 Kilowatt hours per ton. Brick is next (4 × the amount for wood), followed by concrete (5 ×), plastic (6 ×), glass (14 ×), steel (24 ×) and aluminium (125 ×)' (Van Der Ryn and Cowan, 1996: 95). It should be clear from these simple facts that choosing to construct a building out of steel and glass is pushing the embodied energy count towards its ceiling, and that adding new, rather than recycled, aluminium will send it through the roof. It should be clear, but such simple conclusions are useless unless the purpose and performance of these materials are also taken into account. One has to compare like with like, which suggests a case-by-case comparison of materials for the same structural function.

First, one has to look at a job that wood can do, say supporting a pitched roof, and then compare it with steel and concrete. Under those circumstances, wood probably wins. But given a structural job wood cannot perform, does one then automatically go for concrete over steel? Its embodied energy is less, and it would seem to be an obvious choice. And yet one may very well use less steel than concrete for the same task, and less of a material with more embodied energy would proba-bly even the score between the two materials. And then the steel foundry may be closer to the site than the cement factory, which would save on fossil energy transporting the steel to site.

Obviously, if the energy being consumed in extraction and manufac-ture were clean and freely available, then the amount embodied in any given material would be of no consequence. If we had solved the problem of nuclear fusion, for example, and could produce energy from a glass of water with no radioactive waste, or if we had vast solar energy farms that supplied all our needs, then environmental auditing within building would concentrate on the impact of methods of extraction and construction rather than energy consumption. But such is not, or not yet, the case. It is therefore important that architects are fully aware, not only of the genesis of the building materials they specify, but of their proximity to the site, and their afterlife, if and when the building is demolished. No decision is categorical, merely one of several options in a complex juggling act that is trying to satisfy many, often conflicting, demands – from the client, the users, the environment, the planners, and the architect him or herself.

Materials raise fraught questions about who can lay claim to designing sustainably, and with what justification. Conferences are a vivid indication of the current debate. In 1996, for example, at a conference held at the Centre for Earthen Architecture at the University of Plymouth on *Contemporary Design from Traditional Materials*, architects, academics, scientists, builders and administrators from all over the world gathered to discuss the merits of natural local materials: rammed earth (Plate 20), thatch, stone, adobe, wood. In the same year, a conference was held by the European Commission in Berlin on *Solar Energy in Architecture and Urban Planning*. Architects, academics, scientists, industrialists and politicians gathered to discuss the merits of industrially produced, advanced sustainable building technologies.

The difference in delegates at the two conferences is revealing. In Berlin there were representatives from major corporations and politicians from central government, instead of the builders and local administrators of the Plymouth conference. It is obvious where the power and money lie. There are other differences, however, more germane to this discussion: differences in the choice of materials being promoted. 'Natural' local materials like those championed in Plymouth are usually part of a larger 'low tech' vision that seeks to reduce to a minimum the damage building does to the environment. At their 'greenest', the use of these materials is integrated with recycling schemes, organic cultivation of food, and the use of entirely passive heating and cooling techniques within a rural context, all at a density low enough to allow each household to be autonomous in terms of energy generation and waste disposal.

Though more energy-expensive to produce, advanced technologies can lay claim to doing more than just 'paying back' their environmental cost, in that they can often produce clean energy themselves. A productive photovoltaic system in an energy-efficient building can put electricity back into the grid when surplus to the building's requirements. Individual buildings, organized systematically – especially in urban contexts – could eventually act collectively as a power station. The higher amounts of energy required to produce such systems could thus be 'paid back' by the clean energy made available for others to use. The ability of individual households to produce their own energy also has far-reaching implications for the present distribution of power, in both senses of the word.

The central argument between such advanced systems and 'low tech' ones is over what is referred to as *capital energy cost*, that is, the total energy used in all the stages of a material's manufacture, from raw material to finished product. Even framing the problem is contentious: should we be arguing about how this capital energy cost is to be repaid, or about whether the energy capital should have been spent in certain ways in the first place? Can even rapid repayment with interest (clean energy back into the grid via photovoltaics or wind turbines) ever justify a more environmentally expensive method when less expensive ones are available? Every unit of polluting energy used in the making of, in this case, a building is a debit. It is repaid by saving on the use of polluting energy in the later running of the building, but it is never removed. What has been burned can never be unburned. The problem with the idea of repayment is that one can justify any amount of capital energy cost, as long as one can eventually repay it. The very high capital energy cost of buildings made of steel, smart glass, and even aluminium, could be justified by their later energy productivity when up and running.

What, then, is an acceptable length of time for energy repayment? It may take anything from eight to eighty years to pay back the energy expended making a building. Would an agreed-upon time serve as a quantifiable criterion for a building's sustainability? At the moment, environmental performance is measured by the burning of so many kilowatts of electricity an hour per square metre of building (kWh/m^2) – in other words it is measured by the energy running costs of the building, and doesn't include life cycle analysis of the building's constituent parts. Meeting energy running targets is at present voluntary. The incentive for a client is to win the seal of approval from the Building Research Establishment, which sets these targets, an approval that increasingly is adding to the desirability of a property in terms of lower running costs and easier sell or rentability. The concept of payback, therefore, will not discourage an architect from specifying materials with high embodied energy, but a limit on payback time might. It is a question that applies to all 'Eco-Tech' architecture claiming sustainability: does the production of surplus clean energy justify the comparatively higher amount of fossil energy required to make the building? Could the same surplus have been produced by a less energy costly design? If one is judging these buildings from the standpoint of their contribution to experimental work in environmental technique, they will be received more favourably than if one is judging them from the standpoint of bottom line fossil energy reduction.

5.5 Grounded

Historically, materials in architecture have been means to a representational, as well as a constructional, end: smoothed, polished and ordered into states far from their original ones. With synthetic materials, the distance from their origins is even greater, and it becomes impossible to discuss their 'nature'. Yet one should not exaggerate the difference between natural and synthetic materials. They all have physical properties, and these properties are often discovered through the act of building (Plate 21).

Lucretius understood materials to have primary and secondary properties, or characteristics, which, he says, must be distinguished from accidents...; the former are attributes that can neither be detached or separated from an object...and the latter are attributes whose advent or departure will leave the nature or essence of the object intact (Leatherbarrow, 1993: 193).

The primary properties of building materials are those physical characteristics that are present *in situ*, that is, their nature in nature: density,

strength in tension, strength in compression, heat resistance, brittle-
ness, pliancy, weight per unit of measure. The secondary properties are
those that appear when the material is modified through our interventions: cutting, polishing, baking, etc. The distinction, of course, is non-
existent. The discovery of primary properties is as reliant upon our
intervention as the discovery of secondary ones.

What contemporary interest there is in the materiality of architecture
tends, outside phenomenology, to be an interest in the signification of
building materials, in the meanings that have accrued to marble, iron or
glass, rather than their environmental implications. Viewed this way, as
representative of a particular aspect of a particular culture at a particular time, materials have become oddly dematerialized (Plate 22). The
'dematerialization' of architecture thus refers not only to an increasing
'lightness of being', but to the restriction of the consideration of materials to materials-as-signs, not signs-and-things. The sign's referent may
lie originally in the 'nature of the thing', but the fact of the thing and its
material consequences are an irrelevance in this context.

A sophisticated analysis like that by David Leatherbarrow and Mohsen
Mostafavi, of Herzog and de Meuron's Goetz Gallery, Munich (1992)
(Plate 23) may rely on aspects of the physical properties of stone and
glass, but it is the architects' confounding of the conventional readings
of these materials that interests the writers, not the stone and glass as
things-in-themselves:

*The 'lightweight' glass used in the facade of their Goetz Gallery in
Munich, for example, gives the impression of supporting 'heavy' stone.
The reversed position of these materials contradicts the normative logic
of construction, an apparent irrationality* which transforms the semantic
associations of the chosen materials – *stone/traditional, glass/modern
(Leatherbarrow, 1996: 62).*

It is the game that intrigues:

*In the space of the tension between transparency and opacity, the role
and the meaning of materials are destabilised. The* a priori *iconographies
of the facade are supplanted by the configurational juxtaposition of
materials as facts (Leatherbarrow, 1996: 64).*

These materials, however, are not 'facts'. If they were facts, the stone
would crush the glass beneath it. They are the contradiction of the
'facts' of stone (load-bearing) and glass (non-load-bearing). Or rather,
they read as the contradiction of those facts. This stone is 'in fact' stone
cladding, and the reading of it as anything else is due to the fact of the
supporting structure behind, which allows these semantic games to be
played. The game itself, and the attention paid to it, are perfectly legitimate pursuits within architecture. If nothing else, they force us to
consider architecture's materiality again, if only from the distance of
signification.

The question is, can one combine this interest in the meaning of
materials with an equal interest in the ontology of materials, and can
this ontology have a bearing on anything but 'natural' materials? Peter

Salter believes: 'ways must be found to conform and work with nature to resolve...[architectural] propositions in the landscape' (Salter, 1989: 11) (Plate 24). This is ostensibly easier using less processed rather than more processed materials, but Salter is under no illusions about the effect our interventions have on the 'naturalness' of natural materials. Nevertheless, less processed ones still carry more of an aura of their origins in nature that for Salter, maintains a continuity between the architectural object and the material nature of which it is made:

To propose a space enclosed by natural material is to call forth the material's inherent power and quality as a fragment of nature...the ghost of its natural habitation within the ground... (Salter, 1989: 48).

This is the traditional legitimation of architecture by nature interpreted in a traditional way: through the visible correspondence between what nature is made of and what buildings are made of. The greater the material's 'metamorphosis', however, the less it is possible to maintain this continuity between building and nature, which Salter sees as the architect's duty.

What is important for environmental architecture in Salter's work is not the literalness of the connection with nature, but the fact of the connection, the acceptance of architecture as a material as well as a conceptual practice, embedded in time (through weathering and use) as well as floating in a certain 'atemporality'. Salter's particular version of architectural materiality is an attempt to dodge the dominant means of production within the building industry. Indeed, in his work, the industrial is almost entirely replaced by the craft-based, the one-off, the handmade, the particularized. This is not, however, the only way to re-establish the visibility of architecture's material foundation. The work of Renzo Piano can be seen as achieving an inclusive position between the craft-oriented 'naturalist' materiality of a Salter and the cyber-oriented 'metamorphosed' materiality of a Foster. Like Aalto before him, Piano has adopted a wide palette of 'natural' and synthetic materials that both grounds his architecture in a nature it cannot escape, and a culture that can negotiate, a 'post-imperial' contract with this nature. Environmental architecture that adopts such an inclusive position can express more overtly the continuum from less metamorphosed to more metamorphosed materials, differentiated, not through degrees of closeness to nature, but the amount of fossil energy implicit in those degrees of closeness.

5.6 Conclusion

The concept of life cycle analysis links architectural expression directly to means of material production, and thus to real, as opposed to imaginary, ethical dilemmas, that is, ones directly affecting the well-being of the community in a way that the 'honest' expression of materials or their masking does not. The new truth to materials is not that of 'telling the truth' about them, as in 'what you see is what you get', but of weighing up the environmental and thus social costs of their production. Being able to read clearly what a building is made of is irrelevant within

Plate 1
iGuzzini Illuminazione Headquarters,
Recanati, Italy, MCA.

Plate 2
Inland Revenue Centre, Nottingham,
Michael Hopkins and Partners.

Plate 3
Queens Building, De Montfort University,
Leicester, Short Ford Associates.

Plate 4
Monument Towers, Phoenix, Arizona, Emilio Ambasz and Associates: two twenty-five storey office towers intended to echo the rock formations of Monument Valley. The towers are clad in horizontal fins to deflect any direct sunlight from the interior.

Plate 5
Guggenheim Museum, Bilbao, Spain, Frank O. Gehry and Associates.

Plate 6
Reservoir, Chateau Villandry, the Loire.

Plate 7
Herne-Sodingen Academy Government Training Centre, IBA Emscher Park, Germany, Jourda et Perraudin: exterior view of glazed envelope. The roof is covered in photovoltaic panels.

Plate 9
Moat, Chateau d'Angers, France.

Plate 8
Herne-Sodingen Academy, Jourda et Perraudin: the effect of the photovoltaic panels on the interior.

Plate 10
The Getty Centre, Los Angeles, California, Richard Meier &
Partners: biomorphic shading element.

Plate 11
'The Architecture of Genetic Space', Architectural Association
Diploma project by Tomas Quijano and Marit Rastogi, John
Frazer – Unit Leader.

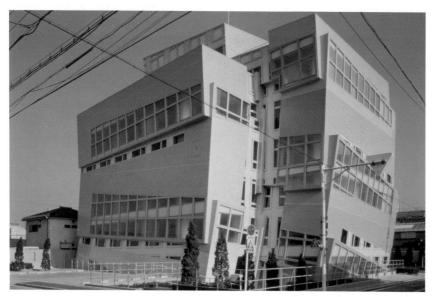

Plate 12
Nunotani Building, Tokyo, Eisenman Architects: shifted elevation.

Plate 13
Reichstag, The New German Parliament,
Berlin, Foster and Partners: cupola and
part of the roof.

Plate 14
Antwerp Courthouse, Belgium, Richard Rogers and Partners: the building is in the
design stage and is intended to have hyperbolic paraboloid roofs constructed of
plywood shells on glulam frames.

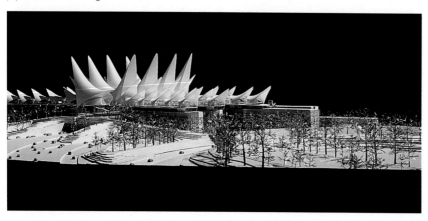

Plate 15
Old Palace, Dungapur, Rajasthan: stair of local slate.

Plate 16
Delphi, Greece: metaphysical architecture.

Plate 17
Old Palace, Dungapur, Rajasthan, first courtyard: indigenous 'modes of construction'.

Plate 18
Temples, Luxor, Egypt: painted.

Plate 19
Temples, Luxor, Egypt: unpainted.

Plate 20
Rammed earth wall, Feldkirch Hospital, Austria, Martin Rauch.

Plate 21
Gary Group Office Building, Culver City, Los Angeles, Eric Owen Moss: courtyard façade.

Plate 22
Norton Residence, Venice Beach, Los Angeles, Frank O. Gehry and Associates.

Plate 23
Goetz Gallery, Munich, Herzog & de Meuron Architekten.

Plate 24
Construction for *Writing the City*, Stockholm, 1998, Peter Salter: clinker built urban marker entered through rammed earth walls.

Plate 25
Business Promotion Centre, Duisburg,
Germany, Foster and Partners.

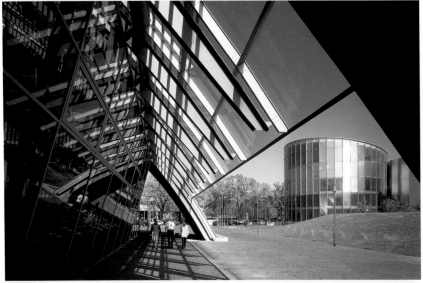

Plate 26
Telematic Centre, Duisburg, Germany:
View from Micro Electronic Centre, Foster
and Partners.

Plate 27
Micro Electronic Centre, Duisburg,
Germany, Foster and Partners.

Plate 28
Tribunal de Grande Instance, Bordeaux, France, 1998, Richard Rogers Partnership: end elevation – loggia and courtrooms.

Plate 29
Tribunal de Grande Instance, Richard Rogers Partnership: interior of one of the criminal courts.

Plate 30
Theatre and Casino: entrance, Potsdamer Platz, Berlin, Renzo Piano Building Workshop.

Plate 31
Mushrabiya, Meharangarh Fort, Jodhpur, Rajasthan.

Plate 32
New Gourna, Egypt, Hassan Fathy.

Plate 33 (left)
Kamiichi Pavilion, Japan Expo, 1992, Toyama, Japan, Peter Salter.

Plate 34 (right)
Water Temple, Hyogo, Japan, Tadao Ando Architect and Associates.

Plate 35 (left)
Nishiyachiyo Town Centre, Emilio Ambasz and Associates: Torii Gate containing offices, restaurants and a museum.

Plate 36 (bottom left)
Torrent Research Centre, Ahmedabad, ABHIKRAM and Brian Ford Associates: stack vents lining external walls, wind-catchers on roof.

Plate 37 (bottom right)
8522 National Boulevard, Culver City, Los Angeles, Eric Owen Moss: an entrance.

Plate 38 (left)
Queens Building, De Montfort Universit, Short Ford Associates: interior.

Plate 39 (below left)
Saudi Arabian National Museum, Riyadh, SITE.

Plate 40 (below right)
Archeolink Prehistory Centre, Oyne, Scotland, Edward Cullinan Architects: 80% of the building fabric is underground.

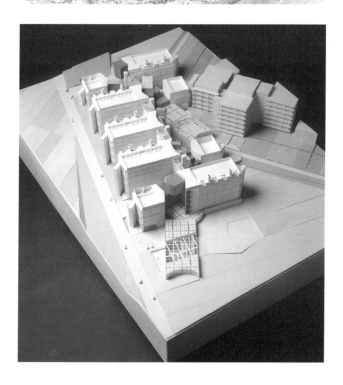

Plate 41 (bottom left)
Bio-centrum, J.W. Goethe University, Frankfurt, Germany, Eisenman Architects.

Plate 42 (bottom right)
Aronoff Centre for Design and Art, University of Cincinnati, Eisenman Architects.

Plate 43
Tennessee Aquatorium, Chatanooga, SITE: a centre dedicated to the history, science and preservation of water.

Plate 44
GSW Headquarters, Berlin, Sauerbruch Hutton Architects: west façade of the main administration building showing the coloured sun screen panels. Behind is an existing 1960's block to which this 85 metre high 'slice' has been added, along with a 10 metre high podium.

Plate 45 (below right)
Magney House, New South Wales (1984), Glenn Murcutt: galavanized corrugated iron holiday pavilion on a treeless site by the sea.

Plate 46 (below left)
Magney House: interior.

Plate 47 (top left)
Paper Gallery, Tokyo (1994), Shigeru Ban Architects: a space for the Miyake Design Studio. The recycled paper tubes bear the entire vertical load.

Plate 48 (top right)
Hall 26, Hanover Messe, Germany, Thomas Herzog and Partner.

Plate 49 (centre left)
Westminster Lodge, Dorset, Edward Cullinan Architects: the first of five residential lodges at Hooke Park, a centre for the ecological use of wood in furniture and construction, built with thinnings from the surrounding woods.

Plate 50 (centre right)
Peckham Library, London, Alsop and Stormer Architects: copper cladding and red 'beret', which shades the clerestory glazing of the central interior 'pod'.

Plate 51 (left)
Peckham Library: one of three pods containing a meeting room, a children's activity centre and an Afro-Caribbean study centre, clad in varnished plywood.

Plate 52
University of Future Generations, near Sydney, Australia (competition entry), Richard Horden & Associates: site model showing the large institutional buildings of the university broken up into smaller ones, and strung around an artificial lake.

Plate 53 (centre left)
Roof-Roof House (1984), Malaysia, T.R. Hamzah & Yeang.

Plate 54 (centre right)
Exhibition (EDITT) Tower, Singapore, Malaysia, T.R. Hamzah & Yeang.

Plate 55 (bottom left)
Tjibaou Cultural Centre, New Caledonia, Renzo Piano Workshop: the 'cases' made of iroko wood.

Plate 56 (bottom right)
Tjibaou Cultural Centre, New Caledonia: traditional Kanak hut under construction.

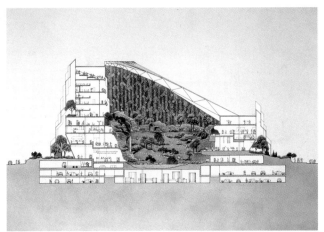

Plate 57 (top left)
Model of the Manoir d'Angoussart, Bierges, Belgium, Emilio Ambasz and Associates: a counter-proposal to the Palladian villa: centrifugal, dispersed.

Plate 58 (top right)
Model of the Schlumberger Research Laboratories, Austin, Texas, Emilio Ambasz and Associates: a computer research facility that can adapt easily to changes in research group size.

Plate 59 (left)
Nichii Obihiro Department Store, Obihiro, Japan, Emilio Ambasz and Associates: the store will cover a two-and-a-half acre site, containing, as well as retail, micro-factories for baking, wine bottling etc., hotels, wedding chapels, health clubs and restaurants.

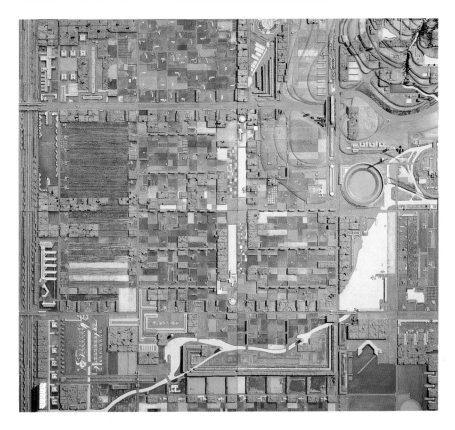

Plate 60
Model of Broadacre City, Frank Lloyd Wright, 1934.

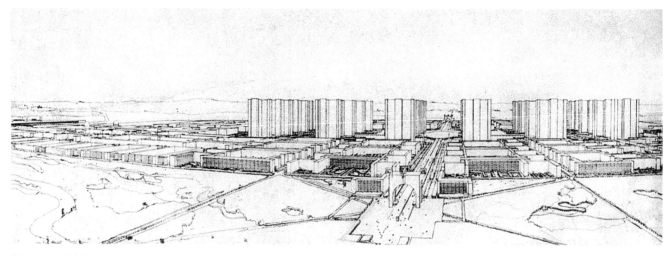

Plate 61 (left)
City of three million inhabitants, Le Corbusier, 1922: green belt around the city.

Plate 62
Beddington Zero Energy Development (BedZED), Croydon, Bill Dunster architects: aerial view from south-east.

Plate 63
Beddington Zero Energy Development (BedZED), Croydon, Bill Dunster architects: section showing mixed use development.

Plate 64
Valencia, Spain: linear park in the old riverbed.

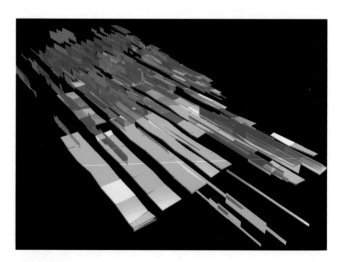

Plate 65
Arabianranta, Helsinki, Finland, 1995–96, OCEAN UK: urban design phases 1–3.

this new dispensation. What is important is the fact of a material's presence, not its readability. Wood may be painted to look like aluminium, but the deception is harmless. What would be genuinely harmful under certain circumstances, and thus unethical, is the use of real aluminium. Nostalgia, then, for a lost meaning in materials is unnecessary. Looked at differently, there is a world of meaning in them, meanings that have the potential, if those on either side of the environmental divide recognized the value of the other's interests, of joining the phenomenon and the sign, and reconciling the 'nature' of materials with the culture of meanings.

PART THREE

6 RULES OF ENGAGEMENT

6.1 Introduction

There is no reason why environmental design's science-based enquiry and architecture's traditional concern with form should not co-exist; indeed, why architectural form should not be enriched by an environmental agenda, as long as that agenda is not prescriptive. The utilitarian ethos that characterizes much of the environmental movement does not sit easily with formal exploration, however. Cast in ethical terms, the debate pitches puritans against aesthetes, the first group asking the second: should 'the formal concerns highly specific to the architectural community...themselves be informed by other concerns specific to a larger community' (Bess, 1996: 379)? This is putting it too mildly for many environmentalists, who would maintain that architecture's 'formal concerns' should be not merely 'informed by', but entirely subordinate to the community's larger concerns.

The view put forward in this book is that the new cannot be excluded from the generation of the sustainable any more than the old can, and that this 'new' is not only new science, but new forms and new ideas. The last two are neither irrelevant nor unethical. On the contrary, they are vital if an architectural shift is to be achieved at the beginning of the twentieth-first century on the scale achieved by the Modern Movement in the middle of the twentieth century. No one who does not appreciate the importance of the visible as an instrument of persuasion, an importance that has increased geometrically during this century, will ever win enough hearts or minds to precipitate the desired 'change for the better':

[A]rchitecture as a subregion of ideology seen from the perspective of signification and culture allows a work at the level of form...that transcends the apparent functionalist determinism (Agrest, 1993: 2, 3).

As long as environmental design permits the self-consciousness required of ideological critique only in the realm of ethics, and not aesthetics, then the possibility of environmental architecture that is culturally as well as environmentally effective will remain a question mark.

This statement will, of course, raise objections from those architects already pursuing sustainability to one degree or another, who will insist that they are already producing a culturally effective architecture, and that consequently there is no question mark over its existence. To some extent, this is true: current production may well come to define the parameters of environmental architecture, and that in itself is a contribution to our culture, architectural or otherwise. The self-consciousness of existing production varies greatly, however. Environmental architecture endeavours to meet a certain level of energy efficiency, and during that process, architectures have emerged which make visible some of the devices of environmental design. There are other architectures, however, that pursue environmental sustainability without this visibility, and do not similarly push environmental design into cultural consciousness.

With a view to increasing the reflexivity, and so the visibility, of environmental architecture, this chapter puts forward three criteria for both identifying and generating it: 'symbiosis', 'differentiation' and 'visibility'. These are examined here as self-conscious positions to be taken up, and in the next chapter, as they are emerging in practice. In one sense, these are not separate criteria at all, but locations on a continuum consisting of different modes of engagement with a new contract of chosen co-operation between architecture and nature (as opposed to the 'unchosen' co-operation of pre-industrial building, in which instrumentality was limited by less powerful technologies). The three criteria, then, are 'rhizomes' rather than stem and branch of a 'tree', to use Deleuze and Guattari's terminology.[1] At the same time, they represent separate enough priorities to be identifiable as discrete areas of concern within this continuum, which may vary in priority. These criteria allow environmental architectures to overlap territories, fulfilling one, two, or all three criteria, and thus avoid classification into what would otherwise be an overly neat taxonomy of a diffused and confusing reality. The criteria also permit other, 'non-environmental' architectures to enter the discussion: an architecture fulfilling the criterion of visibility and no other is not environmentally sustainable, but could be considered to have entered the sphere of influence of environmental architecture. I refer particularly to architects such as Peter Eisenman, Foreign Office Architects, Jeffrey Kipnis and Bahram Shirdel, who are exploring new models of nature in order to generate new forms.

Briefly, the first criterion, 'symbiosis', considers the building in its construction and operation as much as possible as a dynamic system among other dynamic systems, co-operating with them rather than further damaging them. Sustainable building technology, with its use of renewable energies and pursuit of a circular model of consumption, is clearly symbiotic, with the building's operation modelled as closely as

---

1. 'Arborescent systems are hierarchical systems with centres of signifiance [sic] and subjectification...' (Deleuze and Guattari, 1996: 16). 'Such is indeed the principle of roots-trees, or their outcome: the radicle solution, the structure of Power' (p. 17). '...[U]nlike trees or their roots, the rhizome connects any point to any other point...In contrast to centered (even polycentric) systems with hierarchical modes of communication, and preestablished paths, the rhizome is an acentered, nonhierarchical, nonsignifying system without a General and without an organising memory or central automaton, defined solely by a circulation of states' (p. 21).

possible on metabolic processes. The second criterion, 'differentiation', considers whether biological diversity implies cultural diversity, specifically architectural diversity, and what environmental advantage may be gained by pursuing it. The third criterion, 'visibility', considers whether the present range of formal approaches within environmental architecture, from those based on traditional vernacular models to those developing modernism, are the only options. Very few of these take into account the self-conscious expression, as well as enactment, of a new voluntary contract with nature, though the use of vernacular techniques reminds us at least of the old involuntary contract. The criterion of 'visibility' therefore asks whether this push towards conscious signification should not be included in environmental architecture. The issue of visibility pushes beyond architectures-made-sustainable: it marks out the ground on which some environmental architecture doubles back to architecture-as-art, that is, to directed expression. This is not even an oblique reference to an identifiable style, but to an approach that is both environmental action and re-presentation of that action at a reflective distance. The particular form such 'reflexion' took could vary greatly, from something like the freeze-frame imagery of Eisenman's tectonic plates to the landform architecture of Emilio Ambasz, and would be modified by the consideration of matter as physical reality as well as conceptual model. The formal flamboyance of an Eisenman or an Ambasz does not sit well with the utilitarians of environmental design, however, just as the hortatory self-righteousness of some environmentalism alienates those who have so far resisted its moral imperatives. Nevertheless, there is potential for visibly environmental architectures other than environmental functionalism, towards which firms like SITE are feeling their way.

These three criteria are interrogatory rather than prescriptive, a way to direct one's thinking about environmental sustainability in architecture, and by no means everyone would agree that all three are either necessary or appropriate. For many environmentalists, the first, 'symbiosis', is the only necessary measure of environmental sustainability, even if not a fixed measure, and 'differentiation' is subsumed under it. In accepting the remaining criteria as criteria, one is already editing the enquiry, directing the debate down certain avenues and not others, which makes this book normative as well as critical. The enquiry therefore sits both outside and inside its subject, as perhaps most enquiries do. The three criteria are able to perform this double function of analysis and generation because they indicate different kinds of architectural engagement with an environmental agenda, from operation alone through to the representation of the significance of that operation. This engagement *can* have an effect on form at the level of symbiosis, and *will* have an effect on form at the level of visibility. An examination of the relationship between environmental design and architecture has to begin somewhere, and if nothing else, these criteria will provide a basis for the development of others.

In fact, qualifying as environmentally sustainable may prove to be vastly simpler than this set of relationships between a building's operation and its form. It may in the end come down to meeting certain quantified targets of energy efficiency. If you meet them, your building is sustainable. If you don't, it isn't. The arbiter of environmental sustainability in this country is the Building Research Establishment (BRE).

The Environmental Standard award is given to those who pass the BRE's Environmental Assessment Method (BREEAM), which was launched in 1991. There are standards for five types of building, from houses to office buildings, and all of them work on a credit system, some of which the building must earn to qualify, some of which are at the discretion of the architect. The Environmental Standard for houses, for example, tries to minimize any damage new houses may cause to the local and global environment, and promote healthy indoor conditions. The latter may seem irrelevant, but it is where most people in the West spend 90 per cent of their time, exposed to formaldehyde, wood preservatives, bacteria, dust mites, radon, lead, etc. Besides the effect of the built environment upon the climate, the BRE wants us to bear in mind the effects of the climate upon buildings, effects we have contributed to by *NOT* considering the effect of the built environment upon the climate. Global warming may require a greater use of air conditioning and the possible need for better humidity control. It may also mean increased infestation of insects, change in water table levels that might result in unstable ground conditions, and flooding.

Credits are earned across global, local and indoor categories, and the assessment results in a pass or a fail. Some credits are compulsory and some voluntary, and the decision on which should be which is distinctly peculiar. It is compulsory, in order to win an Environmental Standard award, to achieve at least one credit in carbon dioxide reduction. The first credit requires that the production of carbon dioxide from a building be restricted to 29–31 kg/m^2 per year. If the building exceeds this reduction rate, it wins another credit. The same is true for CFCs: the building receives one credit for specifying insulants that have an ozone depletion potential of 0.1 or less, and another if the ozone depletion potential is reduced to zero. These requirements are important, and one would expect to see them. Requiring the provision of space for people to put recycling bins seems less important, especially when at the same time, concern for the ecological value of the site is not required. This seems extraordinary, as it permits voluntary rather than mandatory credits for using brownfield sites, the use of which the government has made a priority.

Other equally important areas of consideration have been deliberately omitted: for example, embodied energy, the use of renewable energy sources, the design of the building and systems for easy maintenance, the use of renewable materials like wood, instead of non-renewable ones, the recycling or reuse of building components, water economy measures, provision of wind shelter and sun shading, etc. The BRE does this because

no clear improvement on current regulations or normal practice can be defined...; there is insufficient evidence of a problem; or...there is no satisfactory way to assess a particular issue at the design stage (Prior and Bartlett, 1995: 2).

It is, however, difficult to see how the design of a building and its systems for easy maintenance, or the reuse or recycling of building components, can be excused for any of these reasons. The most problematic aspect of the award, however, is the fact that it is based on work done at design stage, and not when the building is up and running. Any estimates of energy efficiency are therefore just that: estimates. Anything more requires an analysis of performance in use, again, by the BRE. Inside temperatures all over the building and electric lighting use have to be monitored over a year to judge its performance through all the seasons, and all occupancy variations.

The award, therefore, does not, at present, mean very much: it is voluntary and undemanding, and is not within the BRE's remit to make it anything but voluntary. It is government's business to make the meeting of these targets compulsory, and increasingly, though not as quickly as other European countries like Germany and Sweden, the British government is revising the Building Regulations to change both design and construction methods.[2] In housing, for example, interim provisions are expected to be in place by December 2001, with full implementation following some two years after. These 'energy efficiency provisions' will require significant improvements in housing insulation, which will affect wall construction and window design. Domestic lighting will be addressed for the first time, and for non-domestic buildings, minimum efficiency standards will be introduced for air-conditioning systems. Finished buildings will be required to match the approved designs in terms of targets and house-builders envisage switching from brick construction to steel or wood frame houses. A carbon index is also being considered, which would offer the architect maximum design flexibility by treating the building as a whole, and basing its performance on its overall annual carbon emissions. It is this increasing quantification of environmental sustainability, then, that is beginning to characterize the criterion of symbiosis.

6.2 Symbiosis

Environmental architecture is concerned above all else with the construction and running of the building.[3] This is the *sine qua non* of sustainability, with its own historical antecedents and its own future. Symbiosis means literally 'living together, contributing to each other's support' (OED), in this case, the built environment redirected towards peaceful co-existence with the natural one. Buildings that use renewable energy and recycled or low energy materials fulfil this essential criterion. A symbiotic relationship is only possible if the building fights entropy like a natural system, blurring the line between the man-made and the given. If the built environment is capable of co-operative flexibility rather than oppositional rigidity, then we sustain the environment,

---

2. See the web site of the Department of Energy, Transport and the Regions: www.construction.detr.gov.uk/consult/eep/index.htm
3. One of the most recent and best organized guides to sustainable building methods and materials is by David Anink, Chiel Boonstra, and John Mak (1996): *Handbook of Sustainable Building.*

and the environment sustains us. It is an old relation that is new for us in the West at the turn of a century. Currently, fossil energy goes into a building, and waste and energy are expelled in a linear model of consumption. In nature, ecosystems have evolved to minimize this linear energy loss, forming circular patterns of consumption in which all the parts fit into interlocking wholes that are as efficient as possible: flowers feed bees; bees pollinate flowers; flowers become fruit; fruit feeds birds; birds spread seeds; seeds become flowers; flowers feed birds, etc. (Fig. 6.1). Traditional societies happily followed this model for centuries; our technology enabled us to break out of it. Environmental architecture, then, aims not so much to return the built environment to traditional means of husbanding resources, but to the traditional awareness of the need to husband them. Rejoining the virtuous circle of consumption outside a pre-industrial arcadia is a challenge both inside and outside architecture.

6.2.1 Paradise regained?

Vernacular building is viewed by many as the central paradigm for environmental architecture (Plate 26). Vernacular is a word much used, but to what, exactly, does it refer?

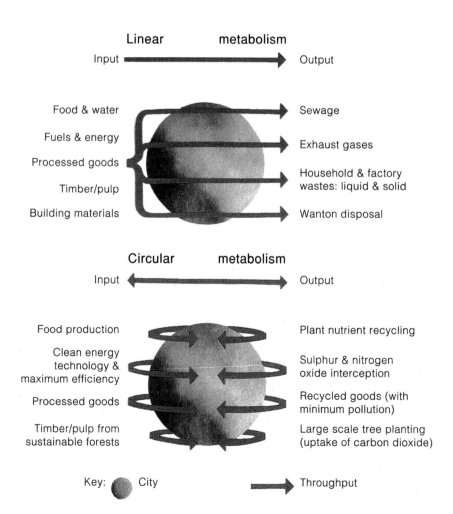

Fig. 6.1
Consumption models, Herbert Girardet.

In topics related to cultures and languages, 'vernacular' means native, indigenous, home-born, by the people, i.e. popular, folkish...(as opposed to literary, metropolitan, civic and artistic), local, provincial or parochial (as opposed to nation-wide, international, scientific or academic) (Gurenc, 1990: 295).

Vernacular building, then, is, in the words of Bernard Rudofsky, 'architecture without architects'. Rudofsky's is an idealized view of vernacular building as 'immutable, indeed, unimprovable' (Rudofsky, 1964: 1). Although this has undergone much scrutiny since, the same romantic celebration of vernacular builders as a touchstone of truth, integrity, participation and anti-élitism pervades much writing on environmental architecture. The craft traditions these craftsmen adhere to, the disciplined acceptance of received techniques and ornament they bow to, and the culture 'of the people' they thus continue are held up in critical contrast to the arrogance and alienation of the cult of expertise, in this case, of the professional architect.[4]

The word 'vernacular' is now more complicated than this, however. In addition to traditional vernacular, based on anonymous craft production passed down from generation to generation, and modified by external influences brought by invasion or trade, there is contemporary vernacular, of the kind Robert Venturi wrote about in *Learning From Las Vegas*, the junk of junk culture – hot dog stands, gas stations, etc. Contemporary vernacular informs some architectural post-modernism, particularly work by Venturi himself. Traditional vernacular informed modernism. In painting, Picasso borrowed from African tribal art; in music, Bartok borrowed from Eastern European folk tunes; in architecture, Frank Lloyd Wright, Alvar Aalto and Le Corbusier all borrowed from indigenous styles.[5]

Those who look to vernacular building as a model for environmental architecture fall into two distinct groups: those who are pursuing an anti-industrial, pro-craft vernacular revival, and those who see it as a source of valuable principles and tried and tested techniques of passive environmental design. The first group wants to return to the craft culture and perceived spirituality of vernacular architecture, an interpretation in tune with the 'mystical' end of environmentalism, in which both nature and architecture are re-animated:

If you stand in front of, or go into, a new building nowadays the usual feeling is one of emptiness. It waits for someone to come along and give it love, cosiness, individuality...Such buildings have not yet started the process of being ensouled *(Day, 1990: 106).*[6]

---

4. '...[V]ernacular architecture [is] the architecture of the ordinary builder, the person with neither pretension nor claim to genius, who has nevertheless availed himself of patterns and principles through which to please his clients...It is my view that we should pay far more attention to the vernacular in architecture than to the masterpieces of the art' (Scruton, 1994: 3).

5. 'Wright's "Prairie Style" was meant to be regional in both derivation and fit. Aalto's work was allied to the building traditions and crafts of Finland...Le Corbusier, especially in his Algerian and Indian work, frequently cited local form and construction techniques as inspirational' (Highlands, 1990: 34, footnote).

6. See also Pearson (1989).

The second group looking to traditional vernacular as a model for architectural practice is interested in a central lesson to be learned from its example: the idea of living within the limits of resources:

The peasant world view...holds that resources available to man are...'limited'. If this is a valid premise, then vernacular architecture may be expected to have been built [according to] the basic principle of 'limitedness'. Rather than a vernacular revival, it is this principle or ethos of 'limited good' that may lead the way to survival (Gurenc, 1990: 296).

Until the advent of modern industrial production, with its vastly increased capacity at seemingly no physical cost to ourselves, the effort of making anything – a house, a city, even a table – was too great to waste. Every object was therefore used, reused and adapted until it wore out, and even then, the parts were recycled. One still sees this in shanty towns, where coke cans and car tyres are reconstituted as shacks. The combination of the machine and fossil fuels made us forget this economical approach. We produced easily and to excess, and we went on producing and consuming as energy costs in the 1980s rose by 100 per cent (Fitch, 1990), and the ozone layer started disappearing. A literal return to traditional vernacular is not called for, however. On a purely practical level, it doesn't necessarily produce ideal dwellings. It does the best it can with what is to hand. In comparison with 'modern urban standards of scale, amenity, safety and permanence,...vernacular architecture is often unsatisfactory' (Fitch, 1990: 267). It is the observance of 'limitedness', an economy of means within an industrial framework, that is of interest. For example, the production of concrete need not cease, but the use of natural aggregates may soon have to. There is a limit to the amount of shoreline and quarries that can be devoured in their extraction, and there are new techniques that allow the use of recycled materials as aggregates instead: old tyres, recycled glass, even crushed concrete from demolished buildings for lower grade construction.

6.2.2 Terra cognita

As important to contemporary architecture is the use of traditional vernacular as a storehouse of ingenious passive environmental techniques developed to mediate between climate and interior. When fossil and nuclear fuels come at such a high environmental price, we cannot afford to dismiss low technology methods using renewable energy. This should not imply a repudiation of modern technology, but does suggest its redirection. What characterizes sustainable building technologies, high or low, is the consideration of the building as one integrated system, not a collection of systems that may be at war with one another: 'There is a breakdown of barriers between building fabric and services design. Both are part of the energy system design' (Evans, 1993: 39).

Before mechanical heating, ventilation and air conditioning (HVAC) systems, the structure and configuration of the building – the fabric –

had to do the mediating between external and internal climates, with heavy or light walls, large or small glazed openings, orientation toward or away from the sun, various shading devices such as shutters, verandahs, overhangs, etc., and ventilation techniques such as cross ventilation, stack vents, wind-catchers, etc. (Fig. 6.2). In the nineteenth

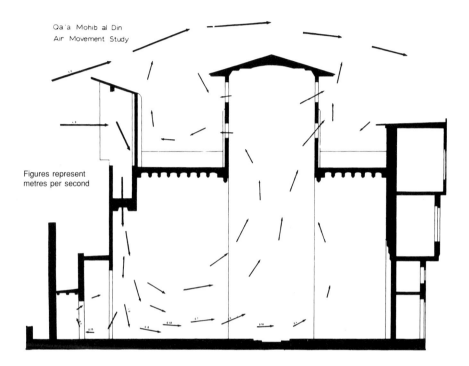

Qa'a Mohib al Din
Air Movement Study

Figures represent
metres per second

Fig. 6.2
House of Qa'a Mohib al Din, Cairo, section showing wind-catcher to bring air into the interior of the house, and qa'a tower to vent hot air to the exterior.

century, as inventions for heating and ventilating buildings were manufactured, the dream of complete control over the interior climate seemed within reach. In the US, the goal was pragmatic: to make the skyscraper, the new temple of commerce, habitable. Architectural histories tend to dwell on structural steel and the invention of the lift as the keys to this new building type, but HVAC systems, electricity, the telephone and even the flush toilet were also vital, as Reyner Banham[7] showed (Banham, 1984: 72). In Europe, however, by the time of the Modern Movement:

---

7. Reyner Banham's *The Architecture of the Well-Tempered Environment* (1984) is a very rare history of the underbelly of modernist architecture: the mechanical, rather than structural systems, that made it possible. He was attacked, during the environmentally sensitized 1970s, for privileging comfort above environmental cost, charges which he failed to rebut successfully, as his admiration for the achievement for those inventors, engineers and manufacturers who made our interior worlds healthier and cleaner outweighed any worries he may have had about the price they exacted from the exterior world. The book is, nevertheless, an invaluable history of an unjustly ignored subject. For those interested in the history of nineteenth-century heating and ventilating technologies, Banham cites an article by Robert Breugmann (1978). In *Journal of the Society of Architectural Historians*, Vol. XXXVII, No. 3, October, 143–66.

The use of this new technology...was not so straightforward:...the promise of improved environmental quality was...ruthlessly sacrificed on the altar of a geometrical machine aesthetic and the honest expression of everything, including the sources of light (Banham, 1984: 124).

This led to a lot of glaring light-bulbs and ferocious headaches. Gropius' Bauhaus was particularly brutal in this regard, with Le Corbusier not far behind. Suddenly double height windows that traditionally faced north were turned towards the south; double glazing was forgotten, and air conditioning wasn't mentioned until Corbusier went to the US in 1935.[8] The vernacular model of differentiated structure to mediate between outside and inside was emphatically repudiated – for ideological rather than practical reasons:

Every nation builds houses for its own climate. At this time of inter-penetration of scientific techniques, I propose: one single building for all nations and climates (Le Corbusier, 1984: 159).

As if this universality of structure were not enough, the interior climate was to be universal as well:

The buildings of Russia, Paris, Suez or Buenos Aires, the steamer cross-ing the Equator, will be hermetically closed. In winter warmed, in summer cooled, which means that pure controlled air at 18c. circulates within forever (Le Corbusier, 1984: 159).

And so it was, and still is, in buildings all over the world, whether you want air at one fixed temperature or not, whether you want to open a window or not. Mechanical systems became essential in mediating between human being and climate to compensate for the building's inadequacies of structure and orientation. The addition of computer controls from the 1970s onwards merely reinforced the commitment to the sealed environment.

Opening up the building to the elements again does not dictate one particular strategy. There are three main ones that are currently being pursued: returning to a position where the building's structure, configu-ration and orientation do all the mediating through passive environmen-tal design; developing an 'ecological high tech', or opting for a hybrid 'both/and' strategy which uses both passive and active systems to control the internal environment.

Dean Hawkes, in his book *The Environmental Tradition*, adapts Ebenezer Howard's famous 'Three Magnets' diagram (Fig. 6.3) to produce three new magnets, not this time addressing the Garden City, but the environment (Fig. 6.4). The 'three magnets of the environment' are the 'exclusive', the 'pragmatic' and the 'selective' (Hawkes, 1996:

8. 'The two big institutional buildings which, with the Villa Savoye, terminate and crown his work of the twenties – the Pavillon Suisse and the *Cite de Refuge* – both have their main glazed elevations facing within a few degrees south and take the full impact of the midday and afternoon sun. Both, in consequence, have presented serious solar heating problems' (Banham, 1984: 152–53).

113). These are three different strategies for designing buildings. The 'pragmatic' is an unconsidered approach. There is no awareness of climate in planning the building's form or orientation. Things happen as they may: windows, for example, are installed for illumination or perhaps façade composition, with no thought for solar gain or heat loss. The second magnet, the 'exclusive', became mainstream modernism's primary strategy, in which the external environment was almost entirely excluded from the building, and an artificial interior environment was created by means of fossil-fuel powered mechanical systems. Hand-in-hand with this approach usually went an inappropriate use of materials: for instance, single-skin glazed curtain walls facing due south in a climate with hot summers, demanding the constant use of air conditioning to maintain internal thermal equilibrium. What Hawkes calls the 'selective' approach has been described in this book as 'symbiotic'. They are two words for the same strategy: reactive designs that take advantage of available renewable energies – sun and/or wind and/or water – and allow the building's fabric to absorb many of the climatic pressures.[9] This can be done entirely passively, or using a combination of passive and active strategies. The return to using structure and configuration to mediate between inside and out is not entirely a return, as it is on a new level

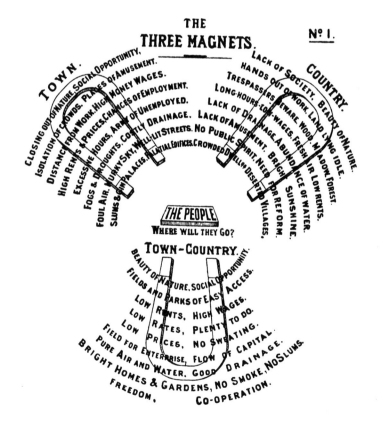

Fig. 6.3
Three Magnets, Ebenezer Howard.

9. 'I proposed...a simple distinction between two modes of environmental control – the "selective" and the "exclusive". This argued the virtues, with respect to environmental quality and energy-saving, of "selective" designs, which use the form and fabric of the building envelope as a filter for the external environment. In combination with user control of envelope, plant and systems, this approach can produce designs that are...environmentally sound and architecturally rich' (Hawkes, 1996: 109).

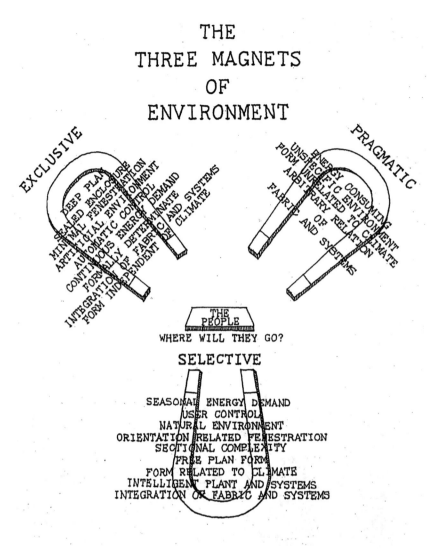

Fig. 6.4
Three Environmental Magnets, Dean
Hawkes.

of scientific understanding. The materials and devices used for the external walls and windows of a building can now control with much greater precision the amount and type of energy flowing through them in either direction (Fig. 6.5).

An example of an exclusively passive approach of architectural interest can be found in the experiments of the American architect and teacher, Ralph Knowles, with what he calls 'solar zoning'. This involves, on the level of planning, sun rights: solar access and, inevitably, solar zoning legislation. On the level of architecture, it involves buildings sculpted into complex shapes to maximize exposure to the sun in cold and temperate climates, and to minimize it in hot ones. Solar zoning is necessary for such an architecture so that no building unreasonably overshadows another, and each has maximum access to usable solar energy. Knowles' solar architecture is arrived at through the calculation of the 'solar envelope'. This he describes as:

a logical and rational construct of time and space defined by the movement of the sun [across a particular site]...The envelope is depen-

Fig. 6.5
Office of the Future, Building Research Establishment, Watford, Fielden Clegg Associates: an active system of computer-controlled sun-tracking louvres are combined with a passive system of stack ventilation.

dent upon the time of day and season, and it is dependent on the shape and orientation of the [site]...[I]t is as much a function of time as it is of space (Knowles, 1981: 87).

This envelope is obviously different, not only in different climatic regions, but at different times of year. Where 'Eco-Tech' overrides these differences, Knowles embodies them. As he says, '[t]he formal implications of changing orientation and scale are dramatic. The crystalline forms emerge as unique' (Knowles, 1981: 105). The use of the word 'crystalline' is indicative of an approach that seeks to meet dynamic change with static configuration, something that will meet average solar conditions for each season and time of day. Most environmentally designed buildings function this way, for example with overhangs calculated to exclude sun in the summer, when its angle is higher, and admit it for solar warming in the winter, when its angle is lower. The other approach, which is to make aspects of the building as dynamic as the climatic conditions they are meeting, requires computers to track the sun's path and adjust louvres, window openings, etc. accordingly.

An exclusively active, that is, mechanized environmental system is in fact extremely rare. Even most 'Eco-Tech' is hybrid, using passive heating, cooling and ventilation techniques as well as machinery. Nevertheless, in contrast to other hybrid systems, 'Eco-Tech' has tended to generalize the solution to the point where a universally applied, technological 'fix' is acceptable. But even that seemingly clear-cut choice raises questions about the level of technology to use. One can see Foster and Partners in their work in the Microelectronic Park in Duisburg, for example, searching for the optimum kinds and levels of technology as they designed three commissions. The Park was meant to signal a shift in the Ruhr valley away from traditional heavy – and polluting – industry to the next generation of technology. Foster's designed three buildings for the park: the Business Promotion Centre (Plate 25 and Fig. 6.6), the Telematic Tower (Plate 26 and Fig. 6.7), and the Microelectronic

Fig. 6.6
Business Promotion Centre, Duisburg, Foster and Partners: typical floor plan.

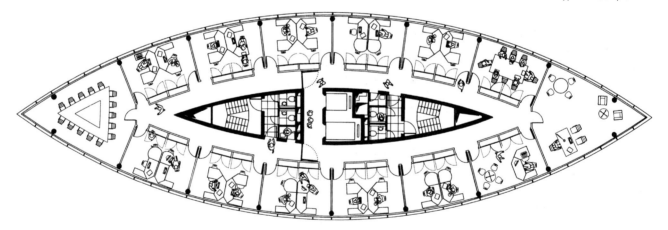

Centre (Plate 27 and Fig. 6.8), which illustrate the impossibility of fixing 'Eco-Tech' to one strategy, at least technically. The Business Promotion Centre, for example, was a sealed building, intended to demonstrate the effectiveness of cutting edge microelectronic controls. It comes under the heading of 'smart' or 'intelligent' buildings.

Smart buildings are 'smart' because some or most of their functions are computer-controlled – internal environment, security, lighting. An automated environmental control system is programmed to adjust the internal climate according to time of day, type of activity, density of people, and season. The last involves

sensors to detect shifts in exterior temperature...These communicate with the central control system to adjust the temperature within individual rooms or among groups of rooms (Downing and Koelker, 1988: 128).

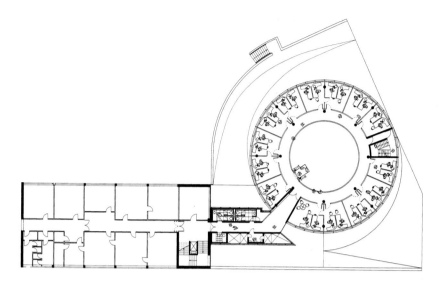

Fig. 6.7
Telematic Centre, Duisburg, Foster and
Partners: typical floor plan.

Such 'smart' buildings have something to teach us in terms of anticipation and flexibility, but not in terms of simplicity and sometimes even
reliability. Instead of the built form absorbing some of the environmental pressures through its constitution and configuration, computer
technology has to cope with it all. This preserves 'modern architecture'
in all its undifferentiated universality at the price of a greater expenditure of energy in materials and control systems. The sophistication of
this technology does, however, allow the building to come much nearer
to the complexity of a natural dynamic system. Walter Kroner of the
Rensselaer Institute fantasizes about a truly intelligent building that 'may
change its colour, envelope configuration, orientation and composition...float in water, rise up and go down into the ground or rotate'
(Kroner, 1988: 159) as the need arises, carrying the dynamic approach
to environmental design to its logical extreme.

Foster and Partners learned a great deal from the Business Promotion
Centre, not least that the simpler the system, the less there is to go
wrong. Consequently, the Microelectronic Centre is much less complicated technically. It is open to the outside so the building can make use

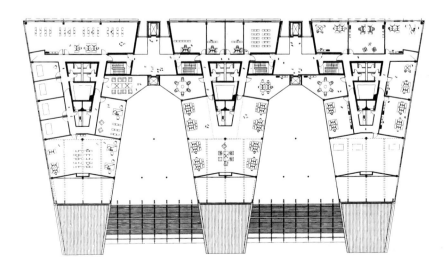

Fig. 6.8
Micro Electronic Centre, Duisburg, Foster
and Partners: upper level plan.

of natural ventilation, but some of the temperature control is achieved through large sun-tracking louvres and low emissivity glazing. This is a more hybrid approach than the one used in the Business Promotion Centre, using a mixture of high and low technologies. Louvres, for example, are traditional shading devices. Sun-tracking louvres are therefore a hybrid of the original low technology and a new advanced technology. Natural ventilation is at the low end of the scale, and low emissivity glazing at the high end – again, a hybrid approach.

What, then, is the problem? Why aren't buildings like this universally welcomed? Is it solely a question of expression, of these buildings doing one thing (trying to operate sustainably) and saying another (celebrating instrumental technology)? Perhaps, but this contradiction is indicative of a more important one environmentally. Though hybridity is emerging as the dominant approach in most environmental architectures, the almost exclusive use of industrially manufactured materials with a high embodied energy content is not. Why pursue hybridization in the building's systems and not in its materials? Foster Associates and Richard Rogers Partnership, both associated with an unrelenting diet of high-performance, industrially produced materials with a high embodied energy content, are already confronting this question. Rogers' Tribunal de Grande Instance in Bordeaux (1998) for instance extends the usual palette of materials with wood (Plate 28). Each of the seven free-standing law courts has a glulam superstructure on a concrete base, clad with cedar strips on the exterior and cold-laid plywood on the interior (Plate 29). Wood is specified for its low heat and cold conductivity and insulation value. It is also specified for its low embodied energy, which makes the simultaneous specification of high embodied energy aluminium in the office block, and copper for the undulating umbrella roof, somewhat inconsistent. Trade-offs have to be made between fossil fuel consumption, architectural effect and structural performance, however. One firm's choices are another firm's bridge too far.

The choice of building materials is crucial, but it should fit into a consistent strategy that covers all aspects of a building's construction and operation. As this is a highly complex process with very little consensus on means or ends, it is hardly surprising that even architects committed to such thinking cannot simply jump into environmental design. They are obliged to evolve their own position. The best go through continual self-appraisal, in which the architecture they have already developed is assessed and edited. The process of editing is a painful one. What is no longer acceptable? What should replace it? How can it be replaced if it has defined an architect's identity? The answers will never be simple, and it will always be a question of 'answers', not one all-embracing answer. As was seen above in Kroner's description, the imitation of nature's operations can require the most advanced technology, not the simplest. This is certainly true in Renzo Piano's design for a theatre and casino in the Potsdamer Platz, Berlin (2000) (Plate 30 and Fig. 6.9). The original intention was to use the wings of the beetle as a model for the roof, not only in its form, but in its operation, with protective outer sections intended to rise and swing away in order to let light and air into the interior of the building. This was a daring idea, and an impossibility without the comparative lightness that certain synthetic materials can provide, and the computer capacity to model the design.

As important in decisions about the level of technology to use is the ability of the building's occupants to operate any system successfully. Hybrid systems can be complicated, combining partial computer control with partial user participation. If the architect or environmental engineer does not explain the system clearly enough, the user can inadvertently sabotage its effectiveness. Madhavi Kohli's case study of the Canning Crescent Mental Health Centre in London describes such an outcome in detail (Kohli, 1998). Designed by MacCormac Jamieson Prichard, the centre was intended from the outset to be passively ventilated. Considerable amounts of air and noise pollution stood in the way of this, and the eventual solution was complicated. Because of heavy traffic on one side of the building, all fresh air is taken in from the opposite side, and piped into the rooms on the traffic side. These outlets are integrated within wall storage units in each bay, as are flues to vent the stale air,

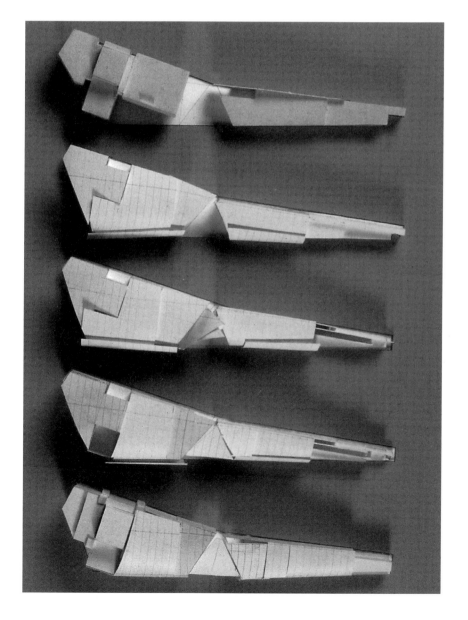

Fig. 6.9
Theatre and Casino: models showing moveable roof section.

which are topped by solar chimneys to speed extraction. Each wing of the building has a set of controls that activates dampers on the air inlets and the solar chimneys. This ventilation system was studied during 1997 by the Building Research Establishment, which found it provided satisfactory internal air quality, in spite of, rather than thanks to, the users:

The drawbacks lie in the users' perception of the system...The cleverly concealed air passages behind the wooden screens of the storage units...are so inconspicuous that for a lay occupant it is difficult to comprehend that the required fresh air is being provided. Their instinctive reaction is to open a window...[They] are suspicious of the system as it reacts slowly and the results of their actions are not physically evident... (Kohli, 1998: 47).

Nor is much help available:

The intricate automatic controls that monitor the actual working of the system have not been clearly understood by the maintenance staff (Kohli, 1998: 49).

This issue of the interface between the environmental system and the user is emerging as one of the central challenges to environmental architecture: how much should one leave to users to control for themselves, and how much to a Building Management System (BMS)? Watching users neglecting to turn off lights when there are already high levels of daylight in a room encourages a greater use of computer control. Machines can be instructed in a way people can't.

Even in an entirely passive environmental system, in which the techniques employed are supposedly quite simple, the users' lack of intuitive understanding can be surprising: for example, roof vents on a conservatory left closed on a sunny summer day, thus heating up the interior of the house. A combination of automatic and user-controlled systems is in some ways the worst of all possible worlds, though the most prevalent. Users tend to assume that partial automation is total automation, and abdicate responsibility for their own areas of control – assuming they know what they are and what to do with them in the first place. User education is a fundamental need of environmental architecture, and one that's seldom answered, in part because it often isn't clear whose responsibility it is. How can it be the architect's after the building has been handed over? How can it be the landlord's if the users are now occupying the building? How can it be the maintenance staff's if no one ever instructed them? There are many cracks to fall through, and many ways of falling through them, given the variety of ways in which buildings are occupied – by owners and tenants public and private. Decisions about the level of intelligence employed in a building's environmental controls thus need to balance user satisfaction in being able to individually tune their immediate environment versus the havoc wrought on the building as a whole if they don't understand fully how to accomplish this. An environmentally designed building is limited in effect if there is no 'mutual support' between user and building.

Environmental symbiosis can thus be achieved to different degrees in different ways, especially if one allows oneself to 'pay back' fossil energy used in the construction and even partial operation of the building. Architects pursuing symbiosis through largely passive environmental design strategies can often produce environmentally determined forms. Their configuration is almost entirely dictated by the exigencies of natural lighting and ventilation, solar access and solar exclusion. Such architecture, however, is not self-consciously re-presenting itself in relation to other, non-environmental architectures, nor to the culture at large. It is, instead, pursuing an operational goal in the most functionally efficient way possible.

A hybrid approach that embraces both the traditional emphasis on differentiated structure, and new sustainable technologies like photovoltaics, can be used in a similarly unreflective way, at least until the architect begins to consider more intently the significance of what he or she is doing. Climate-specific design strategies, when combined with regionally specific materials, can produce environmental architecture that is visibly differentiated climate zone by climate zone. At the level of symbiosis, such architectural differentiation has a greater potential for reducing embodied energy quotients than undifferentiated architecture, unless of course the latter consists of holes in the ground. An architect pursuing sustainability can stop before this, having achieved some degree of symbiosis, and go no further. What if, however, an architect decides to pursue the architectural implications, as well as the greater environmental benefits, of climate-specific design? At this point, the architect is, by default if not deliberation, entering the territory of the second suggested criterion of environmental architecture: differentiation.

6.3 Differentiation

The term 'differentiation' is no longer as straightforward as it was before the new vogue for the organic – organic, not in the sense of parts essential to a bounded whole, but in the sense of certain behaviours of matter mapped by the life sciences that are being imitated by certain architects, 'intricate local behaviours of matter and their contribution to the composition of bodies' (Lynn, 1998: 135). These 'non-static but stable bodies' are not discrete wholes, but instead are constituted through 'the complex interaction of disparate systems' (Lynn, 1998: 137). Here, difference is not a fixed state, but a process, with matter both emerging into identity and submerging into a larger surrounding field.

Is there any connection between this conception of differentiation and the differentiation environmental architecture can and does pursue? Certainly the organic model described above and that described by Kevin Kelly (see Chapter 2) have obvious similarities. The same preference for 'bottom-up' emergence over 'top-down' imposition is apparent in both, and holds the same implications for environmental architecture: multiple affiliations with the immediate environment, out of which a building would emerge and in which it would remain submerged. This is, however, to yoke a particular kind of differentiation, a fluid differentiation or 'morphing', with a particular aspect of environmental architecture

– its differentiated response to the environment. In other words, it is to compare like with not-like. Literal fluidity, or 'morphing' is at present beyond the reach of any architecture, sustainable or otherwise. The tentative dynamism of certain environmental architectures may eventually evolve into structures capable of constant and radical metamorphosis, but will require technological advances we are nowhere near at present.

On the other hand, architecture has traditionally achieved identity 'through multiple affiliations' with its environment, but the built, not the natural one. It has responded to context and convention, and contributed to the constitution of cultural identity. Environmental architecture is hovering on the edge of the new organic model of differentiation, which establishes identity through complex interactions with disparate systems – natural not cultural systems. The question is, could environmental architecture then be a link between this kind of organic differentiation and traditional cultural differentiation?

6.3.1 'You say banana...'

Conventionally, 'differentiation' is found in architecture in the distinctions made between parts of a whole, or between styles. In returning in some form to traditional environmental techniques, must the architect pursuing sustainability also consider returning, in some form, to the vernacular styles that generated these techniques, that is, to a cultural as well as climatic inflection of the building? Is cultural inflection implicit within climatic inflection? There is, after all, an overlapping between traditional techniques of climatic mediation and vernacular styles. Historically, practical devices were slowly embellished and generalized through repetition to become part of an architectural vocabulary, a process Charles Correa has described as one of the generating 'forces' of architecture:

The third force acting on architecture is Climate...[A] very thorough understanding of climate...must go far beyond the pragmatic. For at the deep structure level, climate conditions Culture and its expression...In itself, Climate is the source of myth... (Correa in Curtis, 1996: 650).

The *mushrabiya* is a case in point, its practical function as a sun screen in front of an opening expanded to include a cultural role as well, hiding the women of the Moslem family from view, but allowing them to see out (Plate 31). The devices of modern technology have long since snapped any such connection between climatic function and architectural style. They are not tied to any one set of tectonics or to any one culture.

For some, like Vandana Shiva in her book *Monocultures of the Mind* (1993), there is an obvious connection between physical and cultural monocultures, and between physical and cultural diversity. Addressing the historical origins of Third World agricultural monocultures, she draws a direct parallel between growing one crop and destroying the diversity of a culture that formerly grew many:

The wealth of Europe in the colonial era was to a large extent, based on the transfer of biological resources from the colonies to the centres of imperial power, and the displacement of local diversity in the colonies by monocultures of raw materials for European industry (Shiva, 1993: 78).

This has not only ecological consequences, but cultural ones as well:

The erosion of biodiversity has serious ecological and social consequences since diversity is the basis of ecological and social stability (Shiva, 1993: 73).

Taken out of context, this yoking of the ecological and the social appears arbitrary, but it is defended with an argument that takes as its foundation the origins of culture in nature:

Diverse ecosystems give rise to diverse life forms, and to diverse cultures.

The co-evolution of cultures, life forms and habitats has conserved the biological diversity on this planet. Cultural diversity and biological diversity go hand in hand (Shiva, 1993: 65).

This is incontestable as far as it goes, but does it have much bearing on the urban environment more than half the world's population now inhabits? Different ways of life contingent upon different physical habitats don't have much connection with a universally applied industrialization in which the West dominates the character of production and consumption. Shiva's version of differentiation would require a return to local craft economies, or at least a co-existence of craft and industrial economies that is difficult, but not impossible to achieve, given the political will – and popular demand – to do so. In fact, for certain areas of the developing world, this is just what is happening: Rajasthan, for example, has unmechanized farming in the countryside and Internet facilities in the towns. The problem is that such juxtapositions are representative, not of the end of a cycle, but the middle of one, the end being universal mechanization. In those nations deemed 'post-industrial', the demand for pre-industrial culture takes the form of heritage nostalgia that in no way imagines a real return to pre-modern ways of life.

In architecture, such a return *was* imagined by the Egyptian architect Hassan Fathy. Under the circumstances – rural Egypt in the 1950s and 1960s – this was not as extreme a suggestion as it at first sounds. Fathy's intention was to recover, not just an aesthetic, but an entire way of life, the life before Egypt began to modernize, losing much of its craft culture in the process. The symbol of this recovery was, for Fathy, sundried brick construction, used in Egypt since the pharaohs, and until the advent of breeze block in the 1950s, the basis of every village in the land (Plate 32). The arches, domes and vaults natural to such construction gave rise to an architecture suited to, and characteristic of, its locality, and industrialization meant more than the loss of construction techniques:

Nowadays we never think about what we are losing by not reacting to nature; but if you take the solutions to climatology in the past, such as the windcatcher...and the marble salsabil with carvings of waves on them for the water to trickle over on its way to the fountain, you will find that they create culture. With today's air conditioning, you have removed [that] culture completely (Fathy, 1986: 15).

There is thus a connection between economic organization, technological development and architectural expression. The more universal the first two become, the more problematic a culturally differentiated architecture becomes – or at least one in which the differentiation is essential rather than merely cosmetic. Hence Fathy's insistence on a 'deep' return, that is, one that took into account means of production as well as expression, that embodied a causal relation between the two.

Although during the 1960s and 1970s, in both the West and the Third World, there was a reaction against the reductive universality of modernism, the rebellion sprang from different causes and took different forms. In the West, those who were dissatisfied for the most part enjoyed a high standard of living. This they wanted to keep, while changing its presentation. In the Third World, there was no such popular condemnation of modernity. The resistance to it was centred in an intelligensia largely at odds with a population who thought the gains modernity brought far outweighed the losses. The gains were all to do with a western standard of living and the hardware that delivers it: cars, televisions, refrigerators, hospitals, air-conditioners, etc. Nor was the possession of the technology enough. One must be seen to have achieved such a level of development. Therefore modern architecture, advertising the possession of modern technology, was also required. It was a matter of status. No matter that to devalue one's own culture was to judge it on the West's terms.

Against this, the indigenous intelligensia posited the defence of the architecture of their cultural region as part of a defence and celebration of the difference between indigenous cultures and the dominant culture of the West. Thus it often found itself in the ironic position of siding with conservatives and conservationists in the West to preserve a heritage against its own people's aspirations for a 'modern' (i.e. western) way of life. It was a position summarily rejected by Third World governments at the Rio Earth Summit in 1992. They could not see why they should refrain from raising their living standards through industrialization in order to enable the West to continue unsustainably raising theirs. In the developing world, as long as cultural identity and variety are identified with the pre-modern, and the pre-modern with inferiority, deprivation or sentimentality, then the championing of a differentiation based on the traditional vernacular remains problematic, whatever its environmental, social or economic advantages. Environmental architecture that uses hybrid strategies and mixes western technologies with indigenous traditions therefore has a better chance of acceptance than the entirely traditional.

Whatever the arguments over its significance, or indeed, its existence, post-modernism did clearly address a perceived need to rescue difference from such devaluations. With the publication in 1966 of Robert Venturi's *Complexity and Contradiction in Architecture*, and Aldo Rossi's *Architecture of the City*, the demand that mainstream modernism be enriched by architecture's past began to become ideologically respectable again. This meant using architectural history and/or the vernacular, not implicitly and obliquely, as certain modernists had, but openly and unashamedly. This was done in architectural responses ranging from the literal (Quinlan Terry, Leon Krier) to the ironic (Venturi and Rossi themselves), to the inclusive (Alvaro Siza, Mario Botta). By 'inclusive', I mean the attempt to contain the vernacular and the historical with the modern. Within this interpretation, the work of architects like Siza or Botta is almost indistinguishable in approach from the work of modernists such as Alvar Aalto or Luis Baragan. Aalto, with his incorporation of Finnish and Italian building typologies, and local natural materials, particularly his native pine, and Barragan, with his use of painted render and references to the Mexican *estancia*, are just two examples of modernists inflecting an international architectural language back towards their mother cultures. This was, however, until the 1970s, a minority interest. It was not until historicist post-modernism took hold that such cultural inflection became a permissibly mainstream preoccupation.

Mainstream modernism was abstract, not figurative, and city centres all over the world bear the marks. Such abstraction was built into its foundations. While post-modern historicists objected to abstraction on sentimental or phenomenological grounds, others objected on epistemological grounds. The 'self-transparency' required for designing universally, the assumption that through reasoned reflection the architect could discern and then negate his own bias, attaining an 'objective' view that legitimated his dictation of terms to others, was no longer seen as a possibility by, for example, Jean-Francois Lyotard (1991) and his constituency. Not only that, but the idea that all those attempting it would necessarily arrive at the same conclusions through reasoned reflection was also rejected.

All forms of knowledge, however, whether scientific, philosophical or historical, rely on consensus about their narratives for their legitimation. Without it, such narratives cannot claim to ascendance over competing ones. The Coppernican narrative, for example, was rejected for two hundred years, not because it lacked proof, but because there was a consensus on the earlier Ptolemaic model of the universe. The question is, consensus on the part of whom? What was important for Coppernicus was the narrative's acceptability to the centres of power. Today, in the West, the centres of power are to some degree vulnerable to popular opinion. The public at large, therefore, must be persuaded of the desirability of any narrative. What is deemed desirable at present is what Tafuri dubs 'chaos', and what consumerism celebrates as choice:

it is necessary to persuade the public that the contradictions, imbalances and chaos typical of the contemporary city are inevitable. Indeed the public must be convinced that this chaos contains an unexplored richness, unlimited utilisable possibilities... (Tafuri, 1987: 139).

Frederic Jameson (1984) expresses the view of those who see post-modernism as the most recent development of late capitalism, a capitalism that requires variety rather than uniformity in order to stimulate continuous consumption. Others see post-modernism as a genuine consensual groundswell, a popular, as well as an intellectual, revulsion against the sterility of universality. For both groups, however, the solution of a simple return to the past is as undesirable as it is impossible.

In order to take part in modern civilisation, it is necessary...to take part in scientific, technical and political rationality, something which very often requires the pure and simple abandonment of a whole cultural past...There is the paradox: how to become modern and return to sources; how to revive an old dormant civilisation and take part in universal civilisation (Ricoeur, 1965: 276–77).

There were of course those impatient with any attempt at revival, radical thinkers like Cedric Price who thought the answer to deracination was to embrace it, rather than live in a state of permanent regret for what was irretrievably lost: social and psychological identity created and maintained through identity of place. We are, after all, perfectly capable of defining community in other ways – a community of interests, a cyberspace community, an international community.

The opposition between those who insist there is a direct connection between the material and the cultural and those who insist they are separate spheres is seemingly irreconcilable:

[P]eople are their place and a place is its people, and however readily these may be separated in conceptual terms, in experience they are not easily differentiated (Relph, 1976: 34).

Here, the dialectical relation between people and environment is much like Shiva's model of the emergence of different cultures from different habitats that are then further modified by the emergent cultures. But others ignore the origins of culture within nature as undesirably determinist:

Our everyday world is, from the outset, an intersubjective world of culture...It is a world of culture because, from the outset, the life-world is a universe of significations to us, i.e. a framework of meaning which we have to interpret... (Schutz, 1962: 133).

Certainly it is true that whether architecture or boulders, the 'life-world' is not constituted solely by objects. It is only one of three components Relph identifies in *Place and Placelessness* as essential to the formation of place:

– the static physical setting, the activities, and the meanings – constitute the three basic elements of the identity of places.

The meanings of places may be rooted in the physical setting and objects and activities, but they are not a property of them – rather they are a property of human intentions and experiences (Relph, 1976: 47).

So that although particular configurations of natural landscape or buildings may create identifiable appearances, it is human interpretation that creates a sense of place within them, one that operates on both an individual and a communal level. Place, in this sense, is the 'point' in point of view, the location from which one observes the world, a physical location – a desert rather than a jungle, a slum rather than a middle-class suburb – contributing to a certain psychological and/or social perspective. In this sense, the importance of place is inescapable. However deracinated individuals may be, they were uprooted *from* somewhere. One cannot be deracinated unless one was at some point 'racinated', however tenuously.

Modernism's attempt to construct a universal point of view really foundered, not on its intellectual assumptions, although post-structuralist attacks began here, but on built form. It was the increasing universality of physical place, and the concomitant difficulty of identification of and with it that provoked the most widespread reaction in all cultures. In erasing difference, modernism erased point of view, replacing it with something more amorphous, a 'field of view', perhaps, with no location within it of particular significance, because of no particular difference. If the need to be located – if only to escape it – is inevitable, is it also desirable, or is it a need we should endeavour to resist? Does it necessarily lead to parochialism, if not outright xenophobia? Is its only defence ironically a biological determinism of the kind Shiva deploys ('Cultural diversity and biological diversity go hand in hand' (Shiva, 1993: 65))?

6.3.2 Building 'there'

In architecture, this dilemma became focused on ways in which one might recover 'place' from modernist universal 'space'. For such conflicts between identity and modernity in both the West and the Third World, the critical regionalism developed by Alexander Tzonis, Lliane Lefaivre and Kenneth Frampton held a possible resolution, though not one radicals like Hassan Fathy could ever welcome:

Critical Regionalism has to be understood as a marginal practice, one which, while it is critical of modernisation, nonetheless still refuses to abandon the emancipatory and progressive aspects of the modern architectural legacy (Frampton, 1992: 327).

Here we have a statement entirely in sympathy with the aspirations of the average citizen in any part of the world. Modernism is not repudiated; its benefits are not lost. In fact, it is still the dominant element in the binary 'modern/traditional'.

While opposed to the sentimental simulation of local vernacular, Critical Regionalism will, on occasion, insert reinterpreted vernacular elements as disjunctive episodes within the whole (Frampton, 1992: 327).

This 'swallowing' is viewed with hostility in some quarters, where it is seen as creating a false and reactionary unity:

The internal orders of Neo-Classicism, Neo-Modernism and Regionalism conventionally repress the cultural and contextual discontinuities that are necessary for a logic of contradiction (Lynn, 1998: 110).

Unlike modernism, a hybrid environmental architecture uses pre-industrial technologies in conjunction with industrial and post-industrial ones. Nothing is repressed, but nor are the two systems viewed as contradictory. A Pythagorean modern technology is continuous with vernacular technologies, so that 'affiliations' are created between these modes of operating[10] in the world. Though a false technological unity may be created through 'swallowing' within Critical Regionalism, Frampton quite deliberately repudiates that possibility on a formal level. 'Vernacular elements' are *'disjunctive episodes'* within the modernist whole. This was crucial at a time when reactionary post-modernism was pushing architecture into the false unities of pastiche and kitsch. The 'critical' of 'Critical Regionalism' was a declaration of conscious distance from such illusionism.

The regional – the different – is therefore intended by Frampton to remain different, but how different could it be within a modernist matrix that was dominant aesthetically and technically? It is on this ground that Frampton differs so profoundly from Fathy, and Fathy's western counterpart, Leon Krier. For Frampton, modernism is not to be rejected, but enriched through affiliation with the 'other'. Whether modernism can ever succeed in 'folding' difference into itself without obliterating that difference depends on one's definition of obliteration:

Smooth mixtures are made up of disparate elements which maintain their integrity while being blended within a continuous field of other free elements (Lynn, 1998: 110).

Modernism is the 'continuous field', the regional the 'disparate elements'. Just how invisible this discontinuity can become, and just how tipped in favour of the 'field' of modernism, can be seen in the work of someone like Tadao Ando:

[I]t seems difficult to me to attempt to express the sensibilities, customs, aesthetic awareness, distinctive culture, and social traditions of a given race by means of an open, international vocabulary of Modernism...Detail exists as the most important element in expressing identity... (Ando, 1984: 138).

With ideas such as these, one would expect work as identifiably 'Japanese' as Peter Salter's Kamiichi Pavilion (1993) (Plate 33). Instead, in something like Ando's Water Temple of 1992, the culturally inflected detail is invisible to the foreign eye (Plate 34). Traditionally, there is a

---

10. 'I use the word *affiliative* to describe a system of connections characteristic of a multiplicitous organism...' (Lynn, 1998: 47).

lotus pond by the path to a temple. Here, Ando reinterprets it in a radical way: one descends concrete stairs *through* a lotus pond to the abstract meditation space beneath. A typological idea has been abstracted to the point where it is unreadable as 'Japanese' except to the most informed observers. Compare this with the almost pop version of traditional Japanese architecture seen in Emilio Ambasz's Nishinachiyo Station, with its office towers joined in the form of a gigantic temple arch (Plate 35). It is perhaps no surprise that the first was designed by someone inside the culture, and the second by someone outside. The difference poses a difficult question: should outsiders, especially those from the West, try to preserve, or even re-create, the tradition of the foreign culture within which they have been commissioned to design, particularly in a First World economy like Japan's?

The use of appropriate local elements is an irrelevance in Japan: it is as advanced technologically, and eclectic aesthetically, as the West:

although Japan most certainly constitutes a historically and geographically distinct cultural sphere, contemporary life and culture hardly derive from 'things Japanese' alone. Rather the Japanese actively take in, select and shape diverse elements from foreign cultures into an advanced technological society. Thus with Japanese architecture, the issue is not the architectural possibilities of 'unique Japaneseness'...[but] whether or not works can stand up to...universal standards of evaluation (Taki, 1988: 32).

This is a direct challenge to those regionalists and environmentalists who automatically equate the indigenous with the desirable, and suggests that the primary difference between one culture's architecture and another is not physical location, but level of technology. More often than not clients have looked to a western architect deliberately to avoid difference. Is it appropriate for a western architect to persuade them otherwise, or could such attempts at persuasion themselves be construed as another, if more oblique, form of cultural condescension and/or oppression?

Even if one overcomes this particular dilemma, and decides the end – recognition of the 'other' – justifies the potential political incorrectness, other questions come swiftly on the heels of these: what exactly constitutes a region? Is it local – the towns or countryside surrounding the site? Is it national? Or does it cross national boundaries and embrace the spread of a cultural group? Is it specifically architectural, demanding formal recognition of some kind, or can it be expressed in use? Does regionalism allude to architecture with a capital 'A', or only to the vernacular? In either case, their development has been affected by outside influences. And to what degree is authenticity a concern? Is there objection on more grounds than Ruskinian morality to the application of traditional forms to what are essentially modern buildings? The difficulty with answering any of these questions is the lack of legitimate criteria with which to formulate a response. Upon what grounds does one support or deny the validity of other architectures besides western architecture – not only when building in other cultures, but when building in the West? Upon what grounds does one justify or dismiss the idea of cultural differentiation? Upon what grounds does one choose or reject a particular strategy for expressing differentiation, having decided it is a valid concern?

Critical Regionalism offers another way into differentiation that bypasses such issues of representation, and prefigures more recent writing about architecture from an environmental standpoint in similar language. This aspect of Critical Regionalism focuses more on the relation of the building to physical site than historical context, based on the assumption that the two are bound up in a dialectical relation anyway:

It may be claimed that Critical Regionalism is regional to the degree that it invariably stresses certain site-specific factors, ranging from topography...to the varying play of local light across the structure...An articulate response to climatic conditions is a necessary corollary to this. Hence, Critical Regionalism is opposed to the tendency of 'universal civilization' to optimize the use of air-conditioning etc. It tends to treat all openings as delicate transitional zones with a capacity to respond to the specific conditions imposed by the site, the climate and the light (Frampton, 1992: 327).

In other words, not only does difference arise in architecture on a general level from the use of pre-industrial versus industrial techniques, but a whole range of differentiations can emerge even within industrialized architecture, if it makes itself open to pre-industrial techniques, as hybrid environmental architecture does. The 'delicate transitional zones' or 'buffer zones' that Frampton describes, responding to *specific* conditions of site and climate, are a specific vernacular environmental strategy for mediating between inside and outside. This emphasis on response to specific physical conditions carries important formal implications, but not necessarily to the extent of quotation of specific architectural styles, however 'disjunctive'. In fact, the range of choices open to architects pursuing climatic and/or cultural differentiation is daunting, from an abstract climate-responsive architecture entirely within a modernist vocabulary, to the quotation of historical styles that entirely ignores the conditions of the physical environment. Between these two extremes is a complex inclusive area that stands at the intersection of historical styles and climate, signification and operation, building-as-sign and building-as-thing. Most of those interested in cultural differentiation in the 1970s and 1980s, however, were not speaking the language of environmentalism; they were addressing the problem of the loss of 'place' in the pursuit of 'space'.

6.3.3 No 'where'

With this recognition of architectures other than western and other than modern, western architecture's hegemony was challenged, although under Critical Regionalism, the building crafts of these other architectures did not gain an equal validity. Frampton was not the only one to see this imbalance as unavoidable. The Iraqi-born architect, Rifat Chadirji (Figs. 6.10–12), although on the other side of the western/other divide,

Fig. 6.10
Y. Rafiq Residence, Baghdad, Rifat Chadirji.

encapsulated the new dispensation in a sentence: 'Regionalism...can become a constituent of international culture, a factor of variety within the universal' (Chadirji, 1986: 51).

Regionalism, in other words, cannot reverse this relation, privileging the local above the western-dominated global, because of what Chadirji calls a 'culture gap'. This is effectively a technology gap. The developing world is still largely engaged in what he terms a 'manual-aesthetic mode of production', whereas the developed world has shifted to a 'mechanical-aesthetic mode of production', or even 'cyber-aesthetic'. The result is a gap that 'cannot be bridged by a policy of narrow regionalism, vernacularism, or nationalism because of the characteristics of modern culture' (Chadirji, 1986: 41), that is, its extraordinary invasiveness. He then goes on to discuss Iraq's future, but it could be that of any developing nation:

There is no alternative but to bring the cultural development of Iraq into harmony with this process of internationalisation, while at the same time maintaining the country's traditional characteristics and qualities (Chadirji, 1986: 41).

Chadirji uses the phrase 'cultural development', but again, implicit within this is 'technological development'. Certainly, his own work in Iraq during the 1960s embraces western building technology at the same time it refers to, or directly imitates, forms originally built using indigenous traditional technologies. In fact, as with architects such as Jorn Utzon or Mario Botta, the cultural differentiation in Chadirji's work is achieved primarily on a formal level. In one telling example in his book *Concepts and Influences*, he illustrates two fireplaces (Fig. 6.11) and a shop ceiling he designed for various clients in Iraq. As influences on their design, he shows a sixteenth-century Iranian book cover, a fifteenth-century Afghani shrine interior, and a painting by Mondrian, the point being that his work is a synthesis of regional-traditional and universal-western. This is, however, a synthesis on the level of imagery, imagery contained within the matrix of modern technology. Chadirji does not deny this. He makes his position abundantly clear: you can't beat them, so you have to join them, preserving some traditional forms and techniques as gestures of resistance in the face of the juggernaut. These techniques are environmental: the use of traditional internal courtyards, with water and planting to cool the air moving into the building, the use of clay brick for thermal mass and greater stability of internal temperature (Fig. 6.12).

Architects pursuing environmental sustainability are making similar choices about types and levels of technology, but primarily for reasons of 'greenhouse gas' reduction rather than 'sense of place'. For the Torrent Pharmaceuticals in Ahmedabad, India (Plate 36), Brian Ford studied traditional Mogul cooling techniques by means of deep wells and thermal mass before developing a PDEC (passive downdraft evaporative cooling) system for the centre. PDEC uses micronizers that spray air taken in at the top of the building with a fine mist that causes the air to drop quickly, causing a cool downdraft that cools the floors below as it falls (Fig. 6.13). If one adopts this kind of complex

Fig. 6.11
Fireplace, K. Alousi Residence, Baghdad, Rifat Chadirji.

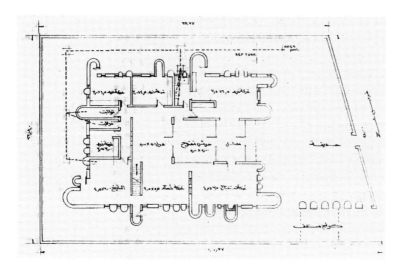

Fig. 6.12
Y. Rafiq Residence, plan showing alcoves for art collection, internal courtyard and clay brickwalls.

inclusive approach to symbiosis, the higher environmental cost of using advanced technologies and industrially produced materials is offset by the simultaneous use of passive vernacular techniques and 'natural' materials. When applied in the culture where they were developed, these vernacular techniques will provide a degree of formal inflection towards that culture. When applied elsewhere, their cultural baggage will be left behind, to accumulate new, more general associations around the environmental. For instance, if wind-catchers, even made of industrially produced materials, are used in a contemporary building in North Africa, they will be read as a deliberate association with the vernacular history of the wind-catcher in that culture. If they are used in Italy, they will be viewed as a 'new' form for a 'new' environmental function.

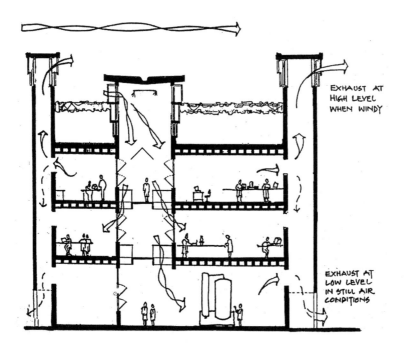

EXHAUST AT
HIGH LEVEL
WHEN WINDY

EXHAUST AT
LOW LEVEL
IN STILL AIR
CONDITIONS

Fig. 6.13
Torrent Pharmaceuticals research centre, Ahmedabad, Abhikram Architects and Brian Ford & Associates: drawing of passive downdraft evaporative cooling (PDEC) strategy: hot air is sprayed with a micronizer assembly at the top of each intake. The cooled air drops down the shaft, entering each floor on the way down.

Materials characteristic of a region are even more crucial to visible differentiation than vernacular techniques. If local materials are used locally, they have not only environmental consequences (less fossil energy to transport them), but cultural ones as well. They 'place' the building in the history of the site, allowing it a correspondence with the surrounding context, a large part of which is made of the same local materials, whether the brick of Sienna, or the recycled pipes of Los Angeles (Plate 37). This attention to materials is a more grounded approach to differentiation than arbitrary borrowings on a formal level, which veer between those too abstract to succeed in their aim of readably placing the building, to those too literal to be anything but pastiche. In enabling the architect to relocate, in environmental terms, the intersection between physical site and cultural place, this second criterion, 'differentiation', opens up the possibility of using the old in new ways:

[W]e think that a naturally conditioned building, in which the stuff of its architecture plays a full role in maintaining comfort within its enclosure, is probably fundamentally reconfigured...[O]ne of the consequences...is a release of further potential for the invention of new forms, [as well as] the reinvigoration of established forms and configurations... (Short, 1997: 1).

If one designs simultaneously considering architecture and environmental sustainability, each will form and re-form the other in a dialectical process that may make detailed and literal obeisance to cultural context, or may make only the most general references in terms of materials and scale or make none at all. This process of reciprocal influence can be seen in Short Ford's Queens Building (1993) for the School of Engineering and Manufacture at De Montfort University, Leicester (Plate 38), which is a combination of passive environmental techniques and Viollet-le-Duc aesthetics. As such, it was one of the first 'green' buildings to be assessed as much in terms of design as sustainability, primarily because the architects insisted that environmental architecture is about architecture (composition, expression, use, style, meaning, etc.) as well as sustainability. In a lecture to the Carnegie Mellon Institute in 1997, Alan Short described the school's double function:

Our hypothesis was that the building could strike a chord with its immediate natural environment and at the same time exploit its inherently more flexible form to plug a hole in the urban landscape... (Short, 1997: 1).

'Plugging the hole' with a provocative historicism is, of course, just one way of addressing a cultural context. What separates the Queens Building from an exercise in pastiche is the new forms that emerged from the environmental agenda: the elaborately articulated stack vents, for example, and the dramatic configuration of internal space to promote air flow for natural ventilation. This invention, if consciously pursued and developed, leads the architect to the third and most contentious (because the least 'necessary') criterion for environmental architectures: visibility.

6.4 Visibility

The reception of architectural meaning may not be that intended by its producer, especially over time, but nevertheless there is usually a conscious attempt on the part of the architect to convey something beyond the function of shelter. The building not only stands, but stands for. The criterion of 'visibility' is therefore the point at which environmental architecture becomes more than the existing plurality made more sustainable, and becomes a self-conscious architecture in its own right ('fundamentally reconfigured'). It is still a plurality, but it has crossed a threshold beyond which form is deliberately manipulated to re-present, as well as present, environmental sustainability. This architecture is reflexive in so far as it is a critique of itself: architecture overcoming architecture – in this case, environmental architecture overcoming conventional practice, and making this project visible in some way.

Some, like James Wines of SITE, are categorical on the subject:

During the past decade, SITE has become increasingly convinced that architecture is urgently in need of a conceptual, philosophical and aesthetic reunion with the natural environment...They propose that buildings today should connect in some physical and iconographic way to their larger context (Wines, 1997: 32).

For SITE, the 'larger context' is interpreted quite straightforwardly as the land surrounding the building, whether urban or rural, generically referred to as 'landscape'. SITE has decided that the way to best represent the new symbiosis between building and landscape is literally to fuse the two as much as possible (Plate 39). In this case, the relation between operation and expression is the reverse of the one usually seen in environmental architecture: the environmental benefit (greater thermal insulation) is a by-product of a reflexive agenda, rather than a certain visibility being the by-product of an environmental agenda.

It is SITE's conviction that environmentally conscious fusions of architecture and landscape architecture should demonstrate their commitment through highly visible aesthetic choices...Clearly, the interactive dialogue between buildings and landscape is an art, as well as an ecological imperative (Wines, 1997: 33).

This is certainly one way of representing a new symbiosis, and the increasingly blurred line between culture and nature: to meld the object and the field. Indeed, so far it seems to be the favoured way of expressing this, with Edouard François, Emilio Ambasz (see Plates 62 and 63), and Edward Cullinan (Plate 40) among others, producing various versions of earthbound architecture.

Having to think about 'nature' at all is a novel experience for many architects. The chapter on nature examined historical and contemporary models of nature that architecture has used. In contemporary practice, the primary difference between environmental architecture, and non-environmental architecture in dialogue with some construct of nature, is the use of models of ordered nature versus models of non-linear nature. Environmental architecture has so far tended to ally itself with classical science, nature-as-order, and traditional architectures. Architecture that deconstructs order and explores non-linearity challenges this view in ways not yet addressed by environmental architecture, ways that might enrich and further develop current sustainable practice.

6.4.1 Dreams of dwelling

Traditionally, an ordered architecture has represented an ordered and meaningful society set in an ordered and meaningful universe, with the relationship between signifier and signified fixed, closed and stable. Environmentalism, when it looks to philosophical justification at all, looks to philosophers who reaffirm something of this traditional western view of culture and nature. This is why certain writings of Heidegger, which were reviewed earlier in the discussion of Norberg-Schulz's architectural phenomenology (see Chapter 5), are referred to again and again. But Heidegger's vision of nature tends to be somewhat nostalgic in its assumptions about dwelling and place, with building fixing us between the sky and the earth, and nature telling us how we should be. The relationship is pre-industrial, arcadian. In a famous, or infamous, passage from his lecture *Building Dwelling Thinking* (1951), Heidegger sets forth his view of building and dwelling:

The nature of building is letting dwell...Only if we are capable of dwelling, only then can we build. Let us think for a while of a farmhouse in the Black Forest, which was built some two hundred years ago by the dwelling of peasants. Here the self-sufficiency of the power to let earth and sky, divinities and mortals enter in simple oneness into things ordered the house (Heidegger, 1971: 160).

Dwelling, therefore, is not just living in a dwelling, it is inhabiting a particular piece of nature in a particularly sympathetic way. This ability, he goes on to say,

placed the farm on a wind-sheltered mountain slope looking south, among the meadows close to the spring. It gave it the wide over-hanging shingle roof whose proper slope bears up under the burden of snow... (Heidegger, 1971: 160).

It is the ability to dwell, to react co-operatively to given circumstances, which creates the dwelling, so that 'the dwelling' is a very particular kind of building, and carries an obvious environmental point.

Such a pastoral scene, however, bears little relation to the nature that others have perceived intuitively for centuries and which is now being empirically analysed by those investigating complexity in nature, nor does it have any bearing on contemporary urban realities. For many, there is no Heideggerian 'dwelling', either as verb or noun. This does not invalidate Heidegger's ideas, but nor does it confirm them as the whole truth. Yes, there is order in nature and the world. But there is also disorder, which, until recently, neither science nor architecture chose to address. Addressing them is, again, to investigate only part of the whole, but they free those doing so to look in directions other than the ones that architecture – and environmentalism – have traditionally pursued. So that, contrary to the phenomenologists' diagnosis of the maladies of the rest of contemporary architecture, it is not that environmental design is over-theorized, but that it privileges the building-as-thing over the building-as-sign to the point that where is only an embryonically self-reflective environmental architecture.

If modernist architects could reflect upon the relation between nature and culture and represent their positions in their designs, there is no reason why 'sustainable architects' cannot and should not do the same. Richard Neutra criticized the 'discrete parts' into which culture dissected nature, when nature was about what he called 'flowing transitions' (see Chapter 2). This flow permeates culture as well as nature, so that not only is nature unstable, at least in part, but culture is also. Experience for many of us is of a world that is out of our control: the traditional city centre and the human community at the centre of that centre displaced by the placeless periphery, the sprawling wastelands on the edge of our cities and the unbounded suburbs beyond. The question finally asked in the 1980s was whether an architecture that represents nothing but order, permanence and stability was still a valid one, given these alternative views of nature and society. If it was not entirely valid, what should architecture be expressing? Would an architecture that redefined architecture's basis be an architecture at all, or would it be an anti-architecture, that is, a critique of all the certainties architecture has traditionally represented?

In his book *De-Architecture* (1987), James Wines writes of the twentieth century's newfound awareness of the instability and indeterminacy of the universe, at the centre of which is the concept of entropy. Wines was one of a number in the 1970s and 1980s who thought this instability should be architecturally represented, that our constructions are, figuratively as well as literally, built on shifting sands:

since art is meant to monitor, to disclose, to illuminate, it can serve as a kind of barometer of entropy. Its relevance will depend on its capacity to express a dialectic of change...When art rejects or denies this role, it becomes hollow and extraneous. Architecture has remained in that situation for most of this century by ignoring the implications of disorder in every possible way. By insisting that a building stand for conditions of determinacy, structure and order...twentieth century architecture has consistently presented a false vision of the contemporary world (Wines, 1987: 125).

Wines, and contemporaries like Bernard Tschumi, demanded an architecture that would address this omission on a formal level. Decay, disruption, demolition, death – these would be expressed in a braver new world of architecture, or perhaps a safer world, for it is often only when a society is confident that it can afford to threaten itself with anarchy and undoing.

6.4.2 Between the lines

In a conscious break with the optimism of architectural modernism, therefore, Tschumi said of his own work: '[it] is not about the way things *should* happen, but the way things are now today. There are no utopias today.' To represent this loss, Tschumi's prize-winning entry for a park to replace the slaughterhouses of La Villette on the north-east edge of Paris was intended to frustrate any expectations we may have of a readable pattern or closure of design: 'relations of conflict are carefully maintained'. In the park, three different organizational systems on the site are overlaid, with none privileged over the others: the point grid, co-ordinate axes and the random curve. For various points on the grid he designed 'follies': large red metal cubes with irregular interior configurations. Some of these cubes have cafés or information centres in them; many are empty, like the traditional follies in the parks of great houses, refusing to serve, to have a use, as conventional architecture has uses. Tschumi's 'point-grid' plan at La Villette is intended as a refutation of modernism's infinitely extendable, infinitely purposeful grid, spreading universal order over varying topographies and cultures. Tschumi's is a leftover space at the edges of modernism's cities: semi-industrial, dispersed, half-deserted. The follies are, he claims, 'open structures for the nomadic suburb', perfect receptacles for an empty and confused mass culture. The park itself is a refutation of the metaphysics of presence architecture has embodied historically:

The project takes issue with a particular premise of architecture, namely, its obsession with presence, with the idea of a meaning immanent in architectural structures and forms which directs its signifying capacity...The La Villette project, in contrast, attempts to dislocate and de-regulate meaning, rejecting the 'symbolic' repertory of architecture as a refuge of humanist thought...its meaning is never fixed but is...rendered irresolute by the multiplicity of meanings it inscribes (Tschumi, 1987: vi–vii).

Bernard Tschumi and Peter Eisenman were the two architects to actively engage with the work of Jacques Derrida, author of perhaps the most provocative and radical of the post-modern critiques, a critique not just of modernism, but of the entire corpus of western philosophy. Deconstruction was intended as a 'close textual analysis' of philosophical and literary works, questioning western culture's foundational assumptions about meaning, language and authorship. In addressing deconstruction in architecture, and discussing architecture's flirtation with deconstruction, one unavoidably distorts and oversimplifies Derrida's ideas, as he claimed the architects and architectural critics who engaged with it were in danger of doing. 'Violated Perfection', the seminal exhibition on deconstruction and architecture at the Museum of Modern Art in 1988, is typical of the distortions of Derrida's work in architectural circles. Within architecture, deconstruction was both a radical refusal to represent order exclusively, and a temporarily fashionable architectural style, confusingly called 'Deconstructivism'. The latter included architects like Zaha Hadid, whose interest lay in the modernist optimism of the Russian Suprematists and not in the essentially scepti-cal and linguistic concerns of Jacques Derrida.

Deconstruction is passé now, its proponents having moved on, as this discussion must, from a concern with binary opposites – order/disorder, closure/indeterminacy, etc. – to ideas of complexity and flow. Deconstruction is, however, the intellectual fount of disjunctive, fragmented form and content within late-twentieth-century architecture, and the paradigmatic polar opposite of environmental design as it is currently constituted. This 'de-architecture' is as much of a challenge to architecture-as-order as non-linear science is to nature-as-order. Neither challenge will go away, and some architects pursuing environmental design may choose to grapple with them formally. As is obvious from such titles as *Of Grammatology* and *Writing and Difference,* deconstruc-tion was emphatically an enquiry into language, not building, but the ideas reinforced those of a number of architects eager to challenge architec-ture's foundations, and already at ease with linguistic theory through earlier borrowings from semiology in the 1970s. For Derrida, the decon-structive project was nothing less than the eradication of transcendence, the tyranny of the metaphysical, from both philosophy and science. This was to be effected through the eradication of the concept of a 'transcen-dental signified' (Derrida, 1987: 19) inscribed within language itself:

all of this concerns putting into question the major determination of the meaning of Being as presence, the determination in which Heidegger recognised the destiny of philosophy (Derrida, 1987: 7).

As cultures define themselves as much through what they suppress as what they express, that is, as much by what is absent as what is present, to reveal this process in its most sacred inscriptions was disrup-tive, to say the least, and intentionally so. The aim was, in part, to '[prevent] any word, any concept, any major enunciation from coming to summarise and to govern from the theological presence of a centre...' (Derrida, 1987: 14). If this sounds like the bleakest kind of relativism, one must remember, surely, that what is being asserted is not the equal value, or valuelessness, of concepts or ideas, but the equal impossibil-ity of legitimating any concept or idea. What is important is the fact that we have constructed their importance, that they are not central by 'divine right', but because we deem them to be so, a fact that is often only apparent if they are 'deconstructed'.

To demonstrate the precarious hold of any choice on legitimacy, Derrida developed what he called a 'double register' in deconstructive practice. Through this he hoped to avoid falling into a crude 'either/or' position in which what was present was supplanted by what was absent. Within traditional metaphysics, meaning is created through difference – light/dark, rough/smooth, male/female, life/death, presence/absence, etc. These terms have meaning in relation to their opposites. Light, for example, has meaning because there is an opposite state of darkness with which to contrast it. What makes such a construction of meaning a target for Derrida's deconstruction is the assigning of privilege to some of these terms, so that traditionally light has been privileged over dark, male over female, presence over absence, culture over nature, and, Derrida's particular focus, speech over writing (because closer to consciousness, and ultimately to God). To begin with, what he calls 'a phase of overturning' is necessary:

To do justice to this necessity is to recognise that in a classical philo-sophical opposition we are not dealing with the peaceful co-existence of a vis-a-vis, *but rather with a violent hierarchy. One of the two terms governs the other (axiologically, logically, etc.), or has the upper hand. To deconstruct the opposition, first of all, is to overturn the hierarchy at a given moment (Derrida, 1987: 41).*

The majority of 'deconstructive' buildings remains within this operation of hierarchy reversal: order is overturned in favour of disorder, stasis in favour of (frozen) flux, closure in favour of the indeterminate. Such an operation Derrida saw as unending and 'structural', because 'the hierar-chy of dual oppositions always reestablishes itself' (Derrida, 1987: 42). In his own work, Derrida pursued a much more difficult, even paradox-ical operation – paradoxical, because although he envisaged the emergence of a new 'concept' from the process of overturning an exist-ing hierarchy, he at the same time refused to allow it to become crystal-lized as such, since 'conceptualisation itself, and by itself alone, can reintroduce what one wants to "criticise" ' (Derrida, 1987: 59). The intention was to keep deconstruction from resembling, let alone becom-ing, another version of the Hegelian dialectic. In this, thesis and antithe-sis always ended in synthesis, a resolution that transcended both previous conditions, usually within a teleological structure, and was precisely the kind of irrational legitimation Derrida sought to expose and avoid:

If there were a definition of differance *[and of deconstruction], it would be precisely the limit, the interruption, the destruction of the Hegelian* relève *wherever it operates*[11] *(Derrida, 1987: 40–41).*

Derrida chooses to operate instead in what he calls 'the interval between inversion, which brings low what was high, and the irruptive emergence of a new "concept"' (Derrida, 1987: 42). While it may be possible to effect this position of perpetual limbo when deconstructing written texts, releasing an endless elaboration of alternative words, meanings and non-meanings, it is almost impossible to do so in archi-tecture. By its very nature, architecture reifies. The 'interval', the fluid polymorphous domain that refuses to become authoritative, is hardened into a fixed 'in-between', either between a specially constructed order and a responding disorder (as in Eisenman's Bio-centrum for the J. W. Goethe University (Plate 41), or between a pre-existing order (the context of the old city, the memory of the beholder) and a newly constructed disorder, as in Coop Himmelblau's explosive attic extension on a nineteenth-century apartment building in Vienna. The latter enacts

---

11. '[R]elève is Derrida's translation of the Hegelian term *Aufhebung*, which means to preserve and negate in a spiritual "lifting up" to a "higher level".' (Derrida, 1987: 99, trans-lator's note).

Derrida's operation most literally, taking an existing building as the 'text' and allowing 'the irruptive emergence of a new "concept"', but in the mere fact of remaining, threatens to become authoritative.

Eisenman said of his work during this period in the 1980s: 'My architecture tries to move away from itself – to be disjunctive with the past, to what I call "between", between its old past and its repressed present' (Eisenman, 1989: 27). This 'past' he refers to is classicism *and* modernism, both of which embody order, even if that order was bent by some – Mannerists, Expressionists – to breaking point. But, says Eisenman,

[t]he way to another architecture is not to suppress the classical but in fact to cut into it. Not to repress but to surgically open up the classical and the modern to find what is repressed (Eisenman, 1989: 29).

Eisenman's Bio-centrum for the J. W. Goethe University, Frankfurt-am-Main (1987), is a demonstration of this technique. In it he established a clear symmetrical order – a 'natural' order, in fact – and then deconstructed it. There is a central circulation spine, off which symmetrically placed modernist blocks are strung, each one given the four basic shapes biologists use to denote the elements of the genetic code – the architectural order reflecting the fundamental physical order of life. In these terms, the operation is entirely traditional, recalling historical imitations of nature as order. But Eisenman then exposes the order as a construct by juxtaposing a contrasting disorder immediately alongside it, a revelation of suppressed mutation and collapse without which order and growth have no meaning. In Eisenman's words: 'A world of unstable forms emerges within the stable structures of modernism.' The juxtaposition creates an 'in-between' that is neither entirely ordered nor entirely disordered, but a complex inclusive condition in which the presence of either half inescapably implies the presence of the absent other. An ordered, predictable nature, then, automatically implies the existence of an equally valid non-linear, unpredictable nature, just as an ordered society carries the existence of its anarchic opposite implicit within it, making meaning from that difference. Eisenman's Bio-centrum is important as an example because it underlines in formal terms, not mere hierarchy reversal, but inclusion. The object of the deconstructive exercise is not, at least in architecture, to replace one partial view with another, say, stasis with flux, but to recognize and represent without privilege both terms of any binary opposition.

Eisenman was acutely aware of the problem of relating architecture to deconstruction:

It's very difficult to talk about architecture in terms of deconstruction, because we are not talking about ruins or fragments. The term is too metaphorical and too literal for architecture. Deconstruction is dealing with architecture as metaphor, and we are dealing with architecture as reality... (Eisenman, 1993: 67).

In becoming 'things', deconstructive interventions gain a permanence, and thus an authority, which Derrida was at pains to avoid. Nor can architectural language come anywhere near the complexity and nuance of verbal language, so that inevitably, the complexities and nuances of deconstruction became reduced to a few basic themes: absence versus presence, order versus disorder, and hierarchy reversal, which did not necessarily extirpate the metaphysical from within architecture, historically so often called upon to house it. Derrida himself worried about this in a letter to Eisenman:

This reference to absence is perhaps one of the things (because there are others) which has troubled me most in your discourse on architecture...because it has authorised many religious interpretations...of your work...The same question brings up others...For example...[w]hether it has to do with houses, museums or laboratories of research universities, what distinguishes your architectural space from that of the temple...? Where will the break, the rupture have been in this respect, if there is one...? (Derrida, 1987: 62).

Ironically, architectural deconstruction performed its own suppression – of architecture as material object and material process. In exposing the imbalance on a formal level between order and disorder, Eisenman and Tschumi reinforced another imbalance: the privileging of cultural form over material fact, essentially, the transcendent over the immanent, the exact opposite of Derrida's intention. A truly deconstructive exercise would expose the privileging of architectural idea over architectural object as well, an exercise that environmental architecture is uniquely well placed to perform, although it is not addressing the same deconstruction of established meanings within architecture.

6.4.3 Open the box

Philosophically, environmentalism seems diametrically opposed to deconstruction, its suppressed binary, in fact. It is, for example, a new meta-narrative, its critique of instrumental rationality a would-be authoritative reading of the world. It is hard to see how it could be otherwise, if reconstruction, rather than perpetual deconstruction, is the aim, as it certainly is among those pursuing sustainability in whatever field. Environmentalism also affirms presence: the presence of the human being at the centre of culture, capable, through reason, of changing the ethos of that culture. It also affirms nature as a thing-in-itself, not a mere cultural construct, with its own needs and imperatives – a signified.

In fact, one would be hard put to find any architect engaged in environmental design willing to follow the 'Deconstructivists' into the formal expression of decay and/or instability. They do not share the same view of the fragility of architectural meaning that derives from the perception of the fragility of either our cultural orders or the natural one. On the contrary, they are interested in shoring up order against the unpredictable disorders of nature *and* society, the disorders of the latter exacerbated by our creation of the disorder of the former. This shoring up is approached, not on the level of expression, but of operation. It is a practical shoring up, ways of acting in the physical world that attempt to restabilize what we have destabilized. 'Deconstructive' architecture is, in some sense, a 'verbal' warning. Environmental design is the heeding of that warning on the level of praxis rather than discourse. However, these practical measures – passive environmental design techniques, the use of renewable energies, life cycle analysis, etc. – are themselves derived from a discourse: the outward and visible signs of an inward and invisible cultural shift. As the creation of a new, more subtle material order in the built environment is the object of environmental design, rather than the expression of the inadequacies of conventional architectural expression (and the partial truth it signifies), environmental architectures and deconstructive architecture would then seem, essentially, to be moving in opposite directions.

Indeed, at its most unrigorous and unreflective, environmentalism could be accused of being wishful at best and utopian at worst, looking back to the garden, or ahead to the heavenly (read sustainable) city, instead of facing the 'reality' of permanent exile from both. Such criticism, however, depends upon whether one considers either future achievable. Karl Mannheim in *Ideology and Utopia*, makes a distinction between ideology and utopia, while at the same time admitting the difficulty of distinguishing between them. Both are 'beyond present reality'. The utopian is 'in principle unrealizable'. The ideological is unrealizable 'only from the point of view of a given social order which is already in existence' (Mannheim, 1972: 176–77). Within this framework, those who still believe in our capacity to change our circumstances (the 'evolution' Derrida so mistrusts) will view environmentalism as an ideology, while those who do not will view it as utopian. I obviously hold with the former, or there would be no point in writing this, and such a position does throw into question the usefulness of referring at all to a project as *emotionally* different as deconstruction.

Perhaps then, what is of use to those within environmental architecture is not the radical deconstructive project itself, but the more reflective and reflexive cultural constructions it can encourage, and of which environmental design is in need if it is to develop as a culturally self-conscious, as well as technically enlightened, enterprise. Some of the techniques of deconstruction are therefore useful, not only for analysing past suppressions in other architectures, but also current ones within sustainable practice itself. One can, for example, perform exactly the same kind of hierarchy reversal exercise on buildings that is performed on texts. In Mies van der Rohe's Seagram Building (1965), for example, what is presented is an extreme of instrumental rationality achieved through industrial technology. There is nothing contingent, unpredictable or ambiguous about the finished form until one begins to analyse what is absent, and uncover how this triumphalism is achieved. Implicit within the explicit form are the organic, the multivalent, the irrational, the open, the disordered, the handmade, the figurative, the particular, the 'other', the immanent. One could go on. The building can only express rationality because there is irrationality; can only represent order because there is disorder, the intellect because there is the body, the 'perfection' of culture because there is the imperfection of nature. It presents itself as the truth because it has absented the other halves of these binaries. If one brings them forward, one can see the building suppressing a different relationship to the environment from the one it presents, a relationship that is symbiotic rather than oppositional, that uses 'natural' materials instead of industrially produced ones, that opens to the elements instead of sealing itself off from them, that is specific to climate, if not culture, rather than claiming universality, that is indeterminate and free-running rather than closed and controlled.

This operation in and of itself, however, is not enough. To stop here is to replace 'either' with 'or', modernity with anti-modernity, culture-as-culture with culture-as-nature (as model, at least). There are certainly those within environmentalism who would endorse this, just as there are those outside it who would find such a shift totally unacceptable. But neither the anti-modernists, who dismiss the advantages and capacities that advanced but less instrumental technologies afford us, nor the modernists, who dismiss the variety and ingenuity available to those architectures not driven by high technology, have an inclusive enough view for environmental architecture. Deconstruction poses a challenge: for environmental architecture to perform a hierarchy reversal on itself, revealing its suppression of the second term in the binary 'operation/representation'. Though environmental architecture cannot lose sight of the materiality of its project, it must not itself be lost sight of either. The particular revaluing of nature to be found in environmental architecture cannot be found anywhere else.

Although Eisenman eventually moved away from conceiving of the building as text, and towards seeing it as an aspect of matter (nature), it was in order to generate richer forms, not grapple literally with the matter he was representing (Plate 42):

[I]t has to do with the adoption of a material model – in the case at hand [Aronoff Centre, University of Cincinatti], the geological paradigm of plate tectonics...– in order to weaken the earlier semiotic one. Semiotic structures are binary, hierarchical, closed...Matter is literally riddled with properties, dissymmetries, inhomogeneities, singularities...Matter is, in short, active, dynamic and creative (Kwinter, 1993: 93).

Nevertheless, Eisenman's demanding and rewarding use of nature-as-complexity is one environmental architecture could at least entertain, if only to dismiss. One hopes, for better reasons than mere prejudice.

6.4.4 A cooking lesson

Arguments about whether theory precedes or succeeds practice are of interest mainly to those claiming authorship. What is of note, regardless of whether they came before or after a new breed of architectural forms, is the extraordinary influence that certain French philosophers have had on certain susceptible architects at the end of the twentieth century. As Derrida dominated the 1980s, so Gilles Deleuze and Felix Guattari dominated the 1990s, drawing to themselves like strange attractors all those ideas about topology, morphology, biology, geology and complexity that are currently swarming amongst the architectural intelligensia. There are different names for this architectural production – Greg Lynn's 'amorfal' architecture, Jeffrey Kipnis's 'New Architecture', Charles

Jencks's 'landform' or 'nonlinear' architecture, John Frazer's 'evolutionary architecture', and Eisenman and others' 'folding'.

These experiments are attacked by many as mere formalism, a label some accept (Lynn) and others reject (Kipnis). The work claims to be 'post-contradictory', that is, beyond the deliberate contradiction of architectural conventions and expectations explored by Deconstructivism, and yet in its turn, through its very novelty, it is a contradiction of the very same conventions and expectations, kicking over the same geometric and metaphysical traces. It claims to affiliate itself with the particularity of the material, especially the topography of the site, and yet does so only as a means to a compositional end, translating the 'real' into abstraction, a set of mathematical relations. These generate forms that are intended as responses, in their deliberate 'anexactitude', to the external pressures of site and the internal imperatives of programme, deforming and reforming fluidly, bending rather than breaking. Whether such dynamism is gained or not, what is lost is the materiality of the material with which such architecture claims to align itself. Topos is numbers, not rock or hill or even tarmac.

The motivations for developing such an architecture vary, but there seems to be, on the one hand, a simple desire for new forms, and on the other, a not so simple desire for new forms. These innovators are no longer able to use the Hegelian vocabulary of *zeitgeist* so prevalent in Modern Movement polemic, and yet much of their discontent appears to stem from an architecture that is once again failing to keep up with developments in other disciplines, particularly the natural and computer sciences. Current architectural production is describing an obsolete model of the world in an obsolete language:

the exact, proportional, fixed, and static geometries, seemingly natural to architecture, are incapable of describing corporeal matter and its undecidable effects...rather than violating the inadequate stasis of exact geometries...architecture must begin with an adequate description of amorphous matter through anexact yet rigorous geometries[12] *(Lynn, 1998: 83).*

The imperative is curious, and the argument circular. Why *must* we employ anexact geometries? Because they allow us to 'describe corporeal matter'. Why *must* we 'describe corporeal matter'? Because it allows us to employ 'anexact' geometries. Without smart materials becoming vastly smarter, discussions of architecture in terms of fluidity, viscosity and continual metamorphosis will remain metaphorical, images unachievable except on the level of use rather than structure. In other words, this 'new architecture' will be as 'evolutionary, flexible, and proliferating' (Lynn, 1998) as the more familiar demountable box

---

12. 'These irreducible yet precise geometries are typically associated with disciplines that are forced to develop models that must remain incomplete. For example, the geologic sciences of the earth cannot develop a single fixed model for the continuous transformation of matter. Therefore geologists employ what Husserl has referred to as "*anexact proto-geometries*"...These descriptions are rigorous, yet many resist being reduced to exact forms and are referred to as anexact' (Lynn, 1998: 84).

with adjustable and/or extendable bits, the modernist warhorse championed by Cedric Price and others. Perhaps less so, as these new arrivals are 'wholes' in a way their predecessors are not necessarily. 'Amorfal' architecture may look like process rather than finished product, but structurally it seems more averse to change than much more conventional demountable construction systems, which look closed, but are in fact designed for constant addition and subtraction, inside and out. These contradictions between intention and effect should not, however, lead to a summary dismissal of this work. On the contrary, its welcoming of new ways of modelling the material world from other disciplines, and the direct, if at this point only figurative, connections it is making between architecture and natural processes, make it emblematic of the kind of conceptual thinking that could be going on within environmental architecture, but is not, as yet.

To better understand why, this new work needs to be explored in more detail, and for the purposes of this argument, I'll discuss it as it appears in the practice of 'folding'. Folding is not, as its detractors claim, merely a formal game, but neither is it productive of the heterogeneous signification-free 'things' its supporters claim for it, with its 'weakness' of form creating a lack of clear boundary between object and site. Jeffrey Kipnis's caveats[13] about theory never preceding practice notwithstanding, it is useful to begin with Gilles Deleuze, or rather with Gilles Deleuze looking at Gottfried Leibniz, because it is from there that a divergence is visible between those who have consciously taken up these ideas (Kipnis, Shirdel, Eisenman, etc.), and those who have spontaneously combusted in a similar direction (SITE, Ambasz, Cullinan, Andrew Wright), though a very different realization.

Deleuze examines the way in which Leibniz challenged the dominant Cartesian view of space and matter, and proposed instead a theory of the fold, something that Eisenman has used in the generation of his more recent work:

Traditionally architecture is conceptualised as Cartesian space, as a series of point grids. Planning envelopes are volumes of Cartesian space which seem to be neutral. Of course these volumes of Cartesian space, these volumes that contain the stylisms and images of not only classical but also modern and post-modern space, are really nothing more than a condition of ideology taken for neutral or natural (Eisenman, 1993: 24).

This uniformity and neutrality of space is of course only true as a conceptual framework, a mental, rather than physical construct. If one insists

---

13. Kipnis makes an important point: architects can produce similar forms for very different reasons, and the heterogeneity is only made homogeneous retrospectively, or if someone is particularly sensitive to emergent conditions, during the development of a new direction. In this case, faithful to Heisenberg, the analysis actually affects the outcome, helping to direct it by making what was unself-conscious as a 'movement' newly self-conscious. 'However invaluable and provocative these studies in philosophy or science are, it must be said that neither provide the impetus for a New Architecture, nor the particulars of its terms and conditions. Rather, these have grown entirely out of architectural projects and developments within the discipline of architecture itself' (Kipnis, 1993: 42).

on treating this neutrality as 'real', then the particularity of the material given is erased; something that environmental architecture refuses to allow.

In 'The Fold: Leibniz and the Baroque' (1993), Deleuze examines the etymology of the word 'fold' or *pli*, which plays a central role in the development of his ideas about Leibniz. The fold informs all matter, organic and inorganic, and informs the Baroque:

The Baroque...endlessly produces folds. It does not invent things: there are all kinds of folds coming from the East, Greek, Roman...Gothic, Classical folds...Yet the Baroque trait twists and turns its folds, pushing them into infinity, fold over fold, one upon the other (Deleuze, 1993: 17).

There are two types of fold, 'the pleats of matter, and the folds in the soul' (Deleuze, 1993: 17). In Leibniz, these two systems are continuous, the one 'etherealizing' into the other. To many of us in the twentieth century, the folds of the soul are something of an irrelevance. The 'pleats of matter', however, are increasingly important. There are two kinds of material fold: organic and inorganic.

An organism is defined by endogenous folds [that are formed by an inner genetic imperative], while inorganic matter has exogenous folds that are always determined from without or by the surrounding environment...Organic matter is not, however, different from inorganic matter...Whether organic or inorganic, matter is all one (Deleuze, 1993: 18).

This material unity makes possible a view of the physical world as an interrelatedness and interdependence that strongly resembles the model put forward by the science of ecology:

Each portion of matter may be conceived as a garden full of plants, and as a pond full of fish. But every branch of each plant, every member of each animal, and every drop of their liquid parts is in itself likewise a similar garden or pond (Leibniz, Monadologie, 67–70 in Deleuze, 1993: 19).

Important for architects, among others, however, is the realization that unity does not mean uniformity. On the contrary, at the heart of matter lies variability, difference. No 'portion of matter' is exactly like any other, multi*pli*cities precede unities:

Complexity...does not consist in the One that is said in many ways, but rather in the fact that each thing may always diverge, or fold, onto others...Thus, while it may be said that for Deleuze there are folds everywhere, the fold is not a universal design or model; and indeed no two things are folded in just the same way (Rajchman, 1993: 116).

No two human beings, no two plots of land, and so, if one wishes, no two artefacts either. One can make things the way nature makes them, through understanding the process mathematically. The model of fluid differentiated folds provides a system of variation within repetition. Or as Eisenman puts it: 'Singularity refers to the possibility in a repetition or a multiple for one copy to be different from another copy' (Eisenman, 1993: 23). Folding is an entirely different way of conceiving of space, and of objects, particularly architectural ones, within space:

Place and time when no longer defined by the grid but rather by the fold, will still exist, but not as place and time in its former context, that is, static, figural space (Eisenman, 1993: 25).

Instead, one will get what Deleuze calls 'a heterogeneous series', which is organized into a system that is 'neither stable nor unstable; in other words, not a dialectical either/or relationship' (Eisenman, 1993: 25); the very thing Derrida was striving for. To find it, ironically, the architect had to move from language to matter.

Eisenman's winning entry for the Rebstock Park competition, a five million square foot residential and commercial development on the edge of Frankfurt is a useful case study (Fig. 6.14). In it, he re-examines the *siedlung*, the Modern Movement's reinvention of the residential block. The *siedlung* was a

new linear type form that could be extended indefinitely in one direction...[t]he siedlung *form...was an ideal incarnation for the social ideas of the time...everyone and everywhere was equal. Whether of spatial modulation or individual identity, difference was homogenised in favour of an implacable idea (Eisenman, 1993: 23).*

It is this 'homogenization', this universalizing, that those interested in folding are seeking to overcome in form, and those in environmental architecture are seeking to overcome in operation. Eisenman's starting point is immediately different from that of the Modern Movement: the

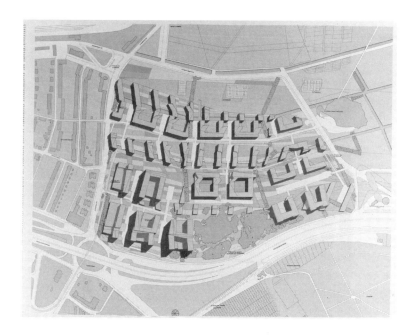

Fig. 6.14
Rebstock Masterplan, Frankfurt, Germany, Eisenman Architects: five million square foot residential and commercial development on the perimeter ring of the city.

ground is no longer a neutral Cartesian point grid, but contains 'a condition of singularity', which is, for him, 'the possibility of the fold' (Eisenman, 1993: 25). Deleuze talks of the folds of inorganic matter being exogenous, formed by external pressures from the surrounding environment. Architecturally, therefore, the inorganic folds of the building can be formed by the external pressures of the site, this time, however, not the physical pressure of shifting tectonic plates, but the mathematics of the topos. 'Rebstock uses the fold as an attempt to produce conditions of a singularity of place and time...' (Eisenman, 1993: 25). Conventional figure-ground distinctions are to dissolve into folds of matter that embrace site and buildings, the buildings merely more intense folds, and more self-conscious ones, than those of the site (Fig. 6.15). 'The ground surface as a membrane which becomes a topological event/structure is also simultaneously the building form' (Eisenman, 1993: 25). Building and topography are only the most obvious of the elements folded into each other. There is also the old – the original version of the *seidlung* – and the new – Eisenman's folded version of it; the site and the rest of Frankfurt; the housing function and the commercial function. All these are intended to be folded into each other. Each fold, whether cultural or topographical, is different. Each building is different. And yet, on such a large scale, the variations are not great enough to escape the repetitiveness they seek to overcome, as folding produces variation without producing difference. It thus uses the site without reflecting the particularity of the site. How could it do otherwise when the site is merely raw material for the mathematical computations that actually generate the design?

This abstraction is evident in a discussion of Eisenman's Centre for the Arts at Emory University, Atlanta. The configuration of the Centre is based

on a grid system that is deformed by the topography of the ravine when extended to the Centre's site. The initial deformation produced by the ravine approximates a fundamental sine wave, similar in amplitude and frequency to the ravine topography. These fundamental lines and their harmonic run to the centre, affecting the site and the four 'bars' which constitute the building.

The harmonic lines compress and deform the continuous surfaces of the bars, folding them in a multiplicity of different configurations (Eisenman, 1993: 31).

The material 'singularity' of the site is thus left far behind as it is abstracted in a mathematical methodology that has used other sources in Eisenman's earlier work: history, traces, texts. As a one-off building, the design is a much richer and more complex abstraction than that produced by mainstream modernism, though the slipstream, in the shape of architects like Scharoun, Aalto and the Constructivists, had already escaped the confines of Euclidean geometry. Folding does then produce undeniable and fascinating formal innovation. What it does not do is produce a new material relation between architecture and site, despite the suggestiveness of the language used. In picking up on

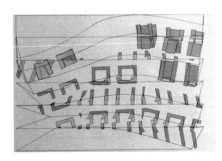

Fig. 6.15
Rebstock Park: folding diagram.

features of the site that are 'secondary', that is, not necessarily regis-
tered by the eye, they could as easily be invented as 'real'. In fact,
topography is already an invention, a system of measurement imposed
upon the ground. Looking at Eisenman's recent work, one gets, not a
lack of clear boundary between object and site, but a much more
exaggerated figure-ground distinction, because his buildings are so
startlingly different from any others in the vicinity. As a result, they are
methodologically folded into the site, but visually, less so than the buildings from which they are supposed to be a departure.

For Kipnis, this difference from conventional architectures is an advantage, and one of the 'two key principles' he identifies for folding:

*(i) an emphasis on abstract, monolithic architectural form that broaches
minimal direct references or resemblance and that is alien to the
dominant architectural modes of a given site (Kipnis, 1993: 47).*

Kipnis re-christens folding 'DeFormation' because one of the defining
characteristics of folding is the deforming of architectural form either by
external pressures from the site (exogenous), or programmatic
pressures from within the building itself (endogenous). The second 'key
principle' is

*(ii) the development of smoothing affiliations with minor organisations
operating within a context that are engendered by the intrinsic geometric, topological and/or spatial qualities of the form (Kipnis, 1993: 47).*

These 'smoothing affiliations' seem to be formal effects flowing from
sites to buildings, or between buildings of the same development, or
between spaces in the same building, which nevertheless preserve
difference in all of these. It is not a question of visible architectural
context influencing design, but 'ad hoc links made with secondary
contingencies', which are 'suppressed or minor organisations that also
operate within the site' (Kipnis, 1993: 48) – like its topography, for
example.

Despite Eisenman's folding of the past of the *siedlung* into the
present of an architecture 'alien to the dominant architectural modes' of
its site, the impetus in some architects interested in dissolving the
distinction between building and site seems to be to move away from
an interpretative dialogue with the site-as-culture, and towards the site
as unmarked ground, with buildings as so many stones upon it, parts of
a landscape that is empty of signification. In describing their design for
Yokohama International Port Terminal, for example, Foreign Office
Architects insist, 'The proposal for the new terminal aims for an artifac-
tual rather than a expressional mediation' between port and city, citizens
and travellers, 'a landscape without instructions for occupation' (Foreign
Office Architects, 1997: 71). This can be seen as a liberating impulse
towards unprescriptive yet richly modulated space. There is a declared
desire to abolish, or at least diminish, social boundary and definition
through the abolition of architectural boundary and definition. Fluid
spaces are intended to provoke more fluid functions and a more fluid
society:

We are trying to develop...processes in which specific domains and organisations are devoid of limits, origins, destination or significance: decoded, unbounded landscapes *rather than overcoded, delimited* places... *(Foreign Office Architects, 1995: 7).*

Landscape, however, is itself heavily coded, and it is only the fixation of the architect upon the built object that allows him or her to view landscape as a blank in which to seek refuge from signification. The seeking of refuge is understandable after the excesses of semiotics, but a refuge from buildings carrying meaning – intended or not – is impossible. Meanings are assigned, whatever the intention of the architect. If nature cannot escape interpretation, architecture certainly can't.

If one moves from a consideration of Delueze/Leibniz in relation to materiality rather than methodology, folding does have the potential to encourage a new relationship between building and site. As with deconstruction, so too with folding, various architects arrived at roughly similar ideas for very different reasons. The American firm SITE is again a case in point, seeking to express the blurring of culture and nature through what James Wines dubs 'passages' rather than folds:

the concept proposes that the wall and floor planes in a building should be seen as fluid, contextually responsive membranes...In terms of architectural construction, plant life and earth elements should be as much a part of the physical substance of shelter as conventional building materials (Wines, 1997: 33).

This sounds like Leibniz and the unity of matter.

From an aesthetic standpoint, the objective is to look at the fusion of structure and landscape as a kind of interactive biographical dialogue, that, when translated into visual imagery, describes their mutual origins in nature (Wines, 1997: 33).

The result is buildings whose walls literally extend into and embrace the landscape, and landscape that enters the buildings in what is intended to reflect the 'fluidity, indeterminacy and chance' of nature (Plate 43). Geological layers are similarly folded so that strata are compressed together, yet still identifiable as layers. SITE has designed 'passages' in urban as well as rural contexts, where the topography is built, rather than planted, but the example they give, of the Saudi Arabian National Museum in Riyadh, shows a self-contained ziggurat (Plate 39). This is hardly surprising: urban sites are not as permeable as green field ones. If one is trying to perform the literal folding of building into site and site into building, rather than just represent it within the confines of the building itself, the extension of these 'passages' is necessarily limited in urban contexts by roads, property lines and existing buildings.

In moving from Eisenman to SITE, one moves from the literal expression of folding (that is, buildings whose appearance is de-formed by, for example, the mathematics of the surrounding topography), to the literal enactment of folding (that is, buildings which are physically integrated with the surrounding land). In the first case, folding works upon the forms of otherwise conventionally constructed and operated buildings. In the second case, folding radically reorganizes the structure and operation of the building, by redistributing its constituent elements.

6.5 Conclusion

It could be reasonably argued that the wilder side of formal experiment is hardly going to win the hearts and minds of a generally conservative public, or for that matter, the generally conservative architectural profession. Folding, however, is not being proposed as the formal template for environmental architecture, but as one way of reflecting upon, and reflecting, a 'new' relation between built and natural environments. Conversely, the focus of environmental design on the precise physical conditions within which the building must exist, and on the particular materiality of which it is constituted, would aid in producing the 'singularity' folding strives for.

Not only the above criterion of 'visibility', but also that of 'differentiation' could find varying degrees of welcome and interpretation in and outside environmental architecture. Differentiation requires that the environmental implications of structure and materials are considered, as well as heating, cooling and ventilation strategies. These strategies are themselves either borrowed directly from those native to the climate zone in question, or serve as inspiration for a more sophisticated system, possibly in another climate zone entirely. At this level of engagement, one has to cease calling this 'existing-architectures-made-more-environmentally-sustainable', and start calling it 'environmental architecture', for it has become something other than what they were, re-formed to some degree by an environmental agenda.

At the level of 'visibility', this re-formation is equally deliberate, but quite possibly in the opposite direction. For example, if an exact geometry of matter is something the architect wants to pursue, then he or she may well end up with a 'universal' form that contains a very particular climatic strategy, that is, with a tension between universal idea and differentiated operation. The examples of folding given above are not 'of' anywhere but an abstracted topography. They speak to a universal condition. Conceptually, this is entirely acceptable within the environmental hermeneutic, but not operationally. This concept of nature would have to be embodied in an energy efficient building to begin to qualify as 'sustainable'.[14]

In various ways, this enquiry has addressed itself throughout to the idea of 'inclusiveness', so that in one sense, this chapter is merely the foregrounding of a methodology that has been informing the arguments of most of the previous chapters, a governing strategy for making architecture sustainable. This obviously affects the content of such an architecture, materially and conceptually. The suggested use of passive and active technologies, of natural and synthetic materials, will obviously

---

14. 'By remaining attentive to the detailed conditions that determine the connection of one part to another, by understanding construction as a "sequence of events", it becomes possible to imagine an architecture that can respond fluidly and sensitively to local difference while maintaining overall stability' (Allen, 1997: 27).

produce different kinds of architecture from that which defines itself through exclusion of one kind or another. The final inclusion of visibility and operation could increase the distance between this kind of environmental architecture and its predecessors geometrically.

7   DOING IT

7.1 Introduction

Discussion can obviously leap much further and faster than practice, which has the inertia of the status quo to contend with. This chapter, therefore, is not about what might be, but about what is developing on the ground in terms of the criteria for engaging with environmental design. A large-scale competition entry by Richard Horden, to which I contributed, demonstrates a level of symbiosis between built and natural environments within a modified modernist framework. This modernist framework makes assumptions about what is environmentally permissible that are problematic to others trying to achieve a greater degree of symbiosis.

In discussing the bioclimatic high-rises of the Malaysian architect Ken Yeang and the Tjibaou Cultural Centre of Renzo Piano as examples of climatic and cultural differentiation respectively, no claims are made for either architect having achieved anything as rigorous as a certain number of kilowatts per square metre, only that they are both pursuing their designs beyond an undifferentiated environmental design. Some of the work may also qualify quantitatively, but that remains to be tested. The fourth example, the work of Emilio Ambasz, is similarly unmeasured – much of it indeed is unbuilt. If built, it would achieve some degree of symbiosis, project by project, and would remain both climatically and culturally undifferentiated, although in some climates, the burying of buildings is climatically appropriate and culturally typical. What much of the work does do is address nature visibly as well as pragmatically, and goes about it quite self-consciously.

This chapter then examines the degree to which different architects have opened themselves up to a process that has the potential to transform their architectural identity. It also examines the validity of the criteria suggested in the previous chapter, i.e. symbiosis, differentiation and visibility. These were posed as questions: how far is it necessary for a design to be pushed to qualify as environmentally sustainable, and does that 'sustainability' include representational as well as operational concerns? None of the criteria, alone or in combination, is a quantified measurement of environmental sustainability, only an indication of intellectual consistency and direction of environmental strategy.

The first two criteria can, on one level, be approached strictly in terms of environmental performance. All three criteria, however, to increasingly greater degrees, affect architectural expression, visibility being simply the last and most noticeable result of such a choice. Moreover, the second, differentiation, if viewed strictly environmentally, can be seen merely as another aspect of the first criterion, that is, as a more effective way of achieving symbiosis. This is why, when setting out these criteria, it was emphasized that the only necessary requirement for environmentally sustainable architecture is the achievement of some acceptable level of symbiosis, quantified in terms of fossil fuel consumption, with differentiation as a further step that encompasses construction as well as operation. Within this utilitarian context, visibility, or more generally, formal experiment, becomes an optional and undesirable extra. Even if one reverses priorities, and privileges the ideological role of environmental architecture over any small contribution it might make to the physical environment through its limited presence, then symbiosis still remains the *sine qua non* of its sustainability. Formal visibility then becomes a vital second criterion, with differentiation as the optional extra.

Does it matter whether 'architectures-made-more-environmentally-sustainable' tell us of their repositioning, beyond the 'accidental' telling that is a by-product of that repositioning? Does it matter that environmental functionalism does not inspire if it performs well environmentally? Does it matter that a response to James Wines' call for 'highly visible aesthetic choices' never materializes? Architects are answering these questions in different ways, some by not asking them in the first place. Carbon dioxide reduction is important, explicitly to environmentalists, and implicitly to the community at large. Those architects who do not consider it to be as important as their other concerns will define symbiosis in their own terms. If that means a lower level of energy efficiency, so be it. They are not willing to follow the implications of environmental design to their transformative conclusions. There is nothing categorical about the examples chosen for this chapter. They merely illustrate possible degrees of transformation in a useful way. Until levels of energy efficiency are quantified and codified as law, these degrees will remain on a sliding scale.

In one of the more recent – and wide-ranging – international surveys of sustainable pluralism to date, David Lloyd Jones's *Architecture and the Environment*, a taxonomy of examples is presented, relating 'to size, form and layout' (Lloyd Jones, 1998: 64), each with a brief environmental assessment. Certain parts of Europe, Japan, and to a lesser extent Australia and the United States, appear to be the areas of greatest environmental design activity, and the wide-ranging examples provide a picture of the actual directions this is taking. Two patterns are immediately apparent: first, that there is no one formally distinct architecture emerging from these concerns; second, that an abstract, industrially based approach dominates, as it does in all other architectures. In other words, despite its partial origin in a rejection of both these aspects of contemporary architecture, environmental architecture is increasingly falling into step with the status quo of form and construction. Environmental strategies re-form already evolved form-making as far as the architect will allow. If the architect – or indeed the client – holds fast to a pre-existing visual identity, such change is minimal.

In office design, even clients whose business requires they demonstrate a commitment to an environmentally led architecture tend to end up with simple 'modern' forms whose environmental behaviour can be more easily modelled and predicted. The requirements for easily calculable passive heating and cooling and natural daylighting can thus dictate the design of the building. Elements emerging as characteristic of passive design – atria, south-facing glazed buffer zones (in cold and temperate climates), fixed or tracking louvres, cooling towers, stack vents, double skins, etc. – tend to be incorporated within reassuringly familiar rectangular forms. These can, however, carry unexpected power, as with Sauerbruch Hutton's neo-modernist GSW Headquarters in Berlin (Plate 44 and Figs. 7.1–2), which hides its environmental strategy within a building type that conventionally denotes a total lack of one.

Fig. 7.1
GSW Headquarters: third floor plan.

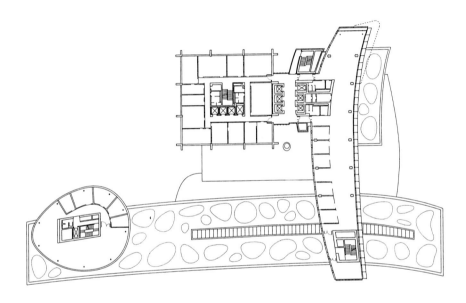

Beyond this, the plurality is remarkable, from the regional – Glen Murcutt's houses in the Australian outback (Plates 45–46) – to the recycled – Shigeru Ban's Paper Gallery (Plate 47) – to the sculptural – Herzog & Partner's Hall 26 (Plate 48) – to the poetic – Fielden Clegg's Earth Centre Canopy (Fig. 7.3) – to the folkish – Edward Cullinan's Westminster Lodge, Dorset (Plate 49) – to the cool – Alsop and Stormer's Peckham Library (Plates 50–51 and Fig. 7.4).

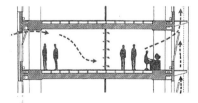

Fig. 7.2
GSW Headquarters: diagram showing cross-ventilation.

If one performed on the Lloyd Jones examples the same analysis that is performed on the examples in this chapter, the same variations in levels of engagement with the environmental agenda would emerge. In Section 7.2 on the symbiosis case study, Richard Horden's competition entry demonstrates the many levels on which the architect must operate in order to achieve not only environmental, but social sustainability as well. If this smacks of social engineering, it is, but client- rather than architect-driven. In Section 7.3 on 'differentiation' case study, Ken Yeang's work was chosen as an example of climatic differentiation because he has thought long and hard about the problem of the bioclimatic skyscraper. He has thus set himself a twofold task: to make more energy efficient a building type originally predicated on mechanical

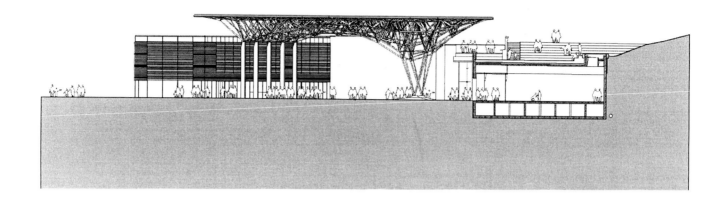

services, and to introduce that re-formed building type into a particularly difficult climate zone – tropical Malaysia. The Renzo Piano example in the same section demonstrates how much further architects can go in allowing environmental considerations to re-form their architectures if they address the overlapping of the climatic and the cultural. Finally, in Section 7.4 on the 'visibility' case study, Emilio Ambasz is taken as an example, one of the very few within environmental design, of the way in which Piano's formal self-consciousness could be turned towards a more explicit and at the same time, more generalized expression of the new contract between (built) culture and nature.

Fig. 7.3
Earth Centre Canopy, Fielden Clegg.

Fig. 7.4
Peckham Library: environmental strategy.

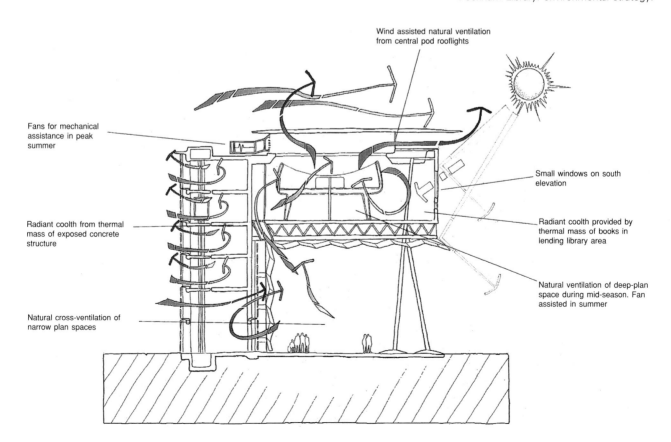

7.2 Symbiosis: Richard Horden

The term 'passive' refers to those environmental design strategies which seek to heat and cool buildings without mechanical help, such as fans, pumps, photovoltaics or any of the other paraphernalia of 'active' systems, however 'clean' those active systems are. The degree of passivity is often determined by the client, whose views on comfort vary from a demand for total control of the internal climate to a willingness to tolerate greater thermal variation. And yet, even in the most rigorously energy-efficient designs, essentially passive systems are often supplemented by active additions like fans, which provide comfort when climatic conditions require. As with everything in environmental design, however, there are degrees of hybridity. Richard Horden's competition design for the 'University of Future Generations' outside Sydney, Australia, followed the requirements of the competition brief and sought to maximize the potential of both passive and active systems in a mix that has become the norm in environmental architecture, with the proportion of active to passive systems the variable in the equation.

The University of Future Generations demonstrates the degree to which an architect committed to the principles of mainstream modernism can allow an environmental agenda to influence his work. This is a particular struggle for anyone seeking, not to repudiate, but to redirect modernity and modernism. Horden is acutely aware of the plurality that is the condition of environmental sustainability at this point in its architectural incarnations, and makes no claims to having even *an* answer, let alone *the* answer to the questions sustainability poses. However, what he has been pursuing as an effect (the experience of nature) now confronts him as a process (the operations of the biosphere) since he chose to engage with environmental design. He is, therefore, pursuing an enquiry that began for him in modernism and ends in a question mark. He doesn't know what effect this enquiry will have on his work, but is open to following where it leads.

The struggle is to accommodate the assumptions of modernism within a narrative of environmentalism that challenges some of those assumptions – for example, the association of ever-advancing technology with material progress, and of material progress with 'the good'. This struggle manifests itself in, for example, Horden's reluctance to commit himself to any particular materials, be they synthetic or 'natural', in case something new and better is on the way from the laboratory, a technology transfer from a moon shot or military research project. This expectation goes hand-in-hand with a faith in material and social progress, and an architecture that should be reflecting a society that is becoming more and more transparent. The modernist dream of transparency is very strong in Horden, as is seen in his admiration for those of his modernist predecessors who achieved the 'flow of nature through the building': Neutra, Ellwood, Lautner, etc. As it was for them, this has until now been for Horden a formal question – the disposition of windows and walls – further enhanced by his pursuit of a light building technology, or 'light tech' as he calls it. This lightness is often difficult to achieve, since having to design big does not always sit well with wanting to build light. Combining them often requires the use of industrially produced materials, putting the architect in a dilemma: building light(er) uses less material, and therefore less energy, but the materials necessary to accomplish this often have a higher embodied energy content than heavier ones.

A possible solution to this was explored in the University of Future Generations, the brainchild of the Ecodesign Foundation. The university was to be built sustainably, operate sustainably and teach various aspects of sustainability, both through its courses – design, agriculture, business management, etc. – and through the transparency of its operation – a living lesson. Horden organized the scheme along entirely different lines from his other work. He had to consider questions he did not usually ask himself: what forms of energy should he use? What was he to do with waste? At what technological level were the buildings to function? Did he have to abjure modernity and take up an arcadian anti-industrialism, or could he merely modify his previous position? The brief called for the design of a private university on a 120 hectare site an hour north of Sydney for 4500 on-campus students and 4500 'electronic distance' students, 30 per cent of whom would be Australian, 40 per cent Asian and 30 per cent other nationalities. The architecture itself was to be a pedagogical tool, demonstrating as far as possible principles of energy efficiency, cultural diversity and interdependency – the last not only local, but global, and realized electronically. In addition to the emphasis on the physical system of the university was an equal insistence on the integration of the disembodied world of the Internet, for distance learning and exchange. Integration was also to be pursued in an interdisciplinary approach to education, with separate faculties separate in name only. Thought had to be given, therefore, to three different but interrelated strands: the physical form of the university, its technology and its pedagogy.

Horden's first decision was to 'build light' by breaking up the large institutional buildings typical of universities into many smaller, lighter ones (Plate 52). He gathered an interdisciplinary team, out of which came a remarkable leap from his pursuit of light high technology to one of light sustainable technology. Wood reappeared as a building material for the first time since his boyhood tree houses, chosen because it was available locally and less energy expensive than steel.

The complex and unpredictable interaction between the different aspects of the university became the central concern of Horden's team, interaction they sought to promote through a network of non-hierarchical relationships. The design therefore integrated built form, landscape, education and technology into one strategy of sustainability – as Horden put it, 'lightness in relation to sky, people, technique, earth and water'. This was done by viewing the university as a continuum of systems ranging from the most 'natural' (the untouched ecosystem represented by the protected woods on site) through to the most artificial (the electronic 'ecosystem' of the Internet) (Fig. 7.5). In between was a delicately calibrated system of fields, gardens, buildings and infrastructure to transform this linear continuum into a circular model of consumption. On a physical level, the wastes produced in maintaining the university and its inhabitants were to be returned to nature as cleanly as possible. On an ethical level, the built systems necessary to accomplish this were to be lessons in themselves, demonstrations of solar and wind power, waste recycling and water conservation, requiring the responsible participation of students and staff to close the consumption circle. On a pedagogical level, knowledge was recycled via electronic loops, which gathered it from the world and disseminated it through the world.

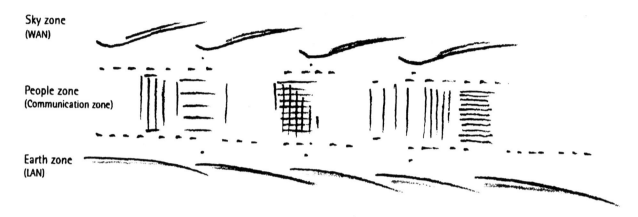

Sky zone (WAN)

People zone (Communication zone)

Earth zone (LAN)

The physical and virtual edges of the 'people zone' (communication zone):
A sequence of layers, filters, screens, displays; responding to internal and external environments and creating 'inside-outside' spaces, virtual and physical spaces and relationships

Four categories were set up to integrate the levels on which the university had to operate: landscape and built form, energy and built form, electronics and built form, and education and built form. All these sought again to set up a circular rather than linear model of operation, whether it was of waste or ideas. Throughout the design, formal organization mirrored technical organization mirrored a version of nature's organization. The university buildings, never more than two storeys high, were strung around the contours of a man-made lake, itself in an ambiguous position conceptually. The buildings, two residential colleges to each of the five faculties, branched off a central street, using the overused analogy of the veins of a leaf branching out from the stem. The cables servicing the electronic life of the campus followed the same system of branching to service the buildings.

Educationally, the central idea was to encourage 'environmental literacy' through direct experience. Students and staff would actively participate in a transparent system of energy consumption and waste recycling, enabling them to see what they consumed, and how this consumption could be rendered self-sustaining through their co-operation. An 'energy card', looking and working like a credit card, was to be introduced, so that individuals and departments could see how much energy they were using each day. To help with this, all high-energy equipment, like computers, was to be fitted with meters to indicate the rate of consumption, encouraging users to avoid peaks of demand. Aesthetically, technically and environmentally, water was to be made highly visible in the daily life of the campus through the artificial lake.

Fig. 7.5
University of Future Generations, Australia, Richard Horden Associates: ideogram.

This was to be the source and end point of both natural and man-made water cycles on site. It was to form a focus for the many buildings surrounding it, as well as providing reed beds for cleaning sewage water, and sustaining an aquatic ecosystem of flora and fauna. Grey water for flushing and cooling was to be collected from roofs and stored in cisterns for subsequent treatment by the building where it had been collected. Heat, electricity, water and waste water would be carried through under-floor ducts and controlled by computer.

In addition to collecting rainwater, the wing-like roofs carried sun-tracking photovoltaic panels, and solar masts capped each of the site's three hills, driving the pumps that brought water up from the lake to run back down through the university to cool the buildings (Figs. 7.6–8). Inside, large networks of computers connected the university to itself and to the world, interweaving as much as possible virtual with physical place. Punctured sliding screens enabled users to control the amount of daylight in different parts of their rooms so they could work at their computers without having to sit in the airless dark. In contrast to the computer technology, temperature was controlled passively, through shading (canopies, sliding screens, trees), cross-ventilation, thermal mass and night and evaporative cooling.

Thermal mass in a construction system that was supposed to 'touch the earth lightly' sounds contradictory. In fact, this mass was concentrated in the floor slabs of rammed earth held in profiled steel trays, with the roof packed with light insulation to protect against solar gain in the hot season and heat loss in the cool season. All the buildings were raised a foot or so above the ground on steel stanchions – high enough to prevent termites eating the timber columns they supported. Raising the buildings gave two advantages: first, it disturbed the site with as little excavation as possible, and vastly reduced the amount of dug earth to be redistributed elsewhere – a serious, or perhaps redundant consideration when so much had already been moved for the artificial lake. And second, it allowed air to circulate under the buildings, which, when run past vegetation and water, was cool enough to condition the interiors. The juxtaposition of electric cabling for the Internet running through rammed earth floors was exactly the kind of inclusive approach to technologies that Horden was aiming for. The construction system for the rest of the buildings was equally hybrid: timber frames allowed panels and screens to be used as in-fill, highly insulated, but light. Large areas of glazing were also possible with such a system, allowing for the visual interpenetration and literal transparency so favoured by modernists.

Symbiosis between the built and natural environments was thus achieved using renewable sources of energy – sun, wind, water – and advanced technology. On a specifically architectural level, what is of interest is Horden's willingness to relinquish his usual palette of high-performance industrially produced materials for a large proportion of wood, a material he had never before specified in his work. The choice was justified environmentally – its use reduced the embodied energy content of the project and greatly increased thermal efficiency – but has obvious architectural consequences: in using a local material, the buildings are to some extent grounded in their locality. They are 'of the place'

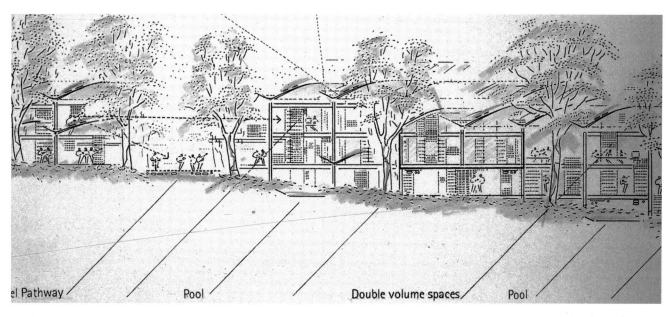

el Pathway   Pool   Double volume spaces   Pool

Roof terraces   Lakeside pathway   Waterside

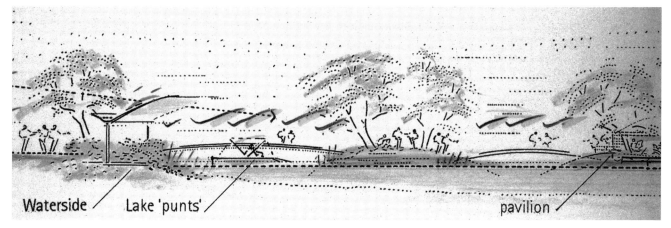

Waterside   Lake 'punts'   pavilion

Figs. 7.6–8
University of Future Generations, Australia, Richard Horden Associates: elevation of student housing running down the hill to the lake.

in a way steel and glass buildings more typical of Horden's work would not have been. They are of the place, however, in only the most general way – the geographical place rather than the cultural place.

This design, then, is one of three strategies for achieving a less exploitative relationship between built and natural environments: the first uses local vernacular techniques to mediate passively between interior and exterior, local, preferably 'natural' materials and low technologies. The second takes vernacular techniques from anywhere and deploys them anywhere, using industrially produced, universally available materials and a hybrid strategy of high and low technologies, with an emphasis on high technologies. The third strategy is inclusive, not just in the use of high and low technologies, but in all aspects of environmental design, using some local techniques and some 'universal' ones, some locally available 'natural' materials and some synthetic ones. Buildings following the first strategy are more regionally identifiable than ones produced from the second and third strategies. Horden's design, following a totally inclusive, hybrid strategy does not 'belong' in Australia the way, for example, Glen Murcutt's work does (see Plates 49–50), nor is it intended to. The goal is physical symbiosis, not cultural inflection.

7.3 Differentiation

7.3.1 Climatic differentiation: Ken Yeang

In the design of his 1984 'Roof-Roof House' (Plate 53), Ken Yeang extracted climatic function from vernacular style in Malaysian architecture. This was the first step towards developing a fully fledged bioclimatic architecture that attempted to assimilate western buildings types such as the high-rise, with traditional passive cooling strategies taken from vernacular Malay houses. Chief among the latter was the idea of roof and verandah serving as a form of 'umbrella' to protect the interior from direct solar gain. The resulting 'Roof-Roof House' does not resemble its vernacular antecedent in form or material, but instead looks like an idiosyncratic piece of International Style architecture, the louvered sunshade over house and pool providing what Yeang calls a 'solar filter', suitable for a warm wet tropical climate:

the architecture of shelter evolved into diverse solutions to meet the challenge of widely varying climates, indicating that the ancients recognised regional climatic adaptation as an essential principle of architecture. In this regard, the climatically responsive building can be seen as having a closer fit with its geographical context (Yeang, 1994: 22).

Yeang has since developed the concept of the building as an environmental filter for all his work in the region. The vernacular origins of this strategy have become more and more remote as Yeang's office has worked increasingly on high-rises, both commercial and residential. Inflecting an alien building type towards one's own culture stylistically as well as environmentally threatens the design with kitsch, so that, apart from the occasional shading screen punctured with the geometric patterns typical of Islamic decoration in earlier work, Yeang makes no overt architectural reference to Malaysian culture. Instead, there is a range of techniques intended to reduce the use of air-conditioning through passive ventilation and cooling used within a series of high-rises that have become increasingly sculptural over twenty years of practice.

As with much commercially oriented environmental architecture, there is a lack of critical assessment of environmental performance. If there are shortcomings in a project, it is not in the interests of a practice to have them noised abroad, as clients are reluctant to be experimented on with new techniques and technologies. The learning curve, therefore, tends to stay in-house. Yeang's publications, like *The Skyscraper Bioclimatically Considered* (1996), give no hint of the difficulties encountered by any architect trying to ameliorate passively the effects of a tropical climate, one notoriously resistant to passive cooling techniques. Nevertheless, Yeang is developing an increasingly adventurous architectural vocabulary for a bioclimatic strategy he has developed through his work on tropical high-rises: vertical landscaping (IBM Plaza, Menara Boustead, Exhibition Tower), air zones (Plaza Atrium, Menara Boustead, BP Tower), wind scoops (Penggiran Apartments, China Towers), sun-path shading (Menara Budaya, Central Plaza, Orchid Tower, Menara Mesiniaga), and increasingly, sculpted elevations that counter the passage of the sun across the building, as in the Exhibition (EDITT) Tower in Singapore (Plate 54).

This last was commissioned by the Singapore Urban Redevelopment Authority, and is intended to begin life as an exhibition tower, with exhibition, retail and performance spaces. Yeang has designed a 'loose fit', however, so that as needs change, so can the use of the building. It is part of a strategy to reduce the enormous drain on resources that high-rises conventionally involve. The structure will be bolted, not welded, for easier demounting, and will carry photovoltaic arrays, heavy planting and rain scoops. The result is an expressionism that struggles against the structural linearity dictated by the engineering demands of the high-rise. The degree to which such designs are energy efficient has yet to be assessed, and to his great credit, Yeang is co-operating fully with a doctoral study[1] examining a problem central to passive cooling in the tropics: the extent to which daylight is sacrificed in the battle against solar gain. The more shading devices employed to prevent direct sunlight from entering the building, the darker the interior becomes; the darker the interior becomes, the more electricity is necessary to artificially light the interior. This is probably less electricity than the amount required to run extra air-conditioning if there were no, or insufficient, solar shading, but it remains a significant energy expenditure.

To what degree, then, is this work climatically differentiated? Does its configuration and articulation visibly indicate its climate zone? Yeang certainly wants his tropical high-rises to declare their intentions; that is, he wants them to be readable *as* tropical. At the same time, however, environmental design is an aspect of his architecture, not its totality:

---

1. Shireen Jahnkassim (1999). *A Comparative Study of the Daylight and Thermal Impacts of Three High-rise Building Envelopes in a Tropical Climate.* School of Architecture and Interior Design, University of Brighton. Unpublished.

The bioclimatic energy-conserving agenda provides us with a set of theoretical principles for shaping buildings which must eventually allow for a permissiveness in poetic interpretation by design (Yeang, 1994: 22).

The tempering of the environmental imperative by architectural considerations is flagged by the use of the term 'energy-conserving'. Such an aim removes any quantified environmental performance levels from the equation. As long as fossil fuel consumption is lowered relative to a conventional high-rise, the amount by which it is lowered cannot be held to account. So that the use of aluminium cladding on the Menara Mesiniaga, for example, is of less importance for its high embodied energy content than for its architectural effect, an effect Alan Balfour queries in his introduction to Yeang's book: '...the recent suite of towers...seem like armoured figures preparing for an as-yet-undefined task, somewhat uneasy with their ecological responsibility' (Balfour, 1994: 7). Yeang's architecture is evolving so quickly that this critique no longer has much relevance. The more recent work is planted, opened up and less metallic, responding to climate as particularly as possible.

The degree to which an 'aclimatic' building type – the high-rise – can ever achieve much of a fit in this climatic context is debatable. That Yeang's work does not always look 'ecological'; that it sometimes looks more like the machinery of which it is at least a partial critique, is indicative of the ever-present potential for a divergence between environmental and formal agendas, a divergence that has aesthetic causes, and material, and therefore environmental, consequences. To pursue climatic differentiation to its logical conclusion is perhaps ultimately to exclude a building type alien to that climate. The 'bioclimatic skyscraper', therefore, may be an oxymoron. All one can hope to achieve is a less environmentally damaging building, rather than perfected coexistence, and this Yeang has certainly already achieved, and continues to push forward with remarkable fertility.

7.3.2 Cultural differentiation: Renzo Piano

It could be argued that the choice of a cultural centre to illustrate cultural differentiation is somewhat biased. Even architects who did not normally concern themselves with such an issue might in such a case, especially if the cultural centre were particularly sensitive, as the Tjibaou Cultural Centre (Plate 55) for the native Kanak population of New Caledonia certainly is. This chapter does not seek to argue the desirability, or not, of cultural differentiation, but to examine the way in which it can emerge from the practice of climatic differentiation, and Renzo Piano's cultural centre is a useful example of the way such integration can be realized by an architect not known for regionalism.

That said, the wooden 'cases' that dominate the design of the Tjibaou Cultural Centre were initially conceived for cultural reasons not climatic ones, and then modified to perform their environmental function more efficiently. They refer, however, to the huts of the Kanaks, who did consider climate first, or rather saw climate as indivisible from their culture. Piano's 'cases' thus evolved from a cone-like shape that echoed the conical roofs of the Kanaks' own huts, to more of a cone cut in half, in order to increase air flow for ventilation (Plate 56). There was in fact no other traditional Kanak building form to reflect, in however abstract a way. Piano and his team

were designing a building for people who were not builders. The Kanaks have been...in New Caledonia...more than four thousand years, and they have never built any buildings...[Their] huts are made from perishable materials, and never passed down to the next generation. Their tradition is not in a single building, but in the topology and the pattern of construction (Vassal, 1998: 107).

Piano thus used his own cultural tradition (one that reifies) to fix and preserve another (unreified) culture. Or rather the French, who own the island of New Caledonia and its valuable nickel deposits, asked him to do this, presumably to appease the Kanaks, who were agitating for independence, and in 1989, lost the leader of their movement, Jean Marie Tjibaou (even his name is an irony), in an assassination.

As is often the case when trying to establish a relationship between the vernacular and the contemporary in architecture, it is the physical location of the indigenous culture, that culture's first cause, which provides the link between the two. The vegetation of the island provides the Kanaks with the material for their villages and their mythologies. In examining building practice, Piano could, and did, extend his research into the cultural framework inside which that practice sits. Or rather an expert in South Pacific cultures, the anthropologist Alban Bensa, in another dubious exercise in western intervention, extended Piano's research. As a result of these investigations, both the site and building plans were derived from Kanak symbolism. Around the building winds the 'Kanak Path', which belongs to a myth from Jean Marie Tjibaou's tribe, and tells of the five stages of Kanak culture, from creation through agriculture to habitat (the villages) to the country of the dead to the spirit world, each of which is closely associated with particular stones, plants and trees.

The cultural centre itself is arranged as another path, reproducing the organizational idea of the Kanaks' 'ceremonial path', which is lined with trees, and ends in the chief's hut (Fig. 7.9). Instead of trees, programmatic functions line the building's ceremonial path, enclosed in the ten 'cases', or huts, that make up the 'village'. The Kanak failed to recognize these cases until they reinterpreted them as resembling the structural framework of their huts, before the thatch is applied. It is an ambiguous business: the very idea of a 'cultural centre' for a culture unfamiliar with such a concept is a paradox. Dangerous, too, is the idea that the architect has managed to become culturally transparent, or worse, and more improbably, has 'become' a Kanak:

This was exactly why I won the competition...My proposal had made the effort to be born there, thinking Kanak...A true acceptance of the challenge inherent in the program took courage: it meant taking off the mental clothes of the European architect and steeping myself in the world of the people of the Pacific (Piano, 1998: 92, 93).

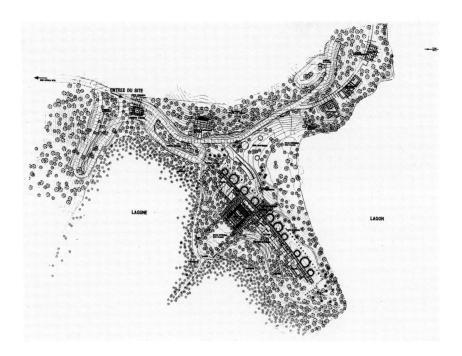

Fig. 7.9
Tjibaou Cultural Centre, New Caledonia:
Renzo Piano Building Workshop: site plan
showing the 'ceremonial path' through
site and building.

Unfortunate though this language is, there are nevertheless sound reasons for attempting to inflect the design towards the culture which it houses:

A proposal based on our own models would simply not have worked in New Caledonia. It was not feasible to offer a standard product of Western architecture, with a layer of camouflage over the top: it would have looked like an armoured car covered with palm leaves (Piano, 1998: 93).

In both the traditional vernacular and the contemporary approach, the strategy is climatic. Passive cooling strategies require that the use of renewable energies is maximized, in this case, the Pacific trade winds, which blow onto the promontory site from the sea. Piano's 'cases', which face south-south-east, are made of iroko wood, with laminated wood elements up to twenty-eight metres high supporting horizontal curved slats that allow free air circulation between themselves and the louvered inner skin. The louvres are computer-operated, designed to open automatically to their full extent when there is a gentle breeze, and begin to close if wind speed increases. If the wind shifts direction, ventilation is through the much lower front of the building, evacuating through the top of the double skin. The design evolved under wind tunnel testing and computer simulations carried out by Ove Arup and Partners and CSTB (Centre Scientifique et Technique de Batiment), but only the building's users will know precisely how the building performs under these varying conditions.

The result is a design that, once cued, may remind the Kanaks of their own minimal built culture, but in no way seeks to imitate it. Piano was adamant about avoiding the slightest hint of kitsch. What he does imitate is the Kanaks' own response to climate: working with, rather

than against it. This is done through a similar attention to passive ventilation, but with very different materials, and at a very different level of
technical complexity. The laminated wood pillars, for example, are set
into a cast steel foundation, which had to be transported across the
Pacific to the site, as did the computers and the louvres. Although to
construct a building of any size and complexity on an unendowed island
would always require imports, for fundamentalists, the choices would
have been different. Doubtless a greater energy saving would have been
achieved, but almost certainly not such a powerful architectural effect.
What is more useful for the 'cause', a worthy but unnoticed building, or
a less environmentally rigorous but more visible one? In this case, the
architect chose in favour of celebrating (inventing?) Kanak culture architecturally, rather than achieving the lowest possible CO_2 emissions.

Because of its attention to the symbolic content of the form, Tjibaou
addresses visibility as explicitly as environmental performance, and
could, with justification, be seen as a good example of the criterion of
visibility. But one can go further in this direction. Environmental design
works by finding particular solutions within a general methodological
framework. Within Piano's design the new contract between nature and
culture has to be inferred from a new relationship between building and
site, that is, the general, and culturally more reflexive, has to be inferred
from the particular. This is a perfectly sound way of going about the
generation of environmental architecture, but it is not the only way to
intensify their ideological effectiveness. In much of the architectural
work of Emilio Ambasz, one can see the possibility of another direction,
one that has the representation of the new contract in all its generality
as its highest priority.

7.4 Visibility: Emilio Ambasz

An Argentinian architect, writer and designer Emilio Ambasz is intensely
aware of the fiction-making role of his profession:

*It has always been my deep belief that architecture and design are both
myth-making acts. I hold that their real tasks begin once functional and
behavioural needs have been satisfied...The architect's or designer's
milieu may change, but the task remains the same: to give poetic form
to the pragmatic (Ambasz, 1991: 24).*

The pragmatic, in this case, is the environmentally sustainable. The
poetic, for Ambasz, is an exercise in hierarchy reversal, bringing nature
out of the shadow of culture within the context of architecture. At first
glance Ambasz's architectural work, most of which comprises projects
rather than built examples, seems to be that of an unreconstructed
arcadian: a return to nature and an obliteration of built culture, burying
it under mounds of earth wherever possible. Many of the projects are
sunk in an imaginary landscape that is like a version of the pampas, not
a tree or a bush or a cow to be seen on an endless undifferentiated
green plain in which buildings appear as geological formations or the
remnants of human interventions that once stood above ground.
Ambasz acknowledges that part of us does and will always want to

return to nature, but his view of this nature is entirely contemporary. He synthesizes Europe's myth of utopia and (north and south) America's myth of arcadia into something new and strange: 'the traditional vision of Arcadia is that of a humanistic garden. America's arcadia has turned into a man made nature, a forest of artificial trees and mental shadows' (Ambasz, 1991: 19). This is a hybrid nature in which the line between nature and culture is lost in varying degrees of fusion.

In the Manoir d'Angoussart, Bierges, Belgium, the house and garden are conceived as an indivisible entity, but made up of diverse architectural elements fanning out from the circular open court of the house (Plate 57). These create multiple perspectives, and a constantly metamorphosing sense of the place, relative to the viewer's position. The whole can never be grasped except from the air. The same disorientation applies to judgements about what is natural and what is artificial. The entrance to the Manoir is a lattice with glazing behind, both in the shape of a pedimented semi-circle, intended to be covered in greenery. One enters the earth in entering the house, 'enterring' oneself, only to emerge outdoors again, into the open court at the building's centre, while still contained within the house.

In the Schlumberger Research Laboratories, Austin, Texas, a computer research facility, the labs are divided into a series of buildings buttressed with earth berms to help integrate them into the landscape and reduce the need for cooling (Plate 58). Again, there is an oscillation between what is 'natural' and what is artificial, the man-made lake one of many ambiguous interventions. Ambasz embraces advanced technology wholeheartedly, but technology that will enable him to achieve his symbiotic goals, an Aristotelean architecture 'without threat' to nature. For him 'new sources of light, electronic and optical fibres, artificial gases, chemically treated materials, bonding agents, mist machines, laser rays, seismographers, ultra-fast cements' (Sottsass, 1991: 11), enable nature to be assimilated into built culture, and built culture into nature.

In Obihiro, Japan, the climate is akin to that of Siberia. Given the hostility of the natural environment, the clients wanted to provide a more benign version of nature inside their store, in the form of a winter garden. This is only possible on such a scale through advanced environmental control and glazing systems. The result is the Nichii Obihiro department store, a two and a half-acre building enclosing a park-within-a-park (Plate 59). An enormous glazed roof shelters a picturesque landscape, complete with waterfall and lake. Around the perimeter, the floors of the store rise. On the exterior face of these floors is a double-glazed façade wide enough to permit more trees and plants to grow between the two layers of glass. Customers approaching the building would see it as both crystalline mountain and wooded hill. The energy embodied in a mountain of high performance glass would probably outweigh any environmental benefit the winter garden might bestow, but here, imagery rather than energy efficiency is paramount. The visible overwhelms the operational. A balance is difficult, but not impossible to achieve, if the environmental and the formal are held in tension in the architect's head, with each informing the other.

Although Ambasz's work is an example of a fully self-conscious, semi-environmental architecture, this is only one way of making visible a new relation between culture and nature. SITE has a different aesthetic approach, as do those experimenting with Folding. It could also be argued that the straightforward expression of the devices of environmental design are the best (because the most obvious) way for environmental architecture to make itself visible, though, like any set of visual elements, their significance would have to be understood by the viewer before the intended meaning could be conveyed. Such expression would, however, achieve only what Eisenman refers to as 'iconicity', that is, representing as well as deploying making its environmental function:

what Vitruvius is talking about is function, not as the literal function, but the propriety of function. The language of function. It has to function, but it also has to deploy the iconicity of function (Eisenman, 1993: 131).

To enter the realm of 'beauty', in Eisenman's terms, and 'visibility' in mine, expression would have to exceed this 'iconicity'. There would have to be a level of formal invention superfluous to configuring an environmental control system as efficiently as possible. Without this 'excess', environmental functionalism cannot achieve the level of reflexivity necessary to re-present itself.

7.5 Conclusion

Do these examples confirm the validity of the three suggested criteria for not only recognizing, but generating, environmental architecture? Are symbiosis, differentiation and visibility useful in developing an understanding of the wide range of practice claiming environmental sustainability? In practice's muddy particularity, perhaps not. Practice is much more ambiguous than any theory trying to articulate, and thereby advance it. For example, Richard Horden's University of Future Generations could have been used as an example of climatic differentiation, Renzo Piano's Tjibao Cultural Centre as an example of visibility, and Ambasz's work as an example of (attempted) symbiosis.

What these criteria do make clear is the relativity of the term 'environmentally sustainable', a relativity more rigorous environmental designers would like to see extirpated through the use of quantified targets for environmental performance. The concerns of design beyond environmental design escape quantification, however, and suggest that the tension between the two is permanent. Yeang speaks for most architects when he says the demands of environmental sustainability are not the only demands, or even the most important ones, when designing a building. Their exact importance depends, for the present at least, on the priorities of the architect, and the three suggested criteria are intended to test the degree to which the environmental agenda is actually incorporated into the work of architects claiming environmental sustainability.

To stop here, however, is to ignore a dimension of this subject that cannot be ignored: the larger system into which any individual building fits, whether urban or rural. One of the reasons no individual architect can have any kind of useful impact on the environment is that he or she is usually working at the scale of the individual building. What, then, is the role of the architect at the scale of the city? And do the criteria applied at the architectural scale have any useful life at this urban scale? The final chapter will, in exemplary fashion, come full circle, and examine both how the new models of nature are feeding new models of urban intervention, and how some architects are imagining the appliction of these new models in the world's cities.

PART FOUR

8 COMPLEXCITY

8.1 Introduction

The temptation to carry the analogy between a non-linear nature and a non-linear architecture to the scale of the city is considerable, and quite a few have succumbed. If anything, the city lends itself more easily to discussions of complex systems because it is itself a complex system, or rather layers of complex systems, some material, some ethereal, with the ethereal seeking to supersede the material. Is there, however, any real environmental advantage to be gained from the imposition of modish conceptual models upon current urban conditions, whether industrial or post-industrial? Can they provide new ways of thinking about urban change that will help us, not only understand, but act on, transformations we feel at present to be uncontrollable and/or undesirable? Current thinking on the future of the city tends to be split between materialists, who concern themselves with sustainable urban forms, whether compact, polynucleated or decentralized, and non-materialists, who proclaim the supplanting of urban space by cyberspace, as if it were a *fait accompli*. Does cyberspace have anything to teach those seeking to give form to the sustainable cities of this millennium. Are there, in the constitution of ephemeral digital systems, models that are of use to those reconstructing material urban systems? Or is cyberspace a passing fashion that has nothing to offer sustainable practice past the usual and dubious claims that computing cuts down on commuting?

The 'sustainable city' is even harder to define than 'environmental architecture', with even more strategies possible inside an even greater variety of parameters. That doesn't, however, stem the flow of manifestos, papers and books from the environmentally minded, all suggesting ways, usually the same ways, of making the cities of the world more able to sustain themselves – and us – in some tolerably equitable and healthy way. At the same time, there is another group of commentators, including architects, foretelling the death of cities, the irrelevance of their materiality – and, by implication, the irrelevance of work done on trying to make them physically sustainable. It is as if cities and their ever-spreading edges, both haemorrhaging energy, both choked with cars, both plagued with buildings as polluting as cars, both afflicted with dereliction and decay, are invisible to these commentators, so that they are able to observe without a trace of irony, 'the necessity for the city as place...has been superseded by the city as condition...From this perspective the city has the appearance of a virtual entity...' (Rhowbotham, 1998: 76–77).

There is in short a new Cartesian mind/body split opening up, but it now involves the city as well as the individual. There are two thin films of life covering the planet: the first, the biosphere, which is organic and material, and the second, the 'cybersphere', which is infomatic and electronic. We are the link between the two, with our feet on the ground and our heads in cyberspace, both embodied and disembodied, here and not here.

8.2 Curvy bits

Generally the new conceptual models are characterized by a materialist view of culture, in this case, not Marxist, but naturalist, that is, to a large degree, culture is considered to work like nature. Manuel de Landa (see Chapter 2) is one of the most extreme and eloquent proponents of this construct:

From the point of view of energetic and catalytic flows, human societies are very much like lava flows; and human-made structures (mineralised cities and institutions) are very much like mountains and rocks: accumulations of materials hardened and shaped by historical processes (de Landa, 1997: 55).

In this model, unconscious processes are privileged over conscious decisions, with 'flows' viewed as common to both culture and nature: 'The city is a field of permanent formal genesis rather than a completion and conservation of a pre-existing state' (Zaera Polo, 1994: 28). What is emerging as a result of this perception is the equivalent of a Gaia theory[1] for cities: that they, like nature, will continuously rebalance themselves, whatever we do to unbalance them. The failures of 'rational' planning have led to its wholesale abandonment in these quarters in favour of a form of *laissez-faire* urbanism that would allow the city to metamorphose according to its own 'natural' imperatives. The same newfound respect accorded to the autonomous workings of nature are here accorded to workings of cities: 'Logistics of context suggests the need to recognise the limits of architecture's ability to order the city, and at the same time, to learn from the complex self-regulating orders already present in the city' (Allen, 1997: 30).

Historically, architects have felt impelled to create new social orders through new formal orders – geometric orders – to control unplanned

---

1. In 1969, the English scientist James Lovelock (Lovelock, 1979) put forward a theory which he named after the Greek goddess of the earth: Gaia. In it, he postulated that the planet operated like a self-regulating organism, capable of re-balancing any environmental imbalances caused by chance or human activity. He illustrated his idea with an invented planet covered entirely in daisies. If the temperature dropped too low to sustain life, the darker daisies would survive more easily, absorbing more solar radiation, and thus more heat. This absorption would slowly raise the temperature of the planet. If the temperature rose too far, the lighter coloured daisies would prevail, reflecting solar radiation and cooling off the planet.

growth. With their ideal cities, Renaissance architects intended to overcome the chaotic medieval town; Haussman intended to render Paris fit for the nineteenth century; Le Corbusier wanted to rationalize it for the twentieth. This kind of intervention unavoidably led to oversimplification, both in form and society envisioned, as not even a team of architects, let alone the self-appointed One, could create by fiat the complexity that accretes over time in any city. And just as it is impossible to consciously design such chaotic richness, so it is impossible to predict its future direction. In the twentieth century, planners tried to predict urban growth patterns using linear models for non-linear phenomena:

Attempts at building mathematical models...which began more than a generation ago were unable to yield realistic predictions even in the narrowest terms...[T]he impact of information and communication technologies and the rise of the network city could not be predicted...In short, conventional science was unable to predict or even sense the emergence of new kinds of cities, new urban forms (Batty and Longley, 1997: 74).

The conventional assumption was that effects could be predicted as a direct consequence of identifiable causes, that there was a linear relation between the two. Complexity theory posits the opposite: that the behaviour of organizations of a certain complexity, whether natural or cultural, escapes direct causality. Simple events can give rise to complex, even chaotic effects that have an indirect, or non-linear relation to their sources.

The danger of this new model is that it puts so much reliance on the city as some sort of 'natural' system. As a result, it has the potential to move us from modernism's excessive faith in the power of the architect to re-form the city (viz. Le Corbusier and Wright) to a potential abdication of responsibility. If it is a system, or collection of systems, with its own imperatives, then its working, are out of our hands, and familiar categories are passé: ' "City", "nature", "centre" and "periphery", once confrontational elements, are now almost obsolete. New readings of the city are required' (Woodroffe et al., 1994: 7). With certain rare exceptions, architects have always lacked the necessary power to transform the city, not because such transformation is the province of unconscious 'strange attractors', but because architects are not, for the most part, big enough players on the political-economic stage. While it may be impossible to predict the trajectory of social change from 'initial conditions', or, at least within a democracy, to halt a social trend once it has begun, the precipitation of a trend is often, at least partially, the result of conscious political and economic acts initiated by those who *are* big players on this stage.

So that although the comparison of non-linear systems in nature with non-linear systems in culture can be fruitful, the literal equation of culture with nature is not. Culture is to some degree self-conscious. Nature is not. It is a profound and crucial difference which the more enthusiastic of the 'new naturists' tend to overlook, seeing culture as an equally 'blind' system, slave to imperatives below individual or collective will. Even if cities grow in ways different from those we predict, and beyond the control we try to consciously exert over them, that is an incentive, surely, not for leaving them to their own devices, but for intervening in cities the way we are realizing we must now intervene in nature: with a willingness to tolerate open-endedness, unpredictability, and bottom-up growth as well as closure, causality and top-down ordinance. It becomes a question of discovering what is controllable – in a democracy, at least – and what is not, and intervening accordingly: 'it is necessary to recognise the complex interplay of interdeterminacy and order at work in the city...Architects need to learn this complexity...' (Allen, 1997: 31). For Stan Allen, then, it is a selective letting go. This is vital because if one lets a city grow the way it wants to, the weak will suffer, that is the poor, the public realm and the environment. On this level, top-down intervention by planners and local and central governments is neither arrogant nor ignorant. It is of active municipal benefit, promoting some degree of protection of the public good across the city as a whole.

Nor can all the new models of nature be so easily transposed to culture. It is novel, for example, to analyse urban growth in terms of fractal mathematics, but does it lead us towards more sensitive urban interventions or towards no action at all? Batty and Longley (1997) maintain that fractals, discovered by Bennoit Mandelbrot[2] in the 1960s, are found not only in natural systems, but artificial ones as well. If true, this blurs the divide between nature and culture, not merely formally, but at a deeper structural level. The essence of fractals is self-similarity: 'the whole is formed from scaled versions of its parts' (Batty and Longley, 1997: 76). The best-known examples are perhaps the snowflake, each projection of which is a mirror image at a smaller scale of the projection from which it projects, and coastlines, which have the added complication of being in one sense immeasurable as a result of this 'scaling': the curve of a headland, for example, is made up of similar curves at a smaller scale, which are in turn made up of similar curves at a still smaller scale.[3] The tree is another example, each branch itself branching into progressively smaller imitations. Our own circulation systems are described as tree-like, and are therefore also fractal. This culture-nature correspondence is easily acceptable on a formal level. There are very strong formal similarities between the branches of a tree and a branching road system, for example. But this is to oversimplify. There are ring roads and motorways that rupture both self-similarity at all scales and the established morphology itself. How are these accounted for? They are not, because they are conscious cultural inventions deliberately designed to interrupt 'natural' growth. Does this mean they are better left unmade? Perhaps, but what then is to replace them if fractal branching is inadequate?

---

2. See Bennoit Mandelbrot (1983). *The Fractal Geometry of Nature*. San Francisco, CA: W.H. Freeman.
3. See the seminal essay by Bennoit Mandelbrot (1967). 'How Long is the Coast of Britain?', *Science*, Vol. 155, 636–38.

And if cities, like road systems, grow fractally, does it provide the planner or architect with a helpful paradigm? Does it help answer dilemmas about density, optimum size, centre and periphery? The fractal is of a similar intensity and complexity at every scale, because it repeats its forms and is organized in the same way at every scale. The city, surely, is more complicated – and more varied – than this. The same forms don't even repeat at the same scale, let alone at different ones: a hospital is different in form from a house; a house is different in form from a theatre. Nor is the intensity of organization the same: a business district is more intense than the outskirts, a popular restaurant more intense than a warehouse. Certain street systems *can* be linked directly to organizational systems in nature like the tree, through a common fractal morphology. The fabric of the city, vastly more differentiated, cannot.

8.3 Cities of the plain

Nor does traditional geometry fare much better under the new dispensation. Although it has served us in the design of cities since cities began, with varying degrees of success, it is, suddenly, inadequate. Why has the nature of the city changed so radically that those means conventionally used both to map and renew it are truly obsolete? What is happening to the city? First, one can't generalize to the extent of discussing The City. At the very least, a distinction has to be made between those, mainly southern hemisphere cities that are still growing as they hit their industrial stride, and those, predominantly northern hemisphere cities that are stable or shrinking in the face of post-industrial pressures. In the latter, new species are emerging in the built environment. One of the most clearly defined is the 'technoburb', a term coined by Robert Fishman in his book *Bourgeois Utopias* (1987), in which he maintains that the conventional division into city and suburbs, primarily in the US, but increasingly in the UK, is outmoded. The old cities are being supplanted by suburbs that have themselves become cities, dubbed 'technoburbs', a 'new kind of decentralised city' (Fishman, 1987: 17). This mutant is made possible by information technology, which, Fishman claims, has 'completely superseded the face-to-face contact of the traditional city' (Fishman, 1987: 184). These 'technoburbs' are not the old dormitory suburbs, dependent economically and culturally on the old industrial city from which they grew. They contain places of employment and entertainment, as well as consumption and education. Travel is increasingly between technoburb and technoburb, rather than technoburb and city, rendering the centre marginal and the margins the new decentred centre.

This resembles Wright's Broadacre City (Plate 60), insofar as the conventional metropolis is dissolved into the landscape. Broadacre too was to contain all the amenities and attractions of the city, but dispersed across a nationwide grid of highways, and buried in fields and woods. Fishman does not expect the city to 'wither away' under the glare of cyber-communication, and acknowledges the magnetic attraction of successful old metropoli, but if accurately observed, the technoburb is a threat to centrists because it is uncontrollable, the product of residential and commercial mass migration that is little affected by planners or governments in democracies, at least within existing legislation. In other words, the sprawl has made itself economically, and if you like that kind of thing, socially, sustainable. It is not, however, environmentally sustainable. Although Fishman denies it, others, like Peter Calthorpe, point out that car traffic has merely moved from clogging and polluting the city to also clogging and polluting the suburbs (or technoburbs). Information technology still only *implies* the 'complete superseding of face-to-face contact'. It is not yet, and may never be, a fact. People still go to work. It is merely that more and more of them go to work from a suburb to a technoburb or from one technoburb to another, rather than in and out of a city.

The periphery has become a new centre, or rather a collection of centres, rendering the term 'centre' meaningless. It is an uncontrolled and perhaps uncontrollable version of Ebenezer Howard's Social City. The crucial difference between this periphery as it is currently proliferating in some post-industrial cities, and Howard's paradigm is its lack of boundaries. Howard's Social City (Fig. 8.1) is specifically constituted to prevent sprawl: growth is redistributed into smaller satellites, themselves organized along the Garden City model. Unlike Broadacre, the Social City maintains a clear demarcation of city and country, with each self-sufficient satellite surrounded by its own agricultural green belt, into which it is forbidden to stray. Howard has been viewed, by Jane Jacobs[4] among

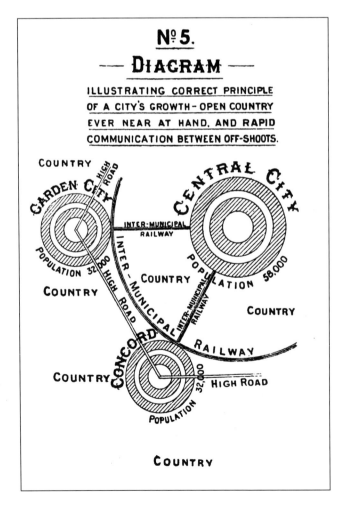

Fig. 8.1
'Correct principle of a city's growth',
Ebenezer Howard, from *Garden Cities of Tomorrow* (1898).

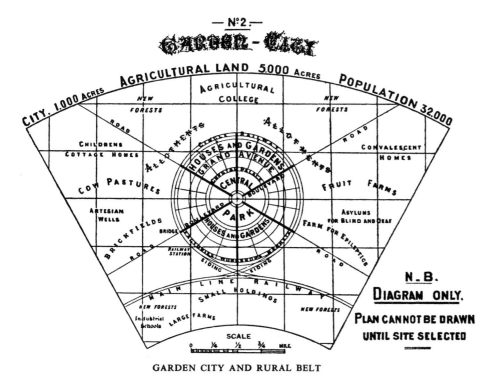

GARDEN CITY AND RURAL BELT

Fig. 8.2
'Garden City and rural belt', Ebenezer
Howard, from *Garden Cities of
Tomorrow* (1898).

others, as an arch-decentrist, but this is to view his low densities as
written in stone. Howard's concerns were, among others, containment
and differentiation. The Garden City was not dense, but, unlike a suburb,
it was clearly bounded (Fig. 8.2). Looking to Howard in the 1990s rather
than the 1960s, there is a useful ambiguity to his model, in that it is both
decentrist, not permitting urban growth beyond a certain size, and
centrist in that it contains growth within limits that preserve contiguous
open land. This avoids the oversimplification of both the centrist and
decentrist models, in which centrists in the northern hemisphere ignore
a continuing decentralizing trend, and decentrists ignore the impossibility of everyone living a rural idyll and the idyll remaining rural.
Nevertheless, the very presence of clear boundaries makes Howard's
Social City a problematic paradigm for an existing sprawl like London's,
or the megalopolis that runs from Boston to New York.

That is perhaps why centrist arguments dominate at present: they
appeal to our atavistic longing to return to a time of clear boundaries,
of city walls demarcating the culture inside from the nature outside as
clearly as our bodies draw – or used to draw – a line between that which
is us, and that which is other. 'Edge City' (Garreau, 1991) has no edge,
but is a blur of built and natural environments at the expense of
metropolitan culture, and therefore of architecture itself:

*Edge City may be the result of Americans striving once again for a new,
restorative synthesis. Perhaps Edge City represents Americans taking
the functions of the city (the machine) and bringing them out to the
physical edge of the landscape (the frontier). There, we try once again*

---

4. Jane Jacobs (1962). *The Death and Life of Great American Cities*. London: Jonathan
Cape.

to merge the two in a newfound union of nature and art (the garden), albeit one in which the treeline is punctuated incongruously by office towers (Garreau, 1991: 14).

A kind of 'organicism' is strongly present within centrist or 'Compact City' thinking (Jenks et al., 1999): the idea of a bounded whole whose parts (organs) are in a harmonious and essential relation to that whole. Interestingly, this idea influenced, not only those, like Camillo Sitte, who admired the towns and cities which found their form over time, emerging 'organically' from their topography and their histories, but also those who supported the idea of total planning, whether Baroque or modernist. The picturesque and the geometric both laid claim to the Albertian definition of the organic as a particular relation between part and whole, and between object (the city) and field. The object had integrity, a coherence within itself. The field did not. The field was the chaos against which, or perhaps within which, architects, engineers and planners organized their hierarchies.

Nor is this kind of hierarchical ordering obsolete. In one of the most important observations in his book, Manuel de Landa emphasizes the need for both types of organization, although the dominance of hierarchical systems throughout western history suggests that we may need a compensatory exaggeration of what he calls 'meshworks', that is, nonhierarchical webs of self-organization, for example California's Silicon Valley:

it is crucial to avoid the facile conclusion that meshworks are intrinsically better than hierarchies...It is true that some of the characteristics of meshworks (particularly their resilience and adaptability) make them desirable, but that is equally true of certain characteristics of hierarchies (for example, their goal-directedness) (de Landa, 1997: 69).

To recognize this is to recognize the need for intervention to promote, for example, social justice, or environmental health, whatever the pattern of growth. One is not, when talking of 'going with the flow' in a social context, discussing weather patterns and their effect on insect populations, one is talking about human beings. What is needed are inclusive strategies, the proportions different in different cases, as the vitality of the mesh evolves through drift, and may drift in a direction that actively harms a sector of the population. Some top-down redirection at that point could be beneficial rather than harmful. Similarly, a rigidity, sterility and/or injustice petrified in a hierarchical system could benefit from an anarchic multiplicity of new possibilities contained within a mesh. In either case, a certain intensity, or rate of energy flow, has to be achieved through the system. This is why, for all its fascinating prefiguring of the dissolution of the city into nature, and for all the ambiguity of a geometric grid that seems to be a dispersed mesh, Frank Lloyd Wright's Broadacre City would tend towards stagnation: the energy in such a low-density model would dissipate in physical distance. It is a single stable state, a timeless arcadia, the city up-ended into a farmyard. Some might argue that information technology could now join the scattered in such a model, but despite apocalyptic predictions about the obsolescence of cities, and face-to-face contact, this does not seem to be coming to pass. If it is, it is happening much more slowly than the prophets anticipated.

8.4 The wild wild Web

The continuing survival of the traditional metropolis depends, to many observers, upon whether the decentralizing pressures of information technology (IT) become dominant or not. Certainly economically, the periphery owes much of its success to IT, which permits firms to do business electronically. Already associated in Anglo-Saxon countries with contributing to the continuing drift away from city centres, IT is deeply embedded in the centrist-decentrist debate. Architects are prominent among those who, like Baudrillard and Richard Sennett, regret the loss of the urbanity of urban life, an urbanity embodied in the material facts of old cities, their morphologies, their densities and the activities they house and encourage. In this regard, Richard Rogers can be heard defending a life of dense and various material and human presence as vociferously as Leon Krier, a life often described as 'real', in contrast to an etiolated existence in the techno/suburb. This is hardly surprising. Despite anxiety about the 'dematerialization' of architecture, and the devaluing of the tectonic, buildings are still 'there', however thin, transparent or temporary, and most are not any of these. Architects still have a vested interest in the 'there', and in conditions which reinforce its position. Traditional cities do just that: the whole is greater than the sum of its architectural parts, but relies upon a large number of those parts being pleasing or stimulating enough to constitute the city as a powerfully magnetic whole. The more diffused the built environment through the proliferation of IT, the less power those architectural 'parts' carry. If we then counter this trend with compaction, how do we do it? By bulldozing the environmentally wasteful and architecturally deprived 'in-between' to create, or recreate, 'compact cities'[5]? Or do we perform a patch-up job on the old centres and new peripheries that retrofits some degree of environmentally sustainability into the existing mess?

The speeches that accompanied the award of the RIBA Gold Medal to the city of Barcelona, and the recently published recommendations of the British Government appointed Urban Task Force[6] are testaments to a preference for concentrating resources and development in existing cities in an effort to stop, or at least slow, further sprawling onto green field sites. With good reason: between 1974 and 1993, derelict land in London rose by 410 per cent (Wickens in Jenks et al., 1999), and dereliction continues. The problem is that for the most part it continues in areas where no one wants to invest. Considerable financial incentives would have to be provided by the state to induce development there. Not only that, but some form of subsidy would also have to be provided to ensure affordable accommodation for more than the few

---

5. For a rehearsal of the arguments for and against compaction as a strategy, see Mike Jenks, Katie Williams and Elizabeth Burton (eds.) (1999), *The Compact City*.
6. See Urban Task Force. *Towards an Urban Renaissance*. E + FN Spon, 1999.

who could pay the prices demanded by a return on private investment. Even if this happened, it would have to be clear to those one was trying to keep in, or tempt back to, the city that the benefits of compaction outweighed the stress of greater intensification: more people, more noise, more demands on services and amenities, and, contentiously, as much or more traffic. Some of those derelict sites would have to be made into parks and sports fields where citizens could decompress, again requiring state intervention, as there is no profit in it.

Compaction tends to be the preferred option for architects, and the diffusing tendencies of IT are greeted with hostility. The replacement of physical collectors by electronic ones is to be resisted, as to embrace them would be professional suicide. This gives architecture two 'opposites' or 'others' to contend with now. The first is traditional – nature as a more powerful object of desire than culture. The second is new – placeless cyberspace as opposed to the 'places' of the city. In her provocative essay, 'Report to Virtual HQ: The Distributed City' (1997), Sarah Chaplin conflates these two 'others', nature and cyberspace:

Once the province of vast untamed and uncharted nature, what is now named as the new frontier is cyberspace/virtual reality/the electronic environment/the Internet... (Chaplin, 1997: 48).

[T]he distributed model for cyberspace is not the urbs *or* civitas*...but the vast Aboriginal landscape... (Chaplin, 1997: 47)*

The Aboriginal landscape is, one assumes, a combination of the *tabula rasa* of the Australian outback, and the intense web of meanings laid over this empty uniformity by the Aborigines. Their song-lines are not cartographic features, but imagined paths conjured out of a physical zone featureless enough to the outsider to be a non-place. Cyberspace, analogously, is an electronic wilderness, a non-place within which we presumably create our own electronic song-lines. It is integrated with the physical world insofar as it is contained within physical objects – computers, cables, disks – and insofar as those physical objects are developed, made, marketed, sold and serviced in physical locations. It is not integrated with the physical world insofar as it promotes a mind-body split, with the mind travelling and the body paraplegic (Virilio 1997).

Can this new non-place, equated with the non-place of wilderness, ever be compatible with phenomena predicated on the ontological 'place' of culture: the city and its architecture? If the spatial analogy of cyberspace with the Australian bush is valid, the answer would seem to be no. After all, the binary opposition 'city vs. country' is merely replaced with a new one: 'city vs. country-or-cyberspace'. But neither Chaplin nor ideological allies like Michael Sorkin can quite bring themselves to write the city's epitaph. Instead, the outmoded city is to survive as the somewhat shrunken space of willed, rather than 'natural', concentration, where people gather, not primarily for business, but for the pleasure of presence: of architecture as well as people.

Such a scenario maintains an assumption of the city's difference from this electronic world, but it is questionable whether cyberspace is precisely the anti-matter to the city's matter. Cyberspace, the medium within which proliferates the connective 'web' between users, is indeed abstract and amorphous, but the interfaces between us and it are highly structured, and remarkably familiar in their configuration. These are, after all, web *sites*. And architecture's conventional palette of Euclidean geometry, comprehensible structure and visual order inform many of the 'places' on the Internet. The square of the computer screen, the orthogonal structure of the 'page', the perspectival representations available for game-playing or planning, and of course CAD itself – all these are familiar territory for architects. They are new versions of the visual constructs they've been familiar with in books, paintings, photographs and films all their lives.

Even so, such common ground as there is between architecture and cyberspace is found within the domain of representation. It is the representations of architecture, and the representations of web sites that mediate between us and cyberspace, which for the most part have a common Euclidean structure. Architecture itself remains obdurately material, and the Web, achingly immaterial. The first houses the second, and the second has no more effect upon the generation of that housing than does any other electrical appliance. To suggest otherwise is wishful at least for the present:

We need a recombinant hybrid architecture such that cyberspace and the city are symbiotically side by side...which makes the architect's new task 'to fuse together material structures and cyberspace organisms into a new continuum' (Ascott, 1995: 39).

Would such a vision, were it were possible, have any environmental and/or social benefit? Strangely and unexpectedly, yes. There is a conceivable future in which the material and the immaterial, urban space and cyberspace, are not separate realms, but entirely embedded in each other, the way neuroscientists now believe thought is embedded in the physical brain, not separate from it. This could happen if the Web became integrated into buildings, not by means of computers sitting in buildings, but by connecting up the building materials themselves.

In Lars Spuybroek's vision, this 'software architecture' looks like the representation, on a gigantic scale, of the many wires and cables required to run computers.[7] Spuybroek calls these horizontal skyscrapers 'softscrapers'. They are connected to the Web and have an interactive relationship with it: they grow, twist and adapt in response to certain information on the Web, and their growing, twisting and adapting in turn modifies that information. There is, in other words, a complete integration of cyberspace and urban space, the immaterial and the material, a future we can only imagine now: architectures and cities that swell and shrink, extend and circle in direct response to what is going on in the collective mind of cyberspace. Responsive and adaptive architecture, responsive and adaptive cities, have potentially enormous environmental benefits. Imagine housing that can multiply to embrace an influx of refugees, an influx first signalled over the Internet. Or the

---

7. See Lars Spuybroek (1998). 'Architects in Cyberspace'. *Architectural Design*.

urban tissue healing itself after a devastating fire, or shoring itself up against immanent flooding – the possibilities are limitless, though such an intense degree of autonomous responsiveness requires very smart materials indeed. It is also important to remember that such ideas dictate no particular aesthetic, certainly not the belligerent presentation of electrical wiring as a 'new architecture'. Non-linear behaviours may or may not be expressed in non-linear forms, as is evident from environmental design.

Nevertheless, there is, then, a possible marriage between cyberspace and urban space on a material level, but one predicated on so much technological advance it seems utopian. Before that, however, in modelling the 'other side' of nature, its dynamic fluctuation, the computer is mapping what environmental design has always addressed: variable conditions in the environment. If the computer can to some degree map the same phenomena in the cities, then it will help us to find a balance between having too much 'faith in design' and too little. Urban compaction may be too facile an answer to urban sustainability, just as a *laissez-faire* approach may be too facile a response to our inability to establish total control over urban complexity. In fact, where the thinking emerging from complexity and the thinking required for environmental design seem to run parallel is in their recognition of the value of case-by-case analysis, rather than dogmatism. While a conceptual, value-laden model of the sustainable city is necessary to define goals, deriving an exclusively top-down urban strategy from it would be too crude, just as an exclusively bottom-up strategy would not protect the weak or the public weal.

The Sustainable City is not the Heavenly City secularized, a universal model for all time. There are more and less – usually less – sustainable cities, all of which have emerged, and continue to emerge, from very different historical/economic conditions. These require particular responses, guided, yes, by general principles and aims, but not determined by them. In some cases, a sprawl rendered less environmentally damaging may be more sustainable socially than bulldozing it and scattering the inhabitants into a hinterland that can't support them. In other cases, compaction may be entirely feasible, achieved through the pressure of economic instruments. On this strategic level, such decisions are out of the hands of architects and engineers, whose remit is more the implementation of them. Nevertheless, as is evidenced by the literature on urban sustainability, architects do think on this level – and should – working out a path between arrogance and timidity, the linear and the non-linear, the city as self-organizing and the city in need of re-organization. If cyberspace can prove a helpful tool both for our understanding of nature and our understanding of the city, then the work of those advancing such models should be welcomed.

Although John Frazer's 'Gröningen Experiment' claims too much for the computer, it is a real, as opposed to utopian instance of the way in which cyberspace can help towards the environmental sustainability of urban space:

The city planning department of Gröningen commissioned a small working prototype demonstration of a predictive urban computer model...Central to the model is the idea that the computer programme inhabits an environment, enters it, reads it, [and] understands its developmental rules. [The model also] grasps [the] topography, latitude and climate [of the place],...– and then starts to solicit suggestions and make proposals...The model becomes an inhabitant. It maintains a discourse with other human inhabitants and tries to understand and interpret their desires, aspirations, urges, expectations, and reactions to their existing environment and projected future environments (Frazer, 1998: 9).

Despite the somewhat worrying description of the model maintaining a discourse with *other* human inhabitants in the Gröningen experiment, citizens can feed information and reactions to this 'cybercitizen'. On the basis of this dialogue, the computer continuously revises its criteria for the evolutionary development of the city. The core of this program is called 'the Evolver', which 'employs the same strategies at each level of interaction', providing 'seeds of genetic algorithms, which learn on the basis of feedback from various sites' (Frazer, 1998: 12). The interface between the Evolver and the citizen is 'the Enabler', which has connections to an interactive map of the city. This can show the city evolving as citizens react to what they see and voice their own desires. Cyberspace thus provides a democratic forum for future development of the town, and enables citizens and planners alike to *see* what their suggestions imply. These desires, however, are bound to conflict with the desires of others. Who – or what – decides between them? Is this decision-making democratic, or ultimately controlled by 'the Evolver', which knows better than we do what is good for us? Despite this caveat, however, the Gröningen Experiment could justifiably be defended as one of the most advanced examples yet of a convergence between urban and cyberspace, assuming this experiment is actually acted upon.

8.5 On edge

At present, any parallel between the material and the ethereal is less between urban centres and cyberspace than the periphery and cyberspace, with the periphery as the built equivalent of Chaplin's 'Aboriginal landscape', a blur of wasteland, barios, industrial parks, malls and suburbs onto which the Net is superimposed, and through which some of it is linked. These peripheries resemble nothing but themselves, not Wright's Broadacre City, not Howard's Social City, and not the zoned outskirts of Le Corbusier's Radiant City. They exist around southern *and* northern hemisphere cities, that is, around industrial and post-industrial cities, and their sprawl is seen by some (Hall, Calthorpe, Fishman) as the byproduct of mismanaged planning, in need of conventional delineation and containment, and by others (Zaera Polo, Garreau, Woodroffe) as the manifestation of a still emerging process:

The evolution from an economy of scale *to an economy of* scope *– from* industrial *to* informational *– shows that production is no longer competitive through a good cost-price relationship, but through its diversification and capacity to adjust to a constantly evolving demand.*

Consequently through this growing disorganisation of the composition of capital, the contemporary city tends to constitute itself as non-organic and complex without hierarchical or linear organisation (Zaera Polo, 1994: 25).

In other words, advanced capitalism needs the amorphous, self-organizing wilderness of the periphery – 'self-organizing' after the wealthy, corporate and/or private, have chosen to go there, or the poor have been forced there. But this is too reductive. It also needs the hierarchical places of the traditional metropolis. If it enriches itself intellectually and economically at the new periphery, it displays and deploys its power at the old centres.

Manuel Castells and Peter Hall, in their book *Technopoles of the World*, are very clear about this. During the course of a worldwide survey of 'technopoles', the French term for places that 'generate the basic materials of the information technology', they found that some of the older metropoli like London and Tokyo were not excluded from qualifying. Such cities, like some peripheries, are economically adaptable, and can 'create conditions that will attract the new sources of wealth, power and prestige' (Castells and Hall, 1997: 481). The city's traditional strength, its ability to concentrate cultural resources and cultural players, facilitates a cross-fertilization between widely disparate professions and interests impossible to duplicate in a peripheral technopole or a technoburb. The work of Castells and Hall indicates that prophecies of metropolitan obsolescence may be premature, and that in some instances at least, the old metropoli will remain 'milieux of innovation'. This gives obvious comfort to those in favour of increased centralization in response to environmentally unsustainable urban sprawl: at least some existing centres are still economically viable, and although the pressure in the West has been to decentralize, there seems, in this analysis, to be a limit beyond which this decentralization will not proceed. Those declaring the death of the city, in other words, must re-examine the assumptions upon which they pass sentence:

massive developments in telecommunications and the ascendance of information industries have led analysts and politicians to proclaim the end of cities...[T]he globalisation of economic activity suggests that place – particularly the type of place represented by cities – no longer matters...These trends...represent only half of what is happening. Alongside the well-documented spatial dispersal of economic activities, new forms of territorial centralisation of top-level management and control operations have appeared. National and global markets...require places where the work of globalisation gets done (Sassen, 1994: 1).

These 'places', according to Saskia Sassen's research, are often the old cities others have dismissed as obsolete. This inclusive view, which takes into account the material base of information technology's dematerialized product, is a necessary counterbalance to the fashionable orthodoxy, and presents economic reasons for concentration, rather than the usual social ones (the desire for face-to-face contact and urban culture).

An economic configuration very different from that suggested by the concept of information technology emerges, whereby we recover the material conditions, production sites, and place boundedness that are also part of globalisation and information technology (Sassen, 1994: 1).

This view also corrects the division of cities into stable northern hemisphere cities, and still-expanding southern hemisphere cities. Instead, there are cities in both hemispheres that have managed to embed the processes of globalization within themselves, and cities that have not:

these trends were...evident during the late 1980s in a number of major cities in the developing world that have become integrated into various world markets: Sao Paulo, Buenos Aires, Bangkok, Taipei, and Mexico City are only a few examples (Sassen, 1994: 54).

What is different between northern and southern hemisphere cities are their very differently constituted peripheries. Technoburbs are for the wealthy north. The edges of most southern hemisphere cities are the places where the desperately poor hang on by their fingernails, trying to claw their way into the prosperous centre from square miles of slums built out of anything they can find to hand – detritus, the ultimate vernacular. These edges are growing just as unpredictably as their counterparts in the West, and self-organizing in equally inventive ways, but they are hardly the promised land that edge dwellers on the Anglo-American axis hope for. Those who want to see where this metamorphosis will lead have in mind the post-industrial periphery, not its industrializing cousin.

The post-industrial periphery has polarized architectural opinion between a minority who accept it on its own terms, and a majority who see it as a threat to conventionally constituted built culture. The majority's opposition is often couched in environmental terms – car use is extended and pollution worsened by sprawl; green field sites are devoured – but the hidden agenda is often cultural. What would be the grounds for objecting if the environmental case were answered and sprawl were democratically desired? The case, surely, would refer to the loss, not of uninhabited 'nature', but of a vast slice of culture: dense urban form and the urbanity that goes with it. Stephen Kieran and James Timberlake envisage an end to this war between centrists and decentrists with a Howardian taking of the best from each:

we will present a case for a symbiotic rather than consumptive relationship between the perimeter and the traditional city, a relationship in which each prospers from the lessons of the other while maintaining its own integrity (Kieran and Timberlake, 1994: 30).

The assertion is unfortunately as far as they get. Apart from a vague reference to the centre incorporating 'certain aspects of the contemporary social and technological programme' of the periphery, and the periphery including 'certain aspects of the social and economic agenda' of the centre (Kieran and Timberlake, 1994: 35), there is no indication of how this is to be implemented, and what its effects might be. If the model is to work as Howard's worked, the taking of the best from each should result in a third entity: a new Garden-City-Garden-Periphery, perhaps, with the environmental promise of decentralization fully realized (very green green field development and solar-powered cars), and the cultural desert blooming. Would this be a newly built synthesis, with its progenitors, centre and sprawl, withering away? Or would this be centre and sprawl themselves transformed? The difficulty of envisaging what might replace the current condition is explanation enough for the enthusiasm with which some have embraced ideas of self-organization.

Meanwhile there are environmentally unsustainable metropoli, and environmentally unsustainable peripheries, and regardless of which is winning where, they are both in need of immediate intervention. Both have energy guzzling built fabrics and too many cars. Both are haemorrhaging fossil energy and polluting at apocalyptic rates. One has only to fly over London or Los Angeles or Buenos Aires or Singapore blazing away at night to see they are fast approaching a supernova state before blackout. Although they have so much in common in terms of environmental problems, however, the actual, as opposed to the conceptual, conditions of both centre and periphery require that choices be made between them. For architects, this does not mean coming down on one side or the other: are you for the metropolis or are you for the edge? Are you for developing 'brown field' sites or 'green field' ones? What is your definition of environmentally sustainable – high-rise-high-density development, or low-rise-low-density development, or some permutation thereof? Instead, it means paying as much attention to the problems of the periphery as those of the centre. As one descends from the Olympian heights of the conceptual to the rigours of the material, the content becomes more banal and more consequential in terms of the effect on our lives. What will architects *do*? More to the point, what *can* architects do? Unless their clients are governments, not very much in terms of practice, a great deal in terms of catalysing models. From Richard Rogers' 'Compact City' to Peter Calthorpe's 'Pedestrian Pockets', architects are producing ideas for more environmentally sustainable cities – and peripheries – ideas that range from modernist brio to 'post-modern' correctness.

8.6 Sustainable heroics?

Typical of the brio is Richard Rogers' 1992 design for Lu Jia Zui, a city-within-a-city in Shanghai: 40 million square feet for 500,000 people, 50 per cent business, 50 per cent residential, and eight times the size of the Canary Wharf development. This circle of skyscrapers, up to 60 storeys high and laid out around a park, was intended to replace an existing suburb (Fig. 8.3). As in Howard's Garden City, boulevards were to radiate from the centre, and a railway was to ring the perimeter. It was to be divided into six neighbourhoods, each no more than ten minutes walk from the next, which meant thirty minutes to the furthest, each neighbourhood served by a station of the light railway. Parking was to be deliberately minimal – only 15,000 underground spaces – to 'encourage' people onto public transportation, particularly the two new metro lines the new city was to receive. In plan, therefore, Lu Jia Zui looks like a repetition of the Garden City diagram, but at Radiant City densities (Fig. 8.4).

Where Lu Jia Zui differed radically from both these precedents was the way in which it was to be deployed. In Le Corbusier's *Ville Contemporaine*, there is reference, not only to what is to all intents and purposes Howard's 'Green Belt', but also to 'Garden Cities' themselves, which Le Corbusier saw as contained suburbs where those working in the industrial zone would live:

Our first requirement will be an organ that is compact, rapid, lively and concentrated: this is the City with its well-organised centre. Our second requirement will be another organ, supple, extensive and elastic; this is the Garden City on the periphery. Lying between these two organs, we must require the legal establishment of that absolute necessity,...a reserved zone of woods and fields, a fresh-air reserve (Le Corbusier, 1987: 166).

Fig. 8.3
Lu Jia Zui masterplan, Shanghai, 1992,
Richard Rogers Partnership: model.

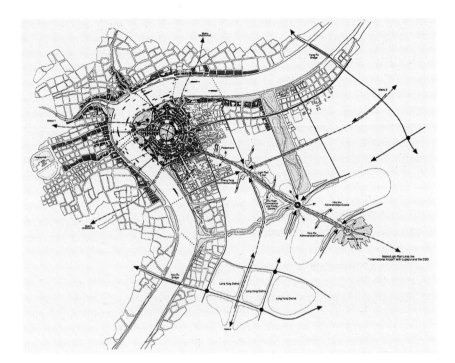

Fig. 8.4
Lu Jia Zui masterplan in city context,
Richard Rogers Partnership.

Here, the idea of a 'natured' city is the same as Howard's, but the density is very different. Howard's Garden City had a maximum of 32,000 inhabitants, with only 25 to 30 people per acre. Le Corbusier's *Ville Contemporaine* was a city for three million, with 1,200 people per acre in the business district, and 120 people per acre in the residential zones, the density offset by the incorporation of parks and the surrounding 'green belt' (Plate 61). Nature, in the form of a horizontal carpet of parks and a vertical tapestry of hanging gardens, was to be reinvented as a source of health and well-being: 'The whole city is a Park' (Le Corbusier, 1987: 177). Though Rogers' Lu Jia Zui makes a similar gesture towards alleviating the intensity of the development with a park at its centre, there is no similar use of a green belt. The new city is used as in-fill for an existing city. The demarcation is not between built fabric and unbuilt land, but between one built fabric and another, the morphology of Lu Jia Zui being conspicuously different from the rest of Shanghai.

High-density living has become a focus of the centrists' platform, for exactly the same reasons Le Corbusier espoused it: to save land, cut distances and thereby polluting journeys. Density is part of the brown field/green field debate, since reclaiming what are predominantly urban brown field sites enables more people to live in those urban locations. If it also brings more congestion and more strain on the infrastructure as well, then the idea carries a hidden environmental price for keeping unbuilt land unbuilt. Does the concept of 'sustainability', whether social or environmental, impose limits on density? Is there such a thing as 'too dense', no matter how energy efficient the settlement? What are the criteria for judging this? Like all matters environmental, context is everything. It is impossible to prescribe beyond the most generalized of aims. Perhaps Rogers' attempt at association with Howard was deliberate, to ease us past the density of the Shanghai project, though what is unbearably dense for one culture (UK) is perfectly normal for another (China).

This density of Lu Jia Zui, however, was defended by one commentator as the way of the future for *all* cities, as populations continue to grow exponentially in the southern hemisphere. The scheme was similarly defended by Rogers in typically modernist language, as a universal panacaea:

Of course, this plan is for China, but it's hard to say how Chinese it is...[I]t is a modern city, and cities all over the world are shaped by the same kind of pressures (Rogers, 1994: 128).

In fact, they're not. Cities in the northern hemisphere, for example are not growing exponentially. Nevertheless, this model of high concentration may well be the most realistic direction for the southern hemisphere.

Whether the land saved from sprawl justifies such intensity depends to some extent on whether or not one holds with the concept of the 'ecological footprint'. Flying in the face of the globalization of markets, the law of the ecological footprint requires that the size of human settlements be governed by their regionally available biomass. They must, in other words, be capable of sustaining themselves to some degree within their own region, in terms of food, energy supply and waste disposal. Bill Dunster's 'BedZED' development (Beddington Zero Energy Development), commissioned by the Peadbody Trust, is a model for a mixed-use prototype flexible enough to be useful in urban, suburban or rural development, and is configured according to the principle of the ecological footprint (Plates 62–63). The fact that the UK imports 80 per cent of its food, with all the fossil energy and global inequity that entails, is unacceptable to Dunster. Coupled with a continuing loss of English agricultural land to unsustainable development, he considers our prospects to be bleak unless we can come up with new ways of organizing ourselves. To this end, BedZED 'proposes a new building type which combines premises for living and working with food production' (Dunster, 1996: 68). What is interesting about this model is the acceptance of the loss of demarcation between city and country, as evidenced by one model for all occasions. It is an attempt to turn this loss to our advantage by transforming what would be parasitic built fabric into self-sustaining built fabric. By housing our activities in compact forms, Dunster ensures arable land is spared or released, and by terracing roofs so they can be 'intensively gardened' to produce vegetables and fruit, more arable land is recreated on top of the footprint of the building:

Initially the...model could be used to recolonise urban wasteland...[but] there is also a need to repopulate the countryside with a compact rural development model... (Dunster, 1996: 68).

A settlement of the density of Lu Jia Zui would require a vast amount of biomass to sustain it. Any world-class city has the same disproportionate ecological footprint. To demand that these cities feed off their own nations rather than the globe is to demand an end to globalization. As the flow of legislation and money is towards greater and greater market integration worldwide, this would require the concerted political will of a majority of nation states to even modify, let alone reverse, a highly unlikely scenario, however desirable socially and environmentally. Nevertheless, as a contribution to the reduction of the rate and amount of imported food and fuel, it is an idea worth exploring, particularly in many developing countries where there is still a large agricultural sector for the domestic market.

8.7 Flowers of the field

In contrast to Rogers' bold interventions, the American urbanist Peter Calthorpe pursues an entirely different approach to prescribing for sustainable cities: he does not prescribe. By adopting a radically inductive method, he stands outside the current centrist/decentrist debates, looking at the existing variety of unsustainable dwelling patterns and suggesting ways of retooling the status quo by developing projects in cities, suburbs and new towns that are 'diverse, centered and walkable'. His solutions are based on a pragmatic, case-by-case analysis of different failures, for which there is no universally applicable solution. Ideologically, this is as far away as one can get from draconian modernist intervention. He advocates ameliorating what is there, not automatically clearing it away and starting again. This amelioration takes many forms, depending on pre-existing conditions:

The specific nature of a metropolitan region will dictate how many and which...growth strategies are necessary and useful. Some regions with a very slow rate of growth may only need incremental infill. Some regions with fast growth and much undeveloped suburban land may benefit from both infill and new growth area projects. Other regions may require all three strategies, including new towns, to absorb massive growth without destroying the identity of existing small towns and urban centres (Calthorpe, 1993: 22).

This approach is much more in keeping with the conservatism of certain strands of architectural post-modernism, but a recognition of the need for different responses to different conditions could as easily be interpreted as maturity, rather than timidity.

Because at this scale, the social and the environmental are so closely intertwined, Calthorpe, like Patrick Geddes (1915) and Ian McHarg (1971) before him, would like to see political and physical topographies treated as one:

At the regional scale, the man-made environment should fit into and along larger natural systems. Urban limit lines or growth boundaries should be set to preserve major natural resources at the edge of the metropolis...Within this regional boundary major natural features and streams should form an internal structure of park-like linkages, trails and cycleways throughout the metropolis. Such open space elements should link and limit individual communities. In these areas the natural systems should be preserved and repaired (Calthorpe, 1993: 20).

This could easily be read as an attempt to return to traditional ways of establishing the location and identity of settlement according to the physical characteristics of the site – 'in the wold', 'on sea'. Although the language is of 'limits' and 'boundaries', with nature used as a means of setting them 'naturally' as opposed to the physical arbitrariness of political boundaries, the idea of the social and the environmental merging into one system of demarcation could just as easily be used as another, perhaps more accessible, version of the conceptual 'blurring' of city and nature found in de Landa or Zaera Polo. Sim Van Der Ryn and Stuart Cowan promote the same kind of strategy as Calthorpe (Van Der Ryn and Cowan, 1996), suggesting that county boundaries should be decided on the lines between one hydrographic basin and another, and not on arbitrary political impositions. In this case, the object is to ensure that human settlement interferes as little as possible with the ecologies upon which they impose themselves, so that we cohabit rather than colonize. If a certain amount of decentralization is allowed, it could be guided according to such ecological criteria, with no expansion, for example, permitted on a flood plain. Had Valencia followed such guidelines, the river running through it wouldn't have overflowed its banks and flooded the city in the 1960s. The fact that the story ended happily, and Valencia now has a park in its old riverbed (Plate 64) doesn't bring back the drowned.

This obeyance to topography and hydrography is easier to imagine when addressing rural development. The datum of a city seems to be a grid or a labyrinth, not soil and subsoil. There is occasionally an inconvenient wetness or coldness or heat from which one flees indoors, not full blown weather systems upon which one's livelihood depends. The connection between the city and the physical given, on top of which it perches and within which it sits, is not often made. To make it might start producing interesting new morphologies of varying intensities, ranging from settlement folded into landscape (the periphery), to landscape folded into settlement (the centre). From here, field theory, as it has manifested itself in architecture, may be helpful for environmentally sustainable urban planning.

'Field' is a term from physics denoting a space under the influence of magnetic, gravitational or electrical forces. Kevin Rhowbotham emphasizes the formal use that can and has been made of this phenomenon within the fine arts, a use that a few architects are now beginning to consider on an urban scale:

Einstein's unified field theory lends itself usefully as a descriptive analogy with regard to the Suprematist project. Here matter which is assumed to inhere ubiquitously in space, identifies itself as fields of relative density or high pressure. Space and object are considered to be made of the same stuff, distinguishable by their relative densities alone...[h]igh pressure denoting objectness, low pressure denoting fieldness... (Rhowbotham, 1999: 30).

This model of greater and lesser intensities could plausibly describe the condition both of the city, its periphery and the countryside. In the city, however, the material dimension cannot be ignored, so that field theory as it is applied to architecture applies to 'forces and events' as they also affect the distribution of material objects:

The infrastructural elements of the modern city, by their nature linked together in open-ended networks, offer [an] example of field conditions in the urban context (Allen, 1997: 24).

The first and most obvious possibility is that one is led away from the difference between built fabric and nature, by which architecture has traditionally defined itself, and towards the kind of actual and conceptual fusion Wines was suggesting in the previous chapter. The difference is that for Allen, this condition already exists, unperceived, or at least unrepresented, whereas for Wines it has to be created:

we think of the figure not as a demarcated object but as an effect emerging from the field itself – as moments of intensity, as peaks or valleys within a continuous field... (Allen, 1997: 28).

SITE's recent rural projects are certainly examples of objects 'emerging from' a literal and figurative field. But where Wines actively encourages an interpretative reading, Allen denies there is one: 'The field is a material condition, not a discursive practice' (Allen, 1997: 27). This may be true of the field itself; it is patently not true of that architecture identifying itself with it. Again, as was discussed above in terms of folding, no architecture so consciously and overtly repudiating Cartesian space can simply 'be'. Nevertheless, the idea of the field allows us to escape not only the usual binary opposites – city/country, bounded/boundless, centralized/ decentralized – but also the privileging of one half over the other. It permits an inclusive view of settlement in which one can think the unthinkable: densifying villages by building intensely on *their* brown field sites, de-densifying cities by putting parks and allotments on some of their brown field sites, ending the war on the fact of the suburbs, and beginning one on the way they're configured.

OCEAN UK's *Arabiananta* urban design for Helsinki (Plate 65) is an example, not of 'mixed use' master-planning, but of melded use and melded forms, producing

maximum integration of all components...An intensified horizontal urbanism evolves a characteristic density and multiplicity...Sectional design policies blend urban public activity surface, built programme mass and landscape systems (OCEAN UK, 1997: 58).

In other words, a fluid and flexible field-within-a-field (the existing urban context) is established, of greater and lesser intensities of built form, out of which 'diverse relationships' emerge, phased to grow in tandem with a step by step clean-up of the polluted site. The design not only 'does the work', it represents the work that is being done.

There is a gap between most of the thinking about field theory in relation to urban design, and the thinking about the sustainable city. The references to nature in the former remain at the level of cultural construct, as ways of generating and explaining formal choices. These forms are of considerable interest, but as examples of knowledgeable environmental intervention, they are entirely lacking in the rigorous focus on the particular physical and climatic conditions of the site. Foreign Office Architects talk of their urban design for the redevelopment of Cartuja Island, Seville, in terms of 'quanta', 'crystals', 'rhizomes' and 'attractors', but again, as yet, this is a layer of new analogies over a development that would operate much more conventionally than, say, Foster, Herzog and Rogers' Solar City in Linz-Pichling, which looks conventional, but will operate (in terms of energy and transportation) in a new way (Fig. 8.5).[8]

8.8 Of mutual benefit

A paradigm entwining social and environmental systems could be fruitful not only in terms of the construction of settlements, but also their operation. 'Industrial ecology', for example, looks at industrial processes as if they were biological ones, shifting production and consumption from a linear entropic model to a circular energy efficient one. Instead of energy being used to produce, say, steel, and its waste being dumped

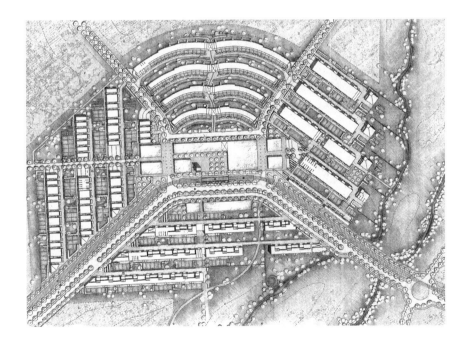

Fig. 8.5
Solar City, Linz, Austria, 1995, Richard Rogers Partnership, Foster and Partners, Thomas Herzog and Partner: general masterplan showing several neighbourhoods centred around a public square, and designed to optimize the use of solar energy.

8. Linz-Pichling is to be a new urban district for the northern Austrian provincial capital of Linz, housing some 25,000 people. Development is organized in compact mixed-use groupings designed by three different architectural firms. The extent of each grouping is determined by the walking distance from the central square, where public transportation joins Linz-Pichling with Linz. This obvious gesture towards minimizing private car use, together with the provision of solar housing, is an attempt to make a new-build development socially and environmentally more sustainable than a conventional dormitory suburb. Whether it will succeed in being anything other than a 'greener' dormitory suburb, with most of the jobs still in Linz, remains to be seen.

as an unwanted byproduct, that waste is used elsewhere, for another industrial process. At present, each manufacturing process tends to operate as if it were the only one in the world. The idea that the waste of one is the raw material of another has yet to become a commonplace. In nature there is no waste because all its 'manufacturing processes' are interrelated through all scales of organization, from the local pond to the globe. What is no longer needed by one organism is used by another. The biosphere was constructed from these relationships, with each further level of complexity emerging from a symbiotic relationship with the levels below.

If industry is to be made sustainable, this model demands serious consideration:

We are just beginning to create fully-fledged industrial ecosystems in which wastes from many different processes become food for others...The most fully realised example to date is in Kalundborg, Denmark. The project encompasses an electric power plant..., an oil refinery, a pharmaceutical plant, a wallboard factory, a sulfuric acid producer, cement manufacturers, local agriculture...and nearby houses. In the early 1980s, [the electric power plant] started supplying excess steam to the refinery and pharmaceutical plant.

It also began supplying waste heat for a district heating system, allowing 3,500 oil furnaces to be shut off. In 1991, the refinery began removing sulphur for its gas, selling it to a sulfuric acid producer...[The electric power plant] is now selling its fly ash to the cement manufacturer and will...sell waste gypsum to the wallboard plant...and the pharmaceutical plant is turning its sludge into fertiliser for local farms (Van Der Ryn and Cowan, 1996: 114).

I quote this at length to demonstrate the potential for an ecology of man-made systems equivalent in idea, if not complexity, to natural ones. The intricate interrelatedness of natural systems that was built up over millions of years has to be approximated within the industrial system as soon as possible through a combination of top-down legislation and bottom-up voluntary arrangements. It is an enormous task, but the Danish example demonstrates that such symbiotic integration of industrial processes is entirely feasible. Not only are they integrated with each other, they are very often integrated with natural ecosystems as well: 'Waste...either cycles back into industrial ecosystems or enters natural ecosystems in non-toxic forms' (Van Der Ryn and Cowan, 1996: 107). There is in such a model the possibility of transforming the exploitative relationship between industry and the biosphere into a co-operative one in which these two form a new techno-biosphere, a synthetic whole in which the man-made operates as far as possible like nature. The financial benefits of having either one enterprise paying another for its waste, or at the very least carting it away for free, are obvious, but industrial ecology requires effort, ingenuity – and proximity – in order for it to work as a system. Financial incentives are needed to speed up what would otherwise be a very slow evolutionary process of self-organizing industrial ecologies.

8.9 Beyond pricing?

How, in a democracy, are citizens to be encouraged to develop such self-organized networks? Ernst von Weizsäcker, in his book *Earth Politics* (1994), suggests a strategy of economic persuasion rather than legislative coercion – carrots rather than sticks:

Cities can work on their ecologies through the awarding of public contracts to sustainable schemes, planning and solar zoning...If abuse of the land and pollution become very expensive, and clean production becomes cheaper, then ideal conditions will be established for a technical revolution in town planning, municipal services and infrastructure (Weizsäcker, 1994: 161–62).

If corporate taxes were to be replaced with environmental taxes, with the biggest polluters in the highest bracket, then, according to Weizsäcker, the city's relationship to its industries would change radically, 'and not necessarily for the worse':

A high tax on land coverage would create an incentive for restoring old, possibly polluted sites rather than building on greenfield ones, which could be assigned very high land development taxes. A national or European tax of this kind would prevent competing localities from underbidding one another: to build anywhere on a greenfield site should be the most expensive option (Weizsäcker, 1994: 162).

Legal penalties thus become the ultimate sanction, rather than first recourse. The appeal of this model is that it uses the devices and desires of capitalism to redirect the exploitative excesses of that system. Building, as a capital-intensive industry and major polluter is obviously heavily implicated in such redirection. The recycling of building materials, for example, would suddenly become economically attractive if there were 'a swingeing tax on primary raw materials'. The idea is for private and public enterprise to evolve their own systems of interdependence within a new framework of energy efficiency, and not for government to try to order them from the top down. The complexity of creating such an 'industrial ecology' by fiat is beyond the capacities of any central authority, but its encouragement is not.

8.10 Conclusion

There is, therefore, a new model for sustainable development which addresses the complexity of decentred centres and intensified decentralization in ways that begin to suggest the possibility of a new vision as powerful as Howard's or Le Corbusier's for their times:

They are cities constituted as constellations of attractors which defy both the gravitational criteria of traditional urban models and the isotropic, centralised modern organisations. Within the emerging urban models, the centre/periphery, full/void and exterior/interior oppositions tend to disappear, evolving towards polycentric, a-hierarchical systems, 'networks', or 'rhizomes', more operative within unstable conditions. The city is built around lines of displacement and connection, operating in a topological rather than geometrical mode. The urban structure turns into a super-conductive topography, capable of continuous reorientation to flows (Zaera Polo, 1994: 26).

This 'topographical' model has implications for construction, operation, and, in architectural terms, representation; a type of development – sometimes more urban, sometimes more rural – that integrates built and natural environments in various sustainable ways. It is on the scale of the city one can see most clearly that this conceptual model and environmental practice are working towards similar formulations from entirely different directions: the integration of built form and land, or built environment and natural environment. To this model, environmental practice could give concrete means of implementation. To environmental practice, this model could give focus and self-consciousness, without which social change is slower, if it happens at all.

CONCLUSION

One of the purposes of this book has been to identify and assess the wide variety of architectures claiming environmental sustainability, and to locate them on a spectrum ranging from the least culturally reflexive to the most. Three criteria were used to accomplish this: symbiosis, differentiation and visibility. The degree to which environmental architecture meets the last two criteria reflects the degree to which these architectures are readable – or not – *as* environmentally sustainable. This indeed was one of the aims of the exercise: to champion formal exploration and expression as allies of environmental design, not decadent obstacles, and to make room for aesthetics as well as ethics in the wide embrace of environmentalism.

The intention was emphatically not to champion a new style of environmental architecture. The examples used of work by Eisenman, Gehry, Fraser, Lynn, etc. are not blueprints for an environmental architecture of the future, but evidence of a regard for nature and a model of nature different to those found in environmental architecture, which for this very reason might enrich it. This means, however, accepting that environmentalism is an ideology among competing ideologies, a view of the world with priorities that are not universally shared, and which is interpreted in very different ways by those who do share it. The built environment is a big polluter. It matters how buildings are built and run, and it matters that environmentalism's view of the world is adopted by all the participants in the building industry, architects included, as soon as possible. This puts a duty of care, not only on the profession, but also on the schools, for training future professionals. Environmental architecture that inspires and excites has therefore as much of a role to play as that which performs virtuously, because the effect of the former is disproportionately large in relation to its numbers. We cannot afford to dismiss the contribution aesthetics can make to environmental ethics at this point in the development of environmental architecture. Making visible brings what is suppressed, lost or emergent forward into cultural consciousness. Through that awareness, emergence is accelerated. To dismiss this making visible as irrelevant is to dismiss not only a means, but the end.

Equally, on the other side of the divide, to dismiss nature as an obsolete subject for culture, specifically architecture, is to miss the profound shift our culture is undergoing. Whether it will shift fast or far enough is another question, but from the sciences to politics to the arts, nature is being re-addressed and reviewed. How could it be otherwise when today culture and nature are mingling promiscuously in more profound and irrevocable ways than ever before? Any architect seeking to make a 'meaningful contemporary architecture' will have to address the blurring of demarcations. This is seen by some as a fall from purity, or at least clarity, as if some taboo has been broken, and what was clean – that is intentional, conscious, clear, superior – is now tainted by the leaking of nature into the *über* category of culture. Our bodies yoke us to the order of nature, and the eagerness with which so many embrace cyberspace is an indication of how firmly embedded in western culture is the unhappiness with this yoke.

Nevertheless, what environmental design is doing, and can do to a much greater extent, is ground architectural practice in the material world in a way architectural phenomenology failed to do. In the past, one could dismiss phenomenology's demands for a return to place-making and tectonics with a clear conscience because such a dismissal could be couched in terms of a refusal of nostalgia and a clear-eyed acceptance of present trends: dispersal, fragmentation, 'etherealization'. One cannot, however, dismiss environmentalism's demands with the same ease. To do so carries much more direct material consequences that affect equally those who long for a lost order and community, and those who celebrate liberation from them. In that equality, a new community has been created: a community of the vulnerable, or what Ulrich Beck calls the 'solidarity of living things':

The toxic threat makes them sense that they participate with their bodies in things...and consequently, that they can be eroded like the stones and trees in acid rain. A community among Earth, plant, animal and human being becomes visible, a solidarity of living things, that affects everyone and everything equally in the threat (Beck, 1992: 74).

The anxiety about the consequences of the present spiral of production and consumption forces a reappraisal of the relation between what is increasingly difficult to discern as culture and nature.[1] Environmental design reflects that reappraisal by enacting subtler ways of making and operating. In part, the success of the new environmental contract, if there is to be any success in the face of ever more invasive instru-mentalities, depends on bottom-up pressure forcing top-down change. Bottom-up pressure is generated not only by threats to our lives – citizens dying of asthma in polluted conurbations, etc – but by ideas and imagery capable of carrying new ideas. In a more reflexive environ-mental architecture, the conceptual and the ontological would be held in tension, suspended in the medium of environmentalism, rather than viewed as mutually exclusive:

The discovery of meaningful architecture should occur in the realm of perception, through the operations of making, of 'concrete poetry' or poesis, derived from the challenge of materials and

---

1. For a discussion of this see Beck (1992), chapter 1.

techniques...Embodied making, involving a mind in *a body...is the opposite of the construction of an object or building through the implementation of conceptual, methodological tools... (Perez-Gomez, 1986: 78–79).*

Environmental architecture could make the endless reiteration of such oppositions an irrelevance, if they are not already, with 'embodied making' entirely compatible with the use of 'conceptual, methodological tools', as they were compatible within classical, and indeed Modern Movement architecture.

'Conceptual, methodological tools', it has been argued here, are as important at this point in the development of environmental architecture as 'embodied making'. They not only frame this making as a cultural as well as a material enterprise, but open up possibilities of formal expression that have not been considered hitherto. The term 'art' is used to denote the lost unity of *techne* in Dalibor Vesely's *Architecture and the Conflict of Expression* (1985), and 'aesthetic expression' is used to denote what is now known as art. The science that burst the bounds of *techne* is condemned by Vesely as instrumental and partial, incapable of revealing 'the truth':

The purpose of my argument has been to show how confusing and illusory is the modern situation: how art, a revelation of the truth of reality preserved in symbolic expression, differs from aesthetic expression, created and experienced as a source of pleasant sensation; and finally, how similar is aesthetic reality to the reality of science and modern technology (Vesely, 1985: 32).

What is regrettable, surely, is not the usurpation of the unity of transcendence by a plurality of aesthetic expressions, but the wholesale commodification of those expressions. The objection that this plurality is one of sterile formalism ('the dissolution of content in aesthetic experience' (Vesely, 1985: 34)) suggests that meaningful expression does not exist outside transcendental symbolism, that without transcendence, all content becomes form, to paraphrase Nietzsche.[2]

In architecture, this is, surely, and always has been, exactly its condition, with or without a transcendent referent: its content is its form is its content. Because it could never literally depict, whether verbally or visually, it was much less easily a means to a clear representational end. On the other hand, exactly because of this lack of a precise match between form and content, its form has always been imbued with *some* meaning, whether produced or received, transcendent or heterogeneous, intended or imposed. Architecture, so embedded in the world, cannot escape carrying meaning, however autonomous it strives to be, and however abstract or alienated it is condemned for being. But it is now many meanings, not one meaning, a Tower of Babel, not a

---

2. Friedrich Nietzsche: 'One is an artist at the cost of regarding that which all non-artists call "form" as content, as "the matter itself". With that, of course, one belongs to an inverted world: for henceforth content becomes something merely formal – our life included' (quoted in Vesely, 1985: 21).

universal language, that architecture carries, and this fragmentation is meaningless to many. Further exacerbating their plight is what they see as the reductive unity of modernism, which leads to such 'aberrations' as works of engineering being hailed as works of art:

Works of engineering – the Eiffel Tower, the Delage automobile, which Le Corbusier compared with the Parthenon, as well as Duchamp's ready-mades or the structures of Mies van der Rohe – are even today discussed, without qualification, as works of art (Vesely, 1985: 32).

It could be argued, however, that such a conflation is a restoration of *techne*, of art and science in one practice. This interpretation is disallowed, however, because industrial production has replaced craft, and the relation of the maker to the made is now 'alienated'. Even so, it is difficult to see how Duchamps and Mies can be included in the same list with the Delage. Are they both tainted with instrumentality? Surely there is ground between transcendent symbolism and autistic formalism, where 'aesthetic expression' is neither empty nor trivial, and architectural forms do carry culturally communicable content?

Environmental architecture can convey its project to those who behold it as much – or as little – as any other architecture can convey a meaning. If it is an environmental functionalism that is being expressed, then the beholder will need to know that the devices that are made visible are the devices of the new environmental contract, just as the beholders of the cathedrals had to be familiar with Christian dogma in order to understand the pictorial signs and symbols that conveyed this meaning. The signified in the second case claims transcendence, and in the first does not, but the two architectures both stand and stand for, regardless. If it is a more generalized view of the new relation between architecture and nature that is being expressed, the same point applies: once one is initiated into the project of an Eisenman or a Lynn or an Ambasz, the meaningless becomes meaningful. One may not agree with that meaning, nor with the way it is conveyed, but meaningful it is, on many levels, some of them a possible source for extending the expressive range of environmental architecture, particularly as critique of conventional architecture, with its unacceptable ways of being in the world.

The examination of the term 'environmental architecture' in this book has produced more complex subdivisions. One of these is environmental architecture as the existing plurality rendered more sustainable. If and when this is achieved, and environmental design is automatically incorporated into the general activity of 'architectural design', the use of the words 'environmental' or 'sustainable' or 'green' to describe these architectures will become redundant. One will no longer have to stipulate 'environmental' architecture because environmental sustainability will be one of the elements understood as present within the term 'architecture', absorbed as one among others. The term 'environmental architecture' may then be used to refer, not to those architectures that operate sustainably, as all will, but to those architectures – and it will again be a plurality – which re-present this sustainable operation aesthetically, those for which the expression of a new co-operative contract between architecture and nature is as important as its enactment.

BIBLIOGRAPHY

AALTO, Alvar (1986). 'Address to the Nordic Building Congress', Oslo, 1938. In Goran Schildt, *Alvar Aalto, The Decisive Years*. New York: Rizzoli.

ADORNO, Theodor and HORKHEIMER, Max (1992). *Dialectic of the Enlightenment* (John Cumming, trans.). London and New York: Verso.

AGREST, Diana I. (1993). *Architecture From Without*. Cambridge, MA and London: MIT Press.

ALBERTI, Leon Battista (1991). *On the Art of Building*. Cambridge, MA and London: MIT Press.

ALLEN, Stan (1997). 'From Object to Field'. In *Architecture After Geometry*, Architectural Design Profile, 127. London: Academy Group.

AMBASZ, Emilio (1991). 'I Ask Myself'. In Emilio Ambasz, *The Poetics of the Pragmatic*. New York: Rizzoli.

ANDO, Tadao (1984). *Tadao Ando: Buildings, Projects, Writings* (Kenneth Frampton, ed.). New York: Rizzoli.

ANINK, David, BOONSTRA, Chiel and MAK, John (1996). *Handbook of Sustainable Building*. London: James & James (Science Publishers).

ARISTOTLE (1911). 'On the Parts of Animals'. In *Aristotle*, Bk. 1, Part 5 (W. Ogle trans.). Oxford: Oxford University Press.

ASCOTT, Roy (1995). 'Technoetic Structures'. In *A.D. Architects in Cyberspace* (Maggie Toy, ed.). London: John Wiley and Sons.

ASCOTT, Roy (1998). 'The Architecture of Cyberception'. In *Architects in Cyberspace*, Vol. 68, No. 11/12. London: Academy Editions.

AUGE, Marc (1995). *Non-Places, Introduction to an Anthropology of Supermodernity*. London: Verso.

BALCOMB, Douglas (1998). 'The Coming Revolution in Building Design'. In *Environmentally Friendly Cities*, Proceedings of PLEA 98 (Eduardo Maldonado and Simos Yannas, eds.). London: James & James (Science Publishers) Ltd.

BALFOUR, Alan (1994). 'Architecture for a New Nation'. In *Bioclimatic Skyscrapers*, London, Zürich and Munich: Artemis.

BANHAM, Reyner (1975). *Theory and Design in the First Machine Age*. London: Architectural Press.

BANHAM, Reyner (1984). *The Architecture of the Well-Tempered Environment*. London: Architectural Press.

BATESON, Gregory (1985). Quoted in Michael Otte, 'Symmetry and Knowledge'. *Daidalos*, 15. Berlin.

BATTY, Michael and LONGLEY, Paul (1997). *The Fractal City.* Architectural Design Profile, 129. London: Academy Group.

BECK, Ulrich (1992). *Risk Society.* London and New Delhi: SAGE Publications.

BENTON, Ted (1993). *Natural Relations: Ecology, Animal Rights and Social Justice.* London and New York: Verso.

BENTON, Ted (1994). 'Biology and Social Theory in the Environmental Debate'. In *Social Theory and the Global Environment* (Michael Reclift and Ted Benton, eds.). London: Routledge.

BESS, Philip (1996). 'Communitarianism and Emotivism'. In *Theorising a New Agenda for Architecture* (Kate Nesbit, ed.). New York: Princeton Architectural Press.

BEUKERS, Adriaan and VAN HINTE, Ed (1999). *Lightness.* Rotterdam: 010 Publishers.

BLOOMER, Jennifer (1993). '...and *venustas*'. *AA Files*, 25. London: Architectural Association.

BLOOMER, Jennifer (1996). 'The Matter of the Cutting Edge'. In *Desiring Practices.* London: Black Dog Publishing Ltd.

BOTTICHER, Karl (1995). *The Principles of the Hellenic and Germanic Way of Building* (1846), in Frampton (1995).

CALATRAVA, Santiago (1993). Quoted in *Santiago Calatrava, Dynamic Equilibrium: Recent Projects.* Zürich: Artemis Verlags AG.

CALTHORPE, Peter (1993). *The Next American Metropolis.* Princeton, NJ: Princeton Architectural Press.

CASTELLS, Manuel (1996). *The Informational City.* Oxford and Cambridge, MA: Blackwell.

CASTELLS, Manuel and HALL, Peter (1997). 'Technopoles: Mines and Foundries of the Informational Technology'. In *The City Reader* (Richard L. Gates and Frederic Stout, eds.). London: Routledge.

CHADIRJI, Rifat (1986). *Concepts and Influences: Towards a Regionalised International Architecture.* London: Routledge & Kegan Paul.

CHAPLIN, Sarah (1997). 'Report to Virtual HQ: The Distributed City'. *Journal of Architecture*, Vol. 2, No. 1, pp. 43–57.

CONNELLY, James and SMITH, Graham (eds.) (1999). *Politics and the Environment.* London and New York: Routledge.

CORNER, James (1994). 'Taking Measures Across the American Landscape'. *AA Files*, 27. London: Architectural Association.

COUSINS, Mark (1994). 'The Ugly'. *AA Files*, 28. London: Architectural Association.

CURTIS, William (1996). *Modern Architecture Since 1900.* London: Phaidon.

DAVION, Victoria (1994). 'Is Ecofeminism Feminist?'. In *Ecological Feminism* (Karen J. Warren, ed.). London and New York: Routledge.

DAWKINS, Richard (1989). *The Selfish Gene.* Oxford: Oxford University Press.

DAY, Christopher (1990). *Places of the Soul.* Wellingborough, Northants: Aquarian Press.

DE LANDA, Manuel (1997). *A Thousand Years of Nonlinear History.* New York: Zone Books.

DELEUZE, Giles (1993). 'The Fold: Leibniz and the Baroque' (Tom

Conley, trans.). In *Folding in Architecture*, Architectural Design Profile, 102. London: Academy Group.

DELEUZE, Gilles and GUATTARI, Felix (1996). *A Thousand Plateaus*. London: Athlone Press.

DERRIDA, Jacques (1987). *Positions* (Alan Bass, trans.). London: Athlone Press.

DOWNING, J. and KOELKER, J. (1988). 'Case Study: Informant-Intelligent Design'. In *Intelligent Buildings* (McClelland, ed.). Berlin and New York: Springer–Verlag.

DUNSTER, Bill (1996). 'Urban Sustainability: Paradox or Possibility?'. *AA Files*, 32. London: Architectural Association.

EAGLETON, Terry (1991). *Ideology*. London and New York: Verso.

EDDINGTON, Arthur (1958). *The Nature of the Physical World*. Anna Arbor: University of Michigan Press.

EISENMAN, Peter (1989). *Deconstruction*. Architectural Design Profile. London: Academy Group; New York: St. Martin's Press.

EISENMAN, Peter (1993). *Arquitectura* (no. 270). Quoted in Jacques Derrida, 'A Letter to Peter Eisenman'. In *RE:WORKING EISENMAN*. London: Academy Editions.

EISENMAN, Peter (1993a). 'Centre for the Arts, Emory University, Atlanta'. In *Folding in Architecture* (Greg Lynn, ed.), Architectural Design Profile, 102. London: Academy Group.

EISENMAN, Peter (1993b). Interview with Alan Balfour. *AA Files*, 25. London: Architectural Association.

EVANS, Barrie (1993). 'Windows as Climate Modifiers'. *The Architects' Journal*, 4 August.

FARMER, John (1996). *The Green Shift*. Oxford. London and Boston: Butterworth Architecture.

FATHY, Hassan (1986). *Natural Energy and Vernacular Architecture*. Chicago: University of Chicago.

FISHMAN, Robert (1987). *Bourgeois Utopias*. New York: Basic Books, Inc.

FITCH, James Marston (1990). 'Vernacular Paradigms'. In *Vernacular Architecture* (Mete Turan, ed.). Hong Kong and Sydney: Avebury.

FOREIGN OFFICE ARCHITECTS (1995). 'Foreign Office Architects'. *AA Files*, 29. London: Architectural Association.

FOREIGN OFFICE ARCHITECTS (1997). 'Foreign Office Architects'. In *A.D. Architecture after Geometry* (Peter Davidson and Donald L. Bates, eds.). London: Academy Group.

FOSTER, Norman (1992). *Foster Associates, Recent Works* (Kenneth Powell, ed.). Architectural Monographs, 20. London: Academy Editions and St. Martin's Press.

FRAMPTON, Kenneth (1992). *Modern Architecture: A Critical History*. London: Thames and Hudson.

FRAMPTON, Kenneth (1995). *Studies in Tectonic Culture*. Cambridge, MA and London: MIT Press.

FRAZER, John (1993). Quoted in 'Interview with John Frazer', by Brian Hatton, *Lotus 79*, pp. 15–25, Elemond Spa, Milan.

FRAZER, John (1998). AD *Architects in Cyberspace*, Vol. 68, No. 11/12. London: Academy Editions.

GARREAU, Joel (1991). *Edge City*. New York: Anchor Books.

GARTNER, Scott (1995). Quoted in Kenneth Frampton, *Studies in Tectonic Culture*. Cambridge, MA and London: MIT Press.

GEDDES, Patrick (1915). *Cities in Evolution*. Williams and Norgate. London.

GINZBURG, Moisei (1982). *Style and Epoch*. Cambridge, MA and London: Opposition Books and MIT Press.

GLEICK, James (1994). *Chaos*. London: Abacus Books.

GROPIUS, Walter (1956). *Scope of Total Architecture*. London: George Allen and Unwin Ltd.

GROPIUS, Walter (1971). *The New Architecture and the Bauhaus* (P. Morton Shand, trans.). Cambridge, MA: MIT Press.

GROSS, Elizabeth (1994). 'Women, Chora, Dwelling'. In *Architecture and the Feminine: Mop-Up Work*, *ANY* (Jennifer Bloomer, ed.). New York: Anyone Corporation.

GURENC, Bozkurt (1990). 'Vernacular Architecture as a Paradigm Case Argument'. In *Vernacular Architecture* (Mete Turan, ed.). Hong Kong and Sydney: Avebury.

HABERMAS, Jurgen (1987). 'Modernity – An Incomplete Project'. In *Postmodern Culture* (S. Ben-Habib, trans.; Hal Foster, ed.). London and Sydney: Pluto Press.

HABERMAS, Jurgen (1987a). *The Philosophical Discourse of Modernity* (Frederick Lawrence, trans.). Cambridge: Polity Press.

HALL, Sir James (1797). 'On the Origins of Gothic Architecture'. In *Transactions of the Royal Society of Arts and Sciences of Scotland*, Edinburgh.

HARAWAY, Donna (1991). *Simians, Cyborgs and Women: the reinvention of nature*. New York: Routledge.

HARRIES, Karsten (1997). *The Ethical Function of Architecture*. Cambridge, MA and London: MIT Press.

HAWKES, Dean (1996). *The Environmental Tradition*. London and New York: E & FS Spon.

HEIDEGGER, Martin (1971). *Building Dwelling Thinking* (A. Hofstadter, trans.). New York: Harper & Row.

HEIDEGGER, Martin (1977). *The Question Concerning Technology and other Essays*. New York and London: Harper Torchbooks and Harper & Row.

HEIDEGGER, Martin (1982). *The Basic Problems of Phenomenology* (A. Hofstadter, trans.). Indiana: Bloomington.

HIGHLANDS, Delbert (1990). 'What's Indigenous?'. In *Vernacular Architecture* (Mete Turan, ed.). Hong Kong and Sydney: Avebury.

HILL, Robert (1998). 'PV cells and modules'. In *Renewable Energy World*, pp. 22–26, July. James & James (Science Publishers) Ltd.

HINSLEY, Hugo (1996). 'Sustaining Architects?'. In *Sustainability Symposium at the AA*, 10 February 1996, *AA Files*, 32 (Autumn). London: Architectural Association.

HOWARD, Ebenezer (1985). *Garden Cities of Tomorrow*. Eastbourne: Attic.

HOWIESON, G. Stirling and LAWSON, Alan (1998). 'Who is Paying the Fuel Price?'. In *Environments by Design* (Sue Ann Lee, ed.), Vol. 2, No. 2. Kingston University Press, Kingston.

IMBERT, Dorothee (1993). *The Modernist Garden in France*. New Haven and London: Yale University Press.

INWOOD, M.J. (1995). *The Oxford Companion to Philosophy* (Ted Honderich, ed.). Oxford and New York: Oxford University Press.

JAMESON, Frederic (1984). 'Postmodernism or the Cultural Logic of Late Capitalism'. *New Left Review*, September/October, 53–65.

JAMESON, Fredric (1985). 'Architecture and the Critique of Ideology'. In *Architecture, Criticism, Ideology* (Joan Ockman, ed.). Princeton, NJ: Princeton Architectural Press.

JENKS, Mike, WILLIAMS, Katie and BURTON, Elizabeth (eds.) (1999). *The Compact City*. London: Routledge.

KELLY, Kevin (1994). *Out of Control*. London: Fourth Estate.

KIERAN, Stephen and TIMBERLAKE, James (1994). 'A Tale of Two Cities'. *The Periphery*, Architectural Design Profile, 108. London: Academy Group.

KIERKEGAARD, Soren (1959). *Either/Or*, Vols. 1 and 2 (David and Lilian Swenson, trans.). New York: Anchor Books.

KIPNIS, Jeffrey (1993). 'Towards a New Architecture'. In *A.D. Folding in Architecture*, Greg Lynn (guest ed.). London: Academy Group.

KNOWLES, Ralph (1981). 'Solar Access, Rhythm and Design'. In *Design Connection* (Ralph Crump and Martin Harms, eds.). New York and London: Van Nostrand Reinhold Co.

KOHLI, Madhavi (1998). *The Use of Natural Ventilation in Contemporary Public Service Buildings in the U.K.*, M.A. Dissertation, Environment and Energy Studies Graduate Program, Architectural Association (unpublished).

KRONER, Walter (1988). 'The Future of Communities, Buildings and Building Systems'. In *Intelligent Buildings* (Stephen McClelland, ed.). IFS Publications, UK, Berlin and New York: Springer–Verlag.

KWINTER, Sanford (1993). 'The Genius of Matter: Eisenman's Cincinatti Project'. In *RE:WORKING EISENMAN*. London: Academy Group.

LAUGIER, Marc Antoine (1977). *An Essay on Architecture* (Wolfgang and Anni Hermann, trans.). Los Angeles: Hennessy and Ingalls, Inc.

LEATHERBARROW, David (1993). *The Roots of Architectural Invention*. Cambridge: Cambridge University Press.

LEATHERBARROW, David and MOSTAFAVI, Mohsen (1996). 'Opacity'. *AA Files*, 32 (Autumn). London: Architectural Association.

LE CORBUSIER (1984). *Precisions*, Paris (1930), in Banham (1984).

LE CORBUSIER (1986). *Towards a New Architecture*. New York: Dover Publications, Inc.

LE CORBUSIER (1987). *The City of Tomorrow*. London: Architectural Press.

LEVINAS, Emmanuel (1997). 'The Old and The New'. In *Time and The Other* (R.A. Cohen, trans.). Pittsburg: Duquesne University Press.

LLOYD JONES, David (1998). *Architecture and the Environment*. London: Laurence King Publishing.

LOVELOCK, James (1979). *Gaia: A New Look at Life on Earth*. Oxford: Oxford University Press.

LYNN, Greg (1993). 'Architectural Curvilinearity: the Folded, the Pliant and the Supple'. In *Folding in Architecture*, Architectural Design Profile, 102. London: Academy Group.

LYNN, Greg (1998). *Folds, Bodies and Blobs*. Brussels: Books-By-Architects.

LYOTARD, Jean-Francois (1991). *The Postmodern Condition: A Report on Knowledge* (Geoff Bennington and Brian Massumi, trans.). Manchester: Manchester University Press.

MACINTYRE, Alasdair (1995). *A Short History of Ethics*. London: Routledge.

MACINTYRE, Alasdair (1996). *After Virtue*. London: Duckworth.

MALLGRAVE, Harry Francis (1995). 'Introduction to Frampton'. In *Studies in Tectonic Culture*. Cambridge, MA and London: MIT Press.

MANNHEIM, Karl (1972). *Ideology and Utopia*. London: Routledge.

MARINETTI, Filippo (1991). *Let's Murder the Moonshine: Selected Writings* (R.W. Flint, ed.). Los Angeles: Sun and Moon Classics.

MARX, Karl (1973). *Grundrisse, Foundations of Critique of Political Economy* (Martin Nicolaus, trans.). Harmondsworth: Penguin.

MATTHEWS, Freya (1994). *The Ecological Self*. London: Routledge.

McCLUNG, William A. (1983). *The Architecture of Paradise*. Berkeley: University of California Press.

McHARG, Ian L. (1971). *Design with Nature*. New York: Doubleday.

MELET, Ed (1999). *Sustainable Architecture*. Rotterdam: NAI Publishers.

MEYER, Leonard B. (1979). 'Toward a Theory of Style'. In *The Concept of Style* (Berel Lang, ed.). Philadelphia: University of Pennsylvania Press.

MOHOLY-NAGY, Laszlo (1986). 'von material zu architektur'. In Goran Schildt, *Alvar Aalto, The Decisive Years*. New York: Rizzoli.

MOLLISON, Bill (1996). *Permaculture, A Designers' Manual*. Australia: Tagari Publications.

MONEO, Raphael (1988). 'The Idea of Lasting: A Conversation with Raphael Moneo', *Perspecta 24*, The Journal of the Yale School of Architecture. New York: Rizzoli International Publications.

MOSTAFAVI, Mohsen and LEATHERBARROW, David (1993). *On Weathering*. Cambridge, MA and London: MIT Press.

MURPHY, Richard, J. and HILLIER, Bill (1997). 'Life Cycle Assessment (LCA)'. In *Green Shift Symposium*. Kingston and London: Kingston University Press.

NEUTRA, Richard (1989). *Nature Near* (William Martin, ed.). Santa Barbara: Capra Press.

NORBERG-SCHULZ, Christian (1980). *Genius Loci: Towards a Phenomenology of Architecture*. London: Academy Editions.

NORBERG-SCHULZ, Christian (1988). *Architecture: Meaning and Place*. New York: Electa/Rizzoli.

NUSSBAUM, Martha (1989). *The Fragility of Goodness*. Cambridge and New York: Cambridge University Press.

OCEAN UK (1997). 'Arabiananta Urban Design (Phases 1–3)'. Architectural Design Profile, 127. London: Academy Group.

PAGE, John (1994). 'Human Use of Renewable Energy to Improve the Global Environment in the Post-Brundtland Era'. In *Global Warming and The Built Environment* (Robert Samuels and Deo K. Prasad, eds.). London and New York: E & FN Spon.

PAGLIA, Camille (1990). *Sexual Personae*. New Haven, CT: Yale University Press.

PAPANEK, Victor (1995). *The Green Imperative*. London: Thames and Hudson.

PEARSON, David (1989). *The Natural House Book*. London: Gaia Books/Conran.

PEPPER, David (1999). *Modern Environmentalism*. London and New York: Routledge.

PEREZ-GOMEZ, Alberto (1983). *Architecture and the Crisis of Modern Science*. Cambridge, MA and London: MIT Press.

PEREZ-GOMEZ, Alberto (1986). 'Abstraction in Modern Architecture'. *Arkkitehti*, Vol. 83, No. 2/3, 97–107.

PERRAULT, Charles (1983). 'Parallele des Anciens et Modernes'. In Perez-Gomez (1983).

PIANO, Renzo (1998). *A+U*, Architecture and Urbanism, 1998: 08, No. 335 (Nobuyuki Yoshida, ed.). Tokyo: A&U Publishing Co. Ltd.

PORPHYRIOS, Demetri (1982). *Sources of Modern Eclecticism: Studies on Alvar Aalto*. London: Academy Editions.

PRIGOGINE, Ilya and STENGERS, Isabelle (1985). *Order Out of Chaos*. London: Flamingo.

PRIOR, Josephine and BARTLETT, Paul (1995). *Environmental Standard: Homes for a Greener World*. Building Research Establishment, Watford: Garston.

QUANTRILL, Malcolm (1987). *The Environmental Memory*. New York: Schocken Books.

RAJCHMAN, John (1993). 'Perplications'. In *RE:WORKING EISENMAN*. London: Academy Group.

RELPH, E. (1976). *Place and Placelessness*. London: Pion Ltd.

REYNOLDS, Michael (1993). *Earthship*, Vols. 1–3. Taos, New Mexico: Solar Survival Press.

RHOWBOTHAM, Kevin (1998). 'Networks', *AD*, Vol. 68, No. 11/12. London.

RHOWBOTHAM, Kevin (1999). *Field Event/Field Space*. Serial Books, Architecture and Urbanism, 2. London: Black Dog Publishing Ltd.

RICOEUR, Paul (1965). *History and Truth* (Charles A. Kelbley, trans.). Evanston, Illinois: Northwestern University Press.

RIFKIN, Jeremy (1998). *The Biotech Century: The Coming of Age of Genetic Commerce*. London: Victor Gollancz.

ROGERS, Richard (1994). *The Architecture of Richard Rogers* (Deyan Sudjic, ed.). Blueprint Monograph. London: Fourth Estate and Wordsearch.

ROGERS, Richard (1997). *Cities for a Small Planet*. London: Faber and Faber Ltd.

RORTY, Richard (1980). *Philosophy and the Mirror of Nature*. Oxford: Basil Blackwell.

ROWE, Colin and KOETTER, Fred (1983). *Collage City*. Cambridge, MA and London: MIT Press.

RUDOFSKY, Bernard (1964). *Architecture Without Architects*. London: Academy Editions.

RUSKIN, John (1989). *The Seven Lamps of Architecture*. New York: Dover Publications Inc.

SALTER, Peter (1987). *TS Intuition and Process*. London: Architectural Association.

SANT'ELIA, Antonio (1988). *Complete Works* (Luciano Caramel and Alberto Longatti, eds.). New York: Rizzoli.

SARTRE, Jean-Paul (1969). *Being and Nothingness* (Hazel E. Branes, trans.). New York: Washington Square Press.

SASSEN, Saskia (1994). *Cities in a World Economy*. Thousand Oaks, California: Pine Forge Press.

SCHILDT, Goran (1986). *Alvar Aalto, The Decisive Years*. New York: Rizzoli.

SCHUTZ, Alfred (1962). *Collected Papers*, Vol. 1. The Hague: Martinus Nijhoff.

SCRUTON, Roger (1994). *The Classical Vernacular*. Manchester: Carcanet.

SEMPER, Gottfried (1989). 'Prospectus: Style in the Technical and Tectonic Arts or Practical Aesthetics'. In *The Four Elements and Other Writings* (Harry Frances Mallgrave and Wolfgang Herrmann, trans.). Cambridge: Cambridge University Press.

SHIVA, Vandana (1993). *Monocultures of the Mind*. London: Zed Books.

SHORT, Alan (1997). Address to the Carnegie Mellon Institute at the Heinz Architecture Centre, Carnegie Musuem of Fine Art, Pittsburg, 12 March 1997 (unpublished).

SLESSOR, Catherine (1998). *Eco-Tech*. London: Thames and Hudson.

SOCIETY OF ENVIRONMENTAL TOXICOLOGY AND CHEMISTRY (1993). *Guidelines for Life Cycle Assessment: A 'Code of Practice'*. Brussels: SETAC.

SOPER, Kate (1995). *What is Nature?*. Oxford and Cambridge, MA: Basil Blackwell.

SOTTSASS, Ettore (1991). Quoted in Emilio Ambasz, *The Poetics of the Pragmatic*. New York: Rizzoli.

SPEIDEL, Manfred (ed.) (1991). *Team Zoo*. London: Thames and Hudson.

SPUYBROEK, Lars (1998). 'Architects in Cyberspace', *AD*, Vol. 68, No. 11/12, London: Academy Editions.

STEADMAN, Philip (1979). *The Evolution of Designs*. Cambridge: Cambridge University Press.

STOLNITZ, Jerome (1998). 'The Aesthetic Attitude'. In *Aesthetics: The Big Questions* (Carolyn Korsmeyer, ed.). Oxford: Blackwell Publishers.

TAFURI, Manfredo (1987). *Architecture and Utopia*. Cambridge, MA and London: MIT Press.

TAKI, Koji (1988). 'Fragments and Noise', *AD,* Vol. 58, 516. London.

TSCHUMI, Bernard (1987). *Cinegramme Folie, La Parc de la Villette*. New York: Princeton Architectural Press.

TSCHUMI, Bernard (1988). Quoted in *Deconstruction, AD*, Vol. 58, No. 3/4. London: Academy Press.

VALE, Brenda and VALE, Robert (1991). *Green Architecture*. London: Thames and Hudson.

VAN DER RYN, Sim and COWAN, Stuart (1996). *Ecological Design*. Washington, DC: Island Press.

VASSAL, William (1998). An interview in *Architecture and Urbanism*, 1998: 08, No. 335 (Nobuyuki Yoshida, ed.). Tokyo: A&U Publishing.

VATTIMO, Gianni (1988). 'The End of Modernity, The End of the Project?'. Jon R. Snyder (trans.). Cambridge: Polity Press.

VESELY, Dalibor (1985). 'Architecture and the Conflict of Representation'. *AA Files*, 8. London: Architectural Association.

VIDLER, Anthony (1990). 'The Building in Pain'. *AA Files*, 19. London: Architectural Association.

VIDLER, Anthony (1996). 'Homes for Cyborgs'. In *Ottagono* (Marco de Micelis, ed.). Milan: CO.P.IN.A.

VIOLLET-LE-DUC (1959). *Entretiens sur l'architecture,* Vol. 1 (Benjamin Bucknall, trans.). London: George Allen & Unwin Ltd.

VIRILIO, Paul (1997). *Open Sky* (Julie Rose, trans.). London and New York: Verso.

VITRUVIUS (1960). *The Ten Books of Architecture*. New York: Dover Publications, Inc.

VON WEIZSACKER, Ernst (1994). *Earth Politics*. London: Zed Books.

WALDROP, M. Mitchell (1994). *Complexity*. London: Penguin Books.

WARNKE, G. (1987). *Gadamer: Hermeneutics, Tradition and Reason*. Stanford: Stanford University Press.

WARREN, Karen J. (1990). 'The Power and the Promise of Ecological Feminism'. *Environmental Ethics*, 12.

WAUGH, Patricia (1992). *Postmodernism, A Reader* (Patricia Waugh, ed.). London: Edward Arnold.

WEIL, Simone (1955). *The Need for Roots*. Boston: Beacon Press.

WEIZSACKER, Ernst Ulrich von (1994). *Earth Politics*. London and New Jersey: Zed Books.

WINES, James (1987). *De-Architecture*. New York: Rizzoli.

WINES, James (1997). 'Passages'. In *The Architecture of Ecology*, Architectural Design Profile, 125. London: Academy Group.

WOODROFFE, Jonathan, PAPA, Dominic and MCBURNIE, Ian (1997). 'An Introduction'. In *Architecture After Geometry*, Architectural Design Profile, 127. London: Academy Group.

WORLD WILDLIFE FUND (1990). *Product Life Assessments: Policy Issues and Implications*. Washington: WWF.

WRIGHT, Frank Lloyd (1945). *When Democracy Builds*. Chicago: University of Chicago Press.

WRIGHT, Frank Lloyd (1971). *The Natural House*. London: Pitman.

YEANG, Ken (1994). *Bioclimatic Skyscrapers*. London, Zürich and Munich: Artemis.

YEANG, Ken (1996). *The Skyscraper Bioclimatically Considered*. London: Academy Editions.

ZAERA POLO, Alejandro (1994). 'Order out of Chaos'. In *The Periphery*, Architectural Design Profile, 108. London: Academy Group.

ILLUSTRATION CREDITS

Chapter 1
Plate 1 Jean de Calan, Fig. 1.1 MCA Architects, Plate 2 Dennis Gilbert/VIEW, Plate 3 Peter Cook/VIEW, Fig. 1.2 Brian Ford, Plate 4 Emilio Ambasz & Associates, Plate 5 Susannah Hagan, Fig. 1.3 Eisenman Architects, Figs. 1.4 and 1.5 Greg Lynn, Fig. 1.6 Sergio Los.

Chapter 2
Plate 6 Susannah Hagan, Plates 7–8 Paul Raftery/Arcaid, Fig. 2.1 Julius Shulman, Fig. 2.2 Phaidon Press Ltd., *Leon Battista Alberti*, Franco Borsi, Plate 9 Susannah Hagan, Fig. 2.3 The British Library, Figs. 2.4–7 and Plate 10 Susannah Hagan, Plate 11 John Frazer, Plate 12 Shigwo Ogawa/Shinkenchiku, Plate 13 Nigel Young/Foster and Partners, Plate 14 and Figs. 2.8–9 Eamonn O'Mahony.

Chapter 3
Fig. 3.1 Susannah Hagan, Fig. 3.2 Living City drawing, copyright 1958, 1988, 1998, 2001, The Frank Lloyd Wright Foundation, Scottsdale, AZ, Fig. 3.3 Phaidon Press Ltd., *Modern Architecture since 1900*, William Curtis, Plate 15 Susannah Hagan, Fig. 3.5 RIBA archive, Fig. 3.6 copyright FLC/ADAGP, Paris and DACS, London 2000, Figs. 3.7–9 British Film Institute.

Chapter 5
Plates 16–20 Susannah Hagan, Plate 21 Christoph Kalb, Plates 22–23 Susannah Hagan, Plate 24 Margherita Spiluttini, Plate 25 Peter Salter.

Chapter 6
Fig. 6.1 Herbert Girardet, Plates 26–27 Susannah Hagan, Fig. 6.2 Omar Al-Farook, Fig. 6.4 Dean Hawkes, Fig. 6.5 Alex Hodge, Plate 28 Dennis Gilbert/VIEW, Duisberg, Germany, Fig. 6.6 Foster and Partners, Plate 29 Nigel Young/Foster and Partners, Fig. 6.7 Foster and Partners, Plate 30 Nigel Young/Foster and Partners, Fig. 6.8 Foster and Partners, Plates 31–32 Christian Richters, Plate 33 and Fig. 6.9 Renzo Piano Building Workshop, Plate 34 Susannah Hagan, Plate 35 James Steele, Plate 36 Susannah Hagan, Plate 37 Peter Salter, Plate 38 Hiroshi Ueda, Figs. 6.10–12 Rifat Chadirji, Plate 40 Brian Ford, Plate 41 Susannah Hagan, Plate 42 Peter Cook/VIEW, Plate 43 SITE, Plate 44 David Churchill, Plate 45 Dick Frank Studio, Plate 46 Jeff Goldberg/ESTO, Plate 47 SITE.

Chapter 7
Plate 48 Anette Kisling, Figs. 7.1–2 Sauerbruch Hutton Architects, Plates 49–50 Electa Archive, Plate 51 Hiroyuki Hirai, Plate 52 Dieter Liestner, Fig. 7.3 Fielden Clegg Architects, Plate 53 Dennis Gilbert/VIEW, Plates 54–55 Roderick Coyne, Fig. 7.4 Alsop and Stromer Architects, Plate 56 and Figs. 7.5–8 Richard Horden, Plates 57–58 K.L. Ng, Plates 59–60 W. Vassal, Renzo Piano Building Workshop, Fig. 7.9 Renzo Piano Building Workshop, Plates 61–62 Louis Checkman, Plate 63 Emilio Ambasz & Associates.

Chapter 8
Plate 64 Scot Weidemann, copyright 1994, 2001, The Frank Lloyd Wright Foundation, Scottsdale, AZ, Fig. 8.3 Eamonn O'Mahoney, Fig. 8.4 Richard Rogers Partnership, Plate 65 copyright FLC/ADAGP, Paris and DACS, London 2000, Plates 66–67 Bill Dunster Architects, Plate 68 Susannah Hagan, Plate 69 OCEAN UK, Fig. 8.5 Richard Rogers Partnership.

PROJECT CREDITS

1992–2000 Potsdamer Platz, Berlin, Germany
Client: Daimler-Chrysler AG.
Renzo Piano Building Workshop, architects – B. Plattner, senior partner in charge in association with Christoph Kohlbecker.

Competition, 1992
Design team: R. Baumgartne, A. Chaaya, P. Charles, J. Moolhuijzen with E. Belik, J. Berger, M. Kohlbecker, A. Schmid, U. Knapp, P. Helppi; P. Darmer (models).

Masterplan, 1993
Design team: R. Baumgarten, G. Bianchi, P. Charles, J. Moolhuijzen with E. Belik, J. Berger, A. Chaaya, W. Grasmug, C. Hight, M. Miegeville, G. Carreira, E. del Moral, H. Nagel, F. Pagliani, L. Penisson, R. Phelan, J. Ruoff, B. Tonfoni; P. Darmer (models).

Kohlbecker: M. Kohlbecker, F. Franke, A. Schmid with L. Ambra, C. Lehmann, B. Siggemann, O. Skjerve, W. Marsching, M. Weiss.

Design Development and Construction phase, 1993–2000
Design team: J. Moolhuijzen, A. Chaaya, R. Baumgarten, M. v. der Staay, P. Charles, G. Bianchi, C. Brammen, G. Ducci, M. Hartmann, O. Hempel, M. Howard, S. Ishida (senior partner), M. Kramer, Ph. v. Matt, W. Matthews, N. Mecattaf, D. Miccolis, M. Busk-Petersen, M. Pimmel, J. Ruoff, M. Veltcheva, E. Volz with E. Audoye, S. Baggs, E. Baglietto, M. Bartylla, S. Camenzind, M. Carroll (partner), L. Couton, R. Coy, A. Degn, B. Eistert, J. Florin, J. Fujita, A. Gallissian, C. Maxwell-Mahon, G.M. Maurizio, J. Moser, J.B. Mothes, O. de Nooyer, F. Pagliani, L. Penisson, M. Piano, D. Putz, P. Reigner, R. Sala, M. Salerno, C. Sapper, S. Schaefer, D. Seibold, K. Shannon, K. Siepmann, S. Stacher, R.V. Truffelli (partner), L. Viti, T. Volz, F. Wenz, H. Yamaguchi and S. Abbado, F. Albini, G. Borden, B. Bowin, T. Chee, S. Drouin, D. Drouin, J. Evans, T. Fischer, C. Hight, J. Krolicki, C. Lee, K. Meyer, G. Ong, R. Panduro, E. Stotts; I. Corte, D. Guerrisi, G. Langasco (CAD operators); J.P. Allain, D. Cavagna, C. Colson, O. Doizy, P. Furnemont (models).

Kohlbecker: M. Kohlbecker, J. Barnbrook, K.H. Etzel, H. Falk, T. Fikuart, H. Gruber, A. Hocher, R. Jatzke, M. Lindner, J. Müller, N. Nocke, A. Rahm, B. Roth, M. Strauss, A. Schmid, W. Spreng.

Consultants: P.L. Copat (interior design for debis tower and casino); Boll & Partners/Ove Arup & Partner, IBF Dr. Falkner GmbH/Weiske & Partner (structure); IGH/Ove Arup & Partners, Schmidt-Reuter & Partner (HVAC); Müller BBM (acoustics); Hundt & Partner (transportation); IBB Burrer, Ove Arup & Partners (electrical engineering); ITF Intertraffic (traffic); Atelier Dreiseitl (landscaping and water basins); Krüger & Möhrle (planting); Drees & Sommer/Kohlbecker (site supervision).

1991–98 Tjibaou Cultural Center Nouméa, New Caledonia
Client: Agence pour le Développement de la Culture Kanak.
Renzo Piano Building Workshop, architects – P. Vincent, senior partner in charge.

Competition, 1991
Design team: A. Chaaya (architect in charge) with F. Pagliani, J. Moolhuijzen, W. Vassal; O. Doizy, A. Schultz (models).

Consultants: A. Bensa (ethnologist); Desvigne & Dalnoky (landscaping); Ove Arup & Partners (structure and ventilation); GEC Ingénierie (cost control); Peutz & Associés (acoustics); Scène (scenography).

Preliminary Design, 1992
Design team: A. Chaaya, D. Rat (architects in charge) with J.B. Mothes, A.H. Téménidès and R. Phelan, C. Catino, A. Gallissian, R. Baumgarten; P. Darmer (models).

Consultants: A. Bensa (ethnologist); GEC Ingénierie (cost control); Ove Arup & Partners (structural and MEP engineering concept); CSTB (environmental studies); Agibat MTI (structure); Scène (scenography); Peutz & Associés (acoustics); Qualiconsult (security); Végétude (planting).

Design Development and Construction phase, 1993–98
Design team: D. Rat, W. Vassal (architects in charge) with A. El Jerari, A. Gallissian, M. Henry, C. Jackman, P. Keyser, D. Mirallie, G. Modolo, J.B. Mothes, M. Pimmel, S. Purnama, A.H. Téménidès; J.P. Allain (models).

Consultants: A. Bensa (ethnologist); Agibat MTI (structure); GEC Ingénierie (MEP engineering and cost control); CSTB (environmental studies); Scène (scenography); Peutz & Associès (acoustics); Qualiconsult (security); Végétude (planting); Intégral R. Baur (signing).

1995–96 Finland: Helsinki
ARBIANRANTA
Urban Design Phases 1–3, 1995–96
Landscapes of Potential
Team: Tom Verebes, Michael Hensel, Kivi Sotamaa, Tony Jones, Toni Kauppila, Andrew Yau, Vike Koskelo, Juha Loukola, Ville Rantanen, Tomas Palmgren, Lucas Borer.

Yellow 6: Rachid Molinary, Bill Szustak, Chris Meyer.

Strategic consultant: Ron Kenley.

Transportation consultants: Ove Arup and Partners Consulting Engineers, London: Juan Alayo, Malcolm Simpson.

Ecological consultants: Ove Arup and Partners Consulting Engineers, London.

INDEX

Page references in italics indicate illustrations.

Aalto, Alvar, 18, 22, 84, 92, 103, 119
Aborigines, 176
Abstraction, 119, 196–7
Aesthetics, 6–9, 14, 195
  and ethics, 12–13, 15
Agrest, Diana, 97
Alberti, Leon Battista, 7, 18, 24–5, *25*, 58
Allen, Stan, 168, 170, 188
Alsop and Stormer Architects, 149, *150*
Altruism, 67–70, 71
Ambasz, Emilio, 4, 99, 139, 147, 150, 161–2, 163
  Manoir d'Angoussart, Bierges, 162
  Nichii Obihiro department store, Obihiro, 129, 162–3
  Nishiyachiyo Station, 123
  Schlumberger Research Laboratories, Austin, 129, 162
Amorfal architecture, 138, 139
Anatomical analogy, 29
Ando, Tadao, 123
Animality, 67
Anink, David, 70
Arabiananta, Helsinki (OCEAN UK), 188–9
Arcadians, xv, 48, 50–2
Architectural Association, 71
Architecture, xx
Architecture and the Conflict of Expression (Vesely), 195–6
Architecture and the Environment (Lloyd Jones), 148
Architecture of Paradise, The (McClung), 48, 52
Architecture of the City (Rossi), 119
Aristotle, 24, 25, 68
Aronoff Centre, University of Cincinatti (Eisenman), 5, *5*, 9, 137
Art, 195
Ascott, Roy, 177

Augé, Marc, 65
Austrian Mineral Oil Company, Schwechat (Lynn), 5, *6*

Bachelard, Gaston, 80
Bacon, Francis, 26, 48
Balcomb, Douglas, 70
Balfour, Alan, 158
Ban, Shigeru, 149
Banham, Reyner, 21, 105–6
Baragan, Luis, 119
Bartlett, Paul, 100
Batty, Michael, 169, 170
Baudelaire, Charles, 48
Baudrillard, Jean, 175
Bauhaus, 106
Beauty, 6–9, 13, 163
Beck, Ulrich, 45–6, 194
BedZED (Beddington Zero Energy Development) (Dunster), 185–6
Bensa, Alban, 159
Benton, Ted, xviii, 37, 66, 67, 69, 72–3
Bess, Philip, 97
Beukers, Adriaan, 38
Bio-centrum, J. W. Goethe University, Frankfurt-am-Main (Eisenman), 134
Bio-climatic high-rises (Yeang), 147, 149–50, 156–8
Biomimesis, 38, 39, 41, 43
Bionic, 43
Biosphere, 168
Bloomer, Jennifer, 6, 20–1, 78
Body, 78–9, 80
Boonstra, Chiel, 70
Botta, Mario, 119, 126
Botticher, Karl, 86
Bourgeois Utopias (Fishman), 171
BREEAM, 100
Brennan, A., 66
Broadacre City (Wright), 171, 174

Building, xx
Building Dwelling Thinking (Heidegger), 129
Building Management System, 41
Building materials, *see* Materials
Building Regulations, 101
Building Research Establishment (BRE), xx, 88, 90, 100–1
  Canning Crescent Mental Health Centre, 113
  Office of the Future (Fielden Clegg Associates), *109*
Business Promotion Centre, Microelectronic Park, Duisberg (Foster), *110*, 110–12
Butterfly effect, 36

Calatrava, Santiago, 18, 30, *31*
Calthorpe, Peter, 172, 182, 186–7
Canning Crescent Mental Health Centre (MacCormac Jamieson Prichard), 113
Capital energy cost, 89–90
Carson, Rachel, xvi
Cartuja Island, Seville (Foreign Office Architects), 189
Castells, Manuel, 180
Centre for the Arts, Amory University, Atlanta (Eisenman), 142–3
Centre for Earthen Architecture, 89
Chadirji, Rifat, 124–5, *125*, *126*
Chaos theory, 35–6, 119
Chaplin, Sarah, 176, 179
Cities, 52–5, 167–8, 171–5
  conceptual models, 168–71
  and information technology, 175–9
  periphery, 179–83
  sustainable, 183–9, 191–2
Cities for a Small Planet (Rogers), 60
Citta Nuova (Sant'Elia), 49, *50*, 55
City of Arts and Sciences, Valencia (Calatrava), *31*

City of Tomorrow, The (Le Corbusier), 54

Classical architecture, 26, *28*, 29

Climatic differentiation, 104–15
  Horden case study, 163
  Yeang case study, 147, 156–8

Co-operation, 46

Compact City, 174

Complexity and Contradiction in Architecture (Venturi), 119

Complexity theory, 169

Concepts and Influences (Chadirji), 125

Concinnitas, 25

Consciousness, 81–2

Conservatism, xvi

Constructivism, 58

Consumerism, 68, 73, 119

Contemporary Design from Traditional Materials (Centre for Earthen Architecture), 89

Contrat Social, Du (Rousseau), 68

Coop Himmelblau, 79, 133–4

Correa, Charles, 116–17

Cousins, Mark, 7, 8

Cowan, Stuart, 88, 187, 190

Critical regionalism, 121–5

Crosara infant school, Italy (Los), *7*, 9

Cucinella, Mario, 4, *4*, 9

Cullinan, Edward, 129, 139
  Westminster Lodge, Dorset, 149

Cultural differentiation, 116–21
  Piano case study, 147, 158–61

Culture, 193–4
  arcadians, 50–2
  and nature, 18–19, 21, 36–7, 42–3, 44, 83, 169

Cyberspace, 167, 176–9

Cybersphere, 168

Davion, Victoria, 20

Dawkins, Richard, 37

Day, Christopher, 103

De Landa, Manuel, 36–7, 168, 174, 187

De-architecture, 130, 132

De-Architecture (Wines), 130–1

Deconstruction, 131–5

Deconstructivism, 132, 195

Deep ecology, 65–6

DeFormation, 143

Deleuze, Gilles, 98, 137, 139–40, 141, 142

Dematerialization, 91, 175

Democracy, xviii–xix

Density, 185

Deracination, 120–1

Derrida, Jacques, 131–5, 141

Descartes, René, 48

Differentiation, xx, xxiii, 98, 99, 115–16, 145, 148, 193

critical regionalism, 121–5
  and culture, 116–21
  Horden case study, 163
  Piano case study, 147, 150, 158–61
  technology and materials, 125–8
  Yeang case study, 147, 149–50, 156–8

Disequilibrium, 41

Domination, 46

Downing, J., 110

Dunster, Bill, BedZED, 185–6

Dwelling, 129–31

Eagleton, Terry, 14

Earth Centre Canopy (Fielden Clegg), 149, *150*

Earth Politics (Weizsacker), 191

Eco–Tech, 39, 60–1, 90
  and passive environmental techniques, 109, 110

Ecological footprint, 185

Economic sustainability, 3

Ecosystem, 18

Eden, 50

Edgar J. Kaufman Desert House, Palm Springs California (Neutra), *23*

Edge City (Garreau), 173, 174

Egypt, 117–8

Einstein, Albert, 34

Eisenman, Peter, 32–3, 38, 77, 98, 99, 131, 197
  Aronoff Centre, University of Cincinatti, 5, *5*, 9, 137
  beauty, 8
  deconstruction, 131, 134–5
  folding, 138, 139–40, 141–3, 145
  iconicity, 163
  Nunotani Headquarters, Tokyo, 33
  Rebstock Park, Frankfurt *141*, *142*

Either/Or (Kierkegaard), 12

Embodied energy, 77, 88, 100

Energy efficiency, 99–101, 148

Entropy, 34–5

Environmental architecture, xv–xxi, 3–15, 197

Environmental rights, 66–7

Environmental Standard, 100

Environmental sustainability, *see* Sustainability

Environmental Tradition, The (Hawkes), 106–7, *108*

Environmentalism, xviii–xix, 193

Essai sur l'architecture (Laugier), 26

Etherealization, 77

Ethical Function of Architecture, The (Harries), 80

Ethics, 12–13, 15, 65–7, 75–6
  being good, 67–70
  being good in buildings, 70–2

materials, 77, 87, 92
  new is good, 72–5

European Commission, 89

Evans, Barrie, 104

Exclusive approach, 106, 107

Exhibition (EDITT) Tower, Singapore (Yeang), 157

Farmer, John, xvi, xx

Fathy, Hassan, 117–8, 121–2

Field theory, 187–9

Fielden Clegg *109*, 149, *150*

Filarete, 53, *54*

Fireplaces, 125, *125*

Fishman, Robert, 171–2

Fitch, James Marston, 104

Fleurs du Mal, Les (Baudelaire), 48

Folding, 138, 139–45

Follies, 79, 131

Ford, Brian, 126, *127*

Foreign Office Architects, 98, 143–4, 189

Form, 9–10, 13, 196

Foster, Norman, 38–9, 60
  Microelectronic Park, Duisberg, 110–11, *111*
  Reichstag, Berlin, 38–9
  Solar City, Linz, 189, *189*

Fractals, 170

Fragility of Goodness, The (Nussbaum), 47

Frampton, Kenneth, 74, 80, 86, 121, 124

Frazer, John, 31, 32, 38, 138, 178–9

Futurism, 55–6, 79

Futurist Architecture (Sant'Elia), 55

Gaia theory, 168

Garden City (Howard), 173, *173*, 183, 184

Garreau, Joel, 173, 174

Gaudi, Antonio *29*, 31, *45*

Geddes, Patrick, 186

Gehry, Frank, 5, 9, 32–3

Gender, 19–21

Genetic architecture, 138

Genius Loci (Norberg-Schulz), 80, 81, 82

Ginzburg, Moisei, 58, 59

Girardet, Herbert *102*

Gleick, James, 36, 39

Godard, Jean-Luc, 3

Goethe, Johann Wolfgang von, 31

Goetz Gallery, Munich (Herzog and de Meuron), 91

Goodin, Robert, 66

Gothic architecture, 27–8, *27*, 29, 85

Green architecture, xvi, 3

Green Architecture (Vale and Vale), 10–11

Green Imperative, The (Papanek), 72
Green Shift (Farmer), xvi, xx
Green utilitarianism, 10–11, 12
Groningen, 178–9
Gropius, Walter, xxi, 60, 106
GSW Headquarters, Berlin (Sauerbruch Hutton), 149, *149*
Guattari, Felix, 98, 137
Guggenheim Museum, Bilbao (Gehry), 9
Gurenc, Bozkurt, 103, 104

Habermas, Jurgen, 46
Hadid, Zaha, 131
Hall, Sir James, 27–8, *27*
Hall, Peter, 180
Hanover Messe (Herzog), 149
Haraway, Donna, 43
Harries, Karsten, 80
Hawkes, Dean, xix, 106–8, *108*
Heavenly City, 53
Heidegger, Martin, 47, 79, 81, 82, 129–30
Helsinki, 188–9
Herzog, Thomas:
    Hall, 26
    Hanover Messe, 149
    Solar City, Linz, 189, *189*
Herzog and de Meuron, 91
High-rises, 147, 149–50, 156–8
Hinsley, Hugo, 74
Hobbes, Thomas, 26
'Homes for Cyborgs' (Vidler), 59
Hopkins, Michael, 4
Horden, Richard, 147, 149, 151–3, *153*, 154, *155*–6, 163
Howard, Ebenezer:
    Garden City, 172, *173*, 182, 183, 184
    Social City, 172, *173*
    'Three Magnets', 106–7, *107*
Howieson, G. Stirling, xix
Husserl, Edmund, 81
HVAC systems, 104–5

Iconicity, 163
Idealism, 17–18
Ideology, 14–15, 136
Ideology and Utopia (Mannheim), 136
Imbert, Dorothee, 22
Inclusiveness, 146
Individuals, 68–9, 73
Industrial ecology, 190–1
Information technology, 175–9
Inland Revenue Centre, Nottingham (Hopkins), 4
Instrumentality, 46–7
International Style, 86
Invention, 74

Iron, 86
Irrationality, 59

Jacobs, Jane, 172
Jameson, Fredric, 14, 78, 120
Japan, 122–3
Jencks, Charles, 138
Jenks, Mike, 174

Kalundborg, Denmark, 190
Kamiichi Pavilion (Salter), 122
Kanaks, 158–61
Kant, Immanuel, 13, 82
Keats, John, 7–8
Kelly, Kevin, 38, 39, 41–2, 115
Kieran, Stephen, 181–2
Kierkegaard, Soren, 12
Kipnis, Jeffrey, 98, 137, 139, 143
Knowles, Ralph, 108–9
Koelker, J., 110
Kohli, Madhavi, 113
Krier, Leon, 119, 122, 175
Kroner, Walter, 111, 112
Kwinter, Sanford, 33, 137

Lacan, Jacques, 79
Lake Shore Drive Towers (Mies van der Rohe), 59
Lamp of Truth (Ruskin), 85–6
Landform, 138
Lang, Fritz, 56–8, *56, 57*
Laugier, Marc Antoine, 18, 26, 27
Lawson, Alan, xix
Le Corbusier, 11, 15, 48, 50
    climate control, 106
    mass production, 31–2
    Modulor, 29
    nature, 20, 22
    and vernacular building, 102–3
    Ville Contemporaine, 53–5, *54*, 169, 184, 185
Learning from Las Vegas (Venturi), 103
Leatherbarrow, David, 79, 90, 91
Lefaivre, Lliane, 121–2
Leibniz, Gottfried, 139, 140, 144
Levinas, Emmanuel, 73
Life cycle analysis (LCA), 77, 87–8, 92
Limits, 72–3
Linz-Pichling, 189, *189*
Living Marxism, 61
Lloyd Jones, David, 148, 149
Longley, Paul, 169, 170
Los, Sergio *7, 9*
Lu Jia Zui, Shanghai (Rogers), 183–5, *183, 184*, 186
Lynn, Greg, 5, *6*, 115, 122, 137, 138, 139
Lyotard, Jean-Francois, 119

McClung, William, 26, 48, 51–2
MacCormac Jamieson Prichard, 113
McHarg, Ian, 186
Machines, 58–9
MacIntyre, Alasdair, 68, 69
Mak, John, 70
Mallgrave, Harry Francis, 80
Man Multiplied and the Reign of the Machine (Marinetti), 55
Mandelbrot, Bennoit, 170
Mannheim, Karl, 136
Manoir d'Angoussart, Bierges (Ambasz), 162
Marinetti, Filippo Tommaso, 55
Marx, Karl, 66, 67, 69
Mass production, 31–2, 85
Materiality, 78–82, 85, 86, 101
Materials, 76, 77–8, 86–93
    and climate control, 111
    Environmental Standard, 100
    true nature, 83–6
Menara Mesiniaga (Yeang), 157, 158
Merleau-Ponty, 81
Meshworks, 174
Metropolis (Lang), 56–8, *56, 57*
Microelectronic Park, Duisberg (Foster), 110–11, *111*
Mies van der Rohe, Ludwig, 59–60, 136
Modern Movement:
    ethics, 65
    Five Points, 11
    materials, 77
    New Architecture, xxi
    siedlung, 141–2
Modernism, 45–6, 147
    arcadians, 50–2
    critical regionalism, 121–2
    makers and breakers, 46–50
    nature, 21–4
    post-imperial, 12, 45, 59–61, 92
    transparency, 151
    universality, 117, 121
    utopians, 52–9
    and vernacular, 119
Modernist Garden in France, The (Imbert), 22
Moewes, 75
Moholy-Nagy, Laszlo, 23, 24
Monocultures of the Mind (Shiva), 116
Morphing, 116
Mostafavi, Mohsen, 91
Murcutt, Glen, 149
Mushrabiya, 116

Nature, 16, 37–42, 44
    arcadians, 50–2
    architecture imitating, 24–31
    blurring and boundaries, 42–3
    and culture, 83, 169

Nature (*cont.*)
  Futurism, 55
  and gender, 19–21
  material reality and cultural
    construct, 16–19
  and materials, 92
  Modern Movement, 46–50
  modernism, 21–4
  re-racinated, 31–3
  relativism, dynamism and
    uncertainty, 33–7
  utopians, 52–9
Neutra, Richard, 22, 23–4, 35, 130, 151
  Edgar J. Kaufman Desert House,
    Palm Springs California *23*
New Architecture, xxi, 138
*New Architecture and the Bauhaus,
  The* (Gropius), 60
Newness, 72–5, 97
Newton, Isaac, 25, 26
Nichii Obihiro department store,
  Obihiro (Ambasz), 162–3
Nietzsche, Friedrich, 196
Nine Laws of God (Kelly), 39, 41–2
Nishinachiyo Station (Ambasz), 123
Nonlinear architecture, 138
Norberg-Schulz, Christian, 80, 81, 82
Nouvel, Jean, 65
Nouvelle alliance, La (Prigogine and
  Stengers), 34
Nunotani Headquarters, Tokyo
  (Eisenman), 33
Nussbaum, Martha, 47–8

OCEAN UK, *Arabiananta*, Helsinki, 188–9
Ode to a Grecian Urn (Keats), 7–8
Office of Metropolitan Architecture
  (OMA), 65
On the Art of Building (Alberti), 24
On Walden Pond (Thoreau), 10
*One Thousand Years of Nonlinear
  History* (de Landa), 36–7
Operation, xx, xxi
  dynamic, 38–9
  symbiosis, 98–9
Organic, 115–16
Organic architecture, 28–9
Out of Control (Kelly), 39, 41–2

Paglia, Camille, 20
Papanek, Victor, 72
Paper Gallery, Tokyo (Ban), 149
Parc de la Villette (Tschumi), 79, 131
Passive downdraft evaporative cooling
  (PDEC), 126, *127*
Passive environmental techniques,
  104–15, 127–8, 151
Peckham Library (Alsop and Stormer),
  149, *150*
Pei, I. M., 65

Perez-Gomez, Alberto, 194–5
Peripheries, 179–83
Permaculturists, 11–12
Perrault, Charles, 25
Perrault, Claude, 25–6
Perronet, J.-R., 29
Phenomenonology, 78–82, 194
Photovoltaics, 21, 89
Piano, Renzo, 92
  Potsdamer Platz, Berlin (Piano),
    112–13, *113*
  Tjibaou Cultural Centre, New
    Caledonia, 147, 150, 158–61,
    160, 163
Place, 121–5
Place and Placelessness (Relph), 120
Plato, 19, 24, 47
Poetics of Space, The (Bachelard), 80
Political ecologists, 66, 70
Post-imperial modernism, 12, 45,
  59–61, 92
Post-modernism, 118–9, 120, 122
Potsdamer Platz, Berlin (Piano),
  112–13, *113*
Pragmatic approach, 106, 107
Price, Cedric, 120, 139
Prigogine, Ilya, 33–4, 35, 36, 37
Principia Mathematica (Newton), 26
Prior, Josephine, 100
Private good, 68–9
Protagoras, 47–8
Public good, 68–9

Qa'a Mohib al Din, Cairo *105*
Quantrill, Malcolm, 53
Queens Building, De Montfort
  University, Leicester (Short Ford),
  4, *5*, 127–8

Radiant City, 183
Rafiq Residence, Baghdad (Chadirji), *126*
Rajasthan, 117–18
Rajchman, John, 141
Rammed earth, 89
Rationalism, xv, 59
Rationality, 136–7
Realism, nature, 17–18
Rebstock Park, Frankfurt (Eisenman),
  141–2, *141*, *142*
Reflectivity, 98
Reflexion, 99
Reflexive modernism, 12, 45, 59–61,
  92
Reichstag, Berlin (Foster), 38–9
Relph, E., 120, 121
Renaissance, 24–5, 168–9
'Report to Virtual HQ' (Chaplin), 176
Rhowbotham, Kevin, 168, 187–8
Ricoeur, Paul, 120
Rifkin, Jeremy, 43

Rogers, Richard, 72
  cities, 60, 175, 182
  dynamic operation, 38
  Lu Jia Zui, Shanghai, 183–5, *183*,
    184, 186
  materials, 39
  Solar City, Linz, 189, *189*
  Tribunal de Grande Instance,
    Bordeaux, 112
  Turbine Tower, Tokyo *40*
Roof-Roof House, Malaysia (Yeang),
  156–7
Rossi, Aldo, 119
Rousseau, Jean Jacques, 68
Rudofsky, Bernard, 103
Ruskin, John, 10–11, 18, 83–4, 85–6

Sagrada Familia, Barcelona (Gaudi), *29*,
  45
Salter, Peter, 91–2, 122–3
Santa Maria Novella, Florence (Alberti),
  25
Sant'Elia, Antonio 49, *50*, 55
Sassen, Saskia, 180–1
Saudi Arabian National Museum,
  Riyadh (SITE), 128, 144
Sauerbruch Hutton, 149, *149*
Schlumberger Research Laboratories,
  Austin (Ambasz), 162
Schutz, Alfred, 120–1
Science, 33–6, 45–6, 48
Scope of Total Architecture (Gropius),
  60
Seagram Building (Mies van der
  Rohe), 59, 136
Selective approach, 106, 107
Self-interest, 68, 71
Semiology, 80, 81
Semper, Gottfried, 83, 84, 85, 86
Sennett, Richard, 175
Seven Lamps of Architecture, The
  (Ruskin), 83–4
Sforzina (Filarete), 53, *54*
Shanghai, 183–5, *183*, *184*
Shape, 9–10, 13, 196
Shelter, 10–11, 14, 83
Shirdel, Bahram, 98, 139
Shiva, Vandana, 116–7, 120–1
Short, Alan, 127
Short Ford Associates, Queens
  Building, De Montfort University,
  Leicester, 4, *5*, 127–8
Siedlung, 141–2
Silent Spring, The (Carson), xvi
Silk, 43
SITE, 99, 139, 188
  passages, 144–5
  Saudi Arabian National Museum,
    Riyadh, 128, 144
  visibility, 128, 129, 163

Sitte, Camillo, 174
Siza, Alvaro, 74, 119
Skeletons, 29, 30, *31*
Slessor, Catherine, 39
Smart buildings, 110–12
Snowflakes, 170
Social City (Howard), 172, *173*
Social sustainability, 3
Socialism, 65–6
Society, 68–9
Socrates, 47
Software architecture, 177
Solar City, Linz (Foster, Herzog and
	Rogers), 189, *189*
*Solar Energy in Architecture and Urban
	Planning* (European Commission),
	89
Solar zoning, 108–9
Soper, Kate, 17, 18, 23, 65–6
Sorkin, Michael, 176
Speidel, Manfred, 8
Spuybroek, Lars, 177
Steadman, Philip, 28, 29
Stengers, Isabelle, 33–4, 35, 36, 37
*Stil in den technischen und
	tektonischen Kunsten* (Semper), 84
Stoa, Athens *28*
Stoffwechsel, 84
Stolnitz, Jerome, 13
Studies in Tectonic Culture
	(Frampton), 74, 80, 86
Sublime, 6–8
Supermodernity, 65
Surrealism, 59
Sustainability, xvi–xvii, xx, xxi, 3–4,
	147
	criteria, 193
	energy efficiency, 99–101
	and newness, 75
	relativity, 163
	University of Future Generations,
		Sydney (Horden), 151
Sustainable cities, 167–8, 178, 183–9,
	191–2
Swallowing, 122
Symbiosis, xx, xxiii, 98–9, 101–2, 148,
	193
	Ambasz case study, 147, 163
	Horden case study, 147, 149,
		151–3, 154, *155*–6
	passive environmental techniques,
		104–15
	vernacular building, 102–4

Tafuri, Manfredo, 12, 119
Taki, Koji, 123
Taylor, Paul, 66

Techne, 47–8, 195, 196
Techno-biosphere, 190–1
Technoburbs, 171–2, 181
Technology, xv–xvi, xvii, 9, 77–8, 195
	materials, 84–5
	as means of control, 56
	modernism, 60
	passive environmental techniques,
		104–15
	symbiosis, 98
	and *techne*, 47
Technopoles of the World (Castells
	and Hall), 180
Tectonics, 80
Telematic Tower, Microelectronic Park,
	Duisberg (Foster), 110–11, *111*
Teletechnologies, 77
Terry, Quinlan, 119
Thatcher, Margaret, 68
*Theory and Design in the First
	Machine Age* (Banham), 21
Thoreau, Henry David, 10
Three Magnets, 106–7, *107*, *108*
Timaeus (Plato), 19
Timberlake, James, 181–2
Tjibaou Cultural Centre, New
	Caledonia (Piano), 147, 150,
	158–61, *160*, 163
Torrent Research Centre, Ahmedabad
	(Ford), 126, *127*
Tower of Babel, 53, 56–7, *56*
Transcendence, 67
Transforming, 74–5
Transparency, 151
Trees, 170
Tribunal de Grande Instance, Bordeaux
	(Rogers), 112
Tschumi, Bernard, 79, 130, 131, 135
Turbine Tower, Tokyo (Rogers), *40*
Type, 84
Tzonis, Alexander, 121

Universality, 68–9, 73, 106, 121
University of Future Generations,
	Sydney (Horden), 147, 149,
	151–3, *153*, 154, *155*–6, 163
University of Plymouth, Centre for
	Earthen Architecture, 89
Uprootedness, 120–1
Urban Task Force, 175
Utopia, 136
Utopians, 48, 50, 52–9
Utzon, Jorn, 126

Vale, Brenda, 10–11, 103
Vale, Robert, 10–11, 103
Valencia, 187

Van Der Ryn, Sim, 88, 187, 190
Van Hinte, Ed, 38
Vassal, William, 159
Vattimo, Gianni, 12–13
Venturi, Robert, 103, 119
Vernacular building, 102–4
	and differentiation, 116–21
	passive environmental techniques,
		104–15
	Roof-Roof House, Malaysia (Yeang),
		156–8
Vesely, Dalibor, 195–6
Vidler, Antony, 59, 79
Ville Contemporaine (Le Corbusier),
	53–4, *54*, 184
'Violated Perfection' (Museum of
	Modern Art), 131
Viollet-le-Duc, Eugene, 84, 85, 86,
	127
Virilio, Paul, 77, 78
Visibility, xx, xxi, xxiii, 97, 98, 99,
	128–9, 145, 146, 148, 193
	Ambasz case study, 150, 161–3
	deconstruction, 131–5, 135–7
	dwelling, 129–31
	folding, 137–45
	Los, 9
	Piano case study, 163
Vitruvius, 18, 29, 51, *51*

Waldrop, M. Mitchell, 35, 36
Warren, Karen J., 19
Waste, 9, 190–1
Water Temple, Hyogo (Ando), 122–3
Weizsacker, Ernst von, 191
Westminster Lodge, Dorset (Cullinan),
	149
What is Nature? (Soper), 18
Wilderness, 176
Wines, James, 128, 130–1, 144, 148,
	188
Women, 19–20
Woodroffe, Jonathan, 169
Wright, Andrew, 139
Wright, Frank Lloyd, 22, 103
	Broadacre City, 169, 171, 174
	Living City 49, *50*

Yeang, Ken, 147, 149–50, 163
	Exhibition (EDITT) Tower, Singapore,
		157
	Roof-Roof House, Malaysia, 156–7
Yokohama International Port Terminal
	(Foreign Office Architects), 143–4

Zaera Polo, Alejandro, 168, 180, 187,
	192